FEMINIST PERSPECTIVES IN

Feminist Perspectives in Philosophy

Edited by

Morwenna Griffiths
and Margaret Whitford

Indiana University Press
Bloomington and Indianapolis

Manufactured in the United States of America

Library of Congress Cataloging-in-Publication Data
Feminist perspectives in philosophy.
    Includes index.
    1. Feminism—Philosophy.   2. Feminism.   I. Griffiths,
Morwenna.   II. Whitford, Margaret.
HQ1154.F4458   1988   305.4'2   87–45774
ISBN 0-253-32172-7
ISBN 0-253-20461-5 (pbk.)

2 3 4 5 6 96 95 94 93 92

Contents

Acknowledgements

The editors would like to thank all the people who contributed directly or indirectly to this volume, particularly all the women who came to the day conferences. Most of the papers in this book developed from workshops at the conferences and have benefited from the lively discussions that took place. We regret very much that we could not include more papers. We would like to give special thanks to Kathleen Lennon for her support and advice.

The editors wish to acknowledge the following for permission to quote from copyright sources:

Edmund Blunden, 'Vlamertinghe', in *Poems of Many Years*, published by William Collins, Sons & Co Ltd. Reproduced by permission of A. D. Peters & Co Ltd.

Franz Kafka, *The Metamorphosis*, translated by Willa and Edwin Muir. Copyright © Schocken Books Inc. 1946, 1948, renewed 1976. Reproduced with the permission of Martin Secker and Warburg Ltd and Schocken Books Inc.

(On pages 53–4) Ten lines from 'Three Women' in *Winter Trees* by Sylvia Plath. Copyright © 1972 by Ted Hughes. Reprinted by permission of Olwyn Hughes and Harper & Row, Publishers, Inc.

John Cottingham, Robert Stoothoff and Dugald Murdoch (eds), *The Philosophical Writings of Descartes*. Reproduced by permission of Cambridge University Press.

MORWENNA GRIFFITHS
MARGARET WHITFORD

Notes on the Contributors

Brenda Almond (formerly Cohen) is Reader in Philosophy and Education at the University of Hull. She is co-founder (with Anthony O'Hear) of the Society for Applied Philosophy and Joint Editor of the *Journal of Applied Philosophy*. She has contributed many articles and reviews to journals of philosophy and is the author of a number of books including *Means and Ends in Education, Education and the Individual* and, most recently, *Moral Concerns*. She is a member of the Council of the Royal Institute of Philosophy and is Vice-President of the Philosophical Society of England.

Alison Assiter is a feminist who teaches philosophy in an interdisciplinary School of Humanities at Thames Polytechnic. She has published in the *British Journal of Sociology, Radical Philosophy, Feminist Review, The Philosopher* and elsewhere. She is author of a forthcoming book, *Sexuality, Fantasy and Personhood*.

Paula Ruth Boddington studied philosophy and psychology at Keele University before going to Oxford, where she took a B.Phil. Since 1982 she has been teaching philosophy at the University of Bristol where she runs a course in feminist theory.

Lorraine Code is a Canada Research Fellow in the Department of Philosophy and the Women's Studies Research Centre at York University in North York, Ontario. She has taught philosophy at Guelph, Queen's, Trent, York and Waterloo universities, all in Ontario, Canada, and has published articles on theory of knowledge, philosophy of language, and feminist philosophy. She is author of *Epistemic Responsibility*. The book has been awarded the Brown University Press First Book Prize Award. She is also co-editor of *Changing Patterns: Women in Canada*, and is currently writing a book on Knowledge and Gender.

Morwenna Griffiths is Senior Lecturer in Education at Oxford Polytechnic, where she teaches courses in philosophy, gender and education. She has published articles on emotion, education and feminism. Her involvement in feminist philosophy came directly from an earlier philosophical interest in emotion and rationality. It developed through a series of day conferences on women and philosophy which she helped to instigate.

Jean Grimshaw lectures in philosophy and cultural studies in the Humanities Department at Bristol Polytechnic. Prior to this she was a schoolteacher for five years, and lectured in the philosophy of education at Redland College, Bristol. She is the author of *Feminist Philosophers: Women's Perspectives on Philosophical Traditions*. She has also published articles and reviews in *Radical Philosophy*.

Joanna Hodge is a temporary lecturer in philosophy at the University of York. She wrote her doctoral thesis in Oxford on the work of Martin Heidegger, which she is currently developing into a book. She has published on political theory and aesthetics in various journals and collections of papers.

Judith Hughes teaches philosophy and international women's studies at the University of Newcastle upon Tyne. She is author of *Women's Choices* (with Mary Midgley). Currently she is developing the ideas in her articles for the publication of a book on the Philosopher's Child. She is married with three teenage children.

Mary Midgley taught philosophy at the University of Newcastle until 1980, when she took early retirement in order to have more time to write. She has been a visiting lecturer at Cornell University and Trent University, Ontario. She is the author of a number of books, including *Beast and Man: The Roots of Human Nature*; *Heart and Mind: The Varieties of Moral Experience*; *Animals and Why They Matter*; *Women's Choices: Philosophical Problems Facing Feminism* (with Judith Hughes); *Evolution as a Religion* and *Wickedness*, and has also published numerous articles in *Philosophy*, *Proceedings of the Aristotelian Society* and elsewhere.

Anne Seller teaches philosophy and women's studies at the University of Kent, and has been a frequent visiting lecturer at the University of Colorado, USA. She has published on philosophy and feminism. She was formally educated at Bedford High School for Girls, and the universities of Leeds and Oxford, but regards her subsequent informal education as the most important part of her biography: she has learned much from the women of Boulder, Colorado, the women involved in the MA in Women's Studies at Kent, the women who made this book, and the women in the peace movement in both Britain and North America, especially the women of Greenham.

Margaret Whitford is Lecturer in French at Queen Mary College, University of London. She has published a book on *Merleau-Ponty's Critique of Sartre's Philosophy*. Her current research is on Luce Irigaray and the implications of structuralist and post-structuralist thought for feminist theory. She has for several years been involved in organising discussion groups on philosophy and feminism.

1

Introduction

Morwenna Griffiths and Margaret Whitford

Philosophy is in urgent need of a feminist perspective. For centuries the practice of philosophy has been overwhelmingly the prerogative of men but it is only recently that feminist analysis has made it possible to see the distorting effect of this historical fact. The articles in this book demonstrate in a variety of ways where the bias occurs and how it might be redressed. They also show that redressing it is a matter of importance to feminists as well as to philosophers.

Feminist ideas are interrelated with philosophical ideas, but most feminist writing would not be recognised as 'philosophy'. Unlike most academic philosophy much of it is personal, polemical, poetical or allusive.[1] Yet part of the practice of feminism is concerned with the essentially philosophical activities of redrawing concepts, reclaiming language, redefining what counts as significant or important, and, as Daly (1984) calls it, 'naming'. The reconceptualisation which feminism is attempting has a direct and vital bearing on central philosophical issues, not only in political philosophy where it might have been expected, but also in epistemology, ontology, philosophy of mind, and ethics. At the same time, in their attempts to rearticulate these basic issues, feminists necessarily take over and use philosophical concepts already available – and in so doing they may import, entailed or entangled in apparently neutral concepts, implications which reiterate and reinforce the assumptions that are being challenged. This point is made explicitly by several of the contributors to this volume (see Mary Midgley, Jean Grimshaw, Joanna Hodge and Anne Seller). Philosophy from a feminist perspective has practical implications for both philosophers and feminists.[2]

The practice and content of Western philosophy are male-dominated and male-biased. This statement is not directed at any one set of philosophers. It is true in general, in spite of the fact that philosophers by no means speak with a single voice, and do not even agree among themselves about what they understand philosophy to

1

be, since the nature of the subject, its preoccupations and methods, is itself a matter of philosophical disagreement. How then could philosophy in general be said to have a male bias? To see this one needs to take a closer look at some of the ways in which philosophy has been conceptualised.

Western philosophy has a long tradition so it is not surprising that it has changed over the centuries both in content and in method. Schools and traditions, with their prescriptions about content, method or both, have risen and fallen, sometimes to rise up again in a new guise. Philosophers of all kinds continually look to thinkers from previous times for inspiration and argument, and schools can often be distinguished by which predecessors they read and discuss. Conversely, bitterly opposed schools can sometimes look to a common ancestor. The result of all this is a web of overlapping – but different – ways of conceiving of the nature of philosophy.

The tradition that is presently characteristic of the English-speaking world, including the United Kingdom, is often called 'analytic'. From about 1955 to 1975 it had a particularly strong hold here in the form of 'conceptual analysis' or 'linguistic philosophy', in which it was axiomatic that any 'empirical' question was not philosophical. Philosophy was held to be a 'second-order subject' concerned only with reason, logic and the clarification of thought. It could be of use to 'first-order', empirically based subjects, but it could learn nothing from them. Plainly, any questions about sex or gender are necessarily non-philosophical, if philosophy is taken to be conceptual analysis in this narrow sense. Any attempt to introduce them into the discourse is immediately blocked by the slogan posing as question – 'but is it philosophy?' Philosophy that limits itself to conceptual analysis can discuss the discourses of those who talk about sex and gender, looking for conceptual coherence and the presence or absence of rational argument. But it cannot treat gender as a theoretical or methodological category, that might structure its own tools and methods of inquiry, and so it cannot examine its own discourse for masculine bias. Unless the category of gender is explicitly seen as of methodological importance, the question cannot even be raised.

Alternative traditions to the analytic one are mostly to be found in Continental Europe (and in some North American universities). Montefiore and Ishiguro (1979) point out:

The universities of Europe which have not been influenced by the analytical tradition . . . have by no means represented any unitary tradition. The disagreements, or even lack of communication, between, for instance, Hegelians, Marxists, phenomenologists and Thomists have often been deep. But these disagreements are 'small' in comparison with the barriers of mutual ignorance and distrust between the main representatives of the analytical tradition on the one hand and the main philosophical schools of the European continent on the other.

(pp. viii–ix)

These barriers have reached towering heights in the twentieth century, although information does slowly trickle through them. It is still true to say that many Continental philosophers would hardly be recognised as such by their English-speaking contemporaries. Montefiore and Ishiguro again:

How unfortunate . . . that they have refused to read or respect one another, the one convinced that the other survives on undisciplined rhetoric and an irresponsible lack of rigour, the other suspecting the former of aridity, superficiality and over-subtle trivialization   (Ibid., p. ix)

Partly as a result of a slow trickle through the barriers, and partly as a result of internal inconsistencies, the analytic tradition has recently shown signs of moving from the strictly aloof position it adopted in the heyday of conceptual analysis. It is now possible, even in respectable academic circles in this country, to recognise that the concepts people use are related to the (changing) circumstances in which they live. The question 'but is it philosophy?' is losing its power to block further discussion. It remains true, however, that it is still deeply contentious to suggest the possibility of points of view in philosophy, let alone that substantial conclusions might be drawn from them. In this volume, the possibility of a women's point of view in philosophy is discussed directly by Paula Boddington from within the analytic tradition. Other contributors who are working within this t̶ ⟨Brenda Almond, Morwenna Griffiths, Mary Midgley and ⟩ consider in what ways central philosophical is different from a women's (or feminist) points of ⟨

Other contributors, like Alison Assiter, Jo⟨ Margaret Whitford, have been influenced by⟨

traditions of Continental Europe. In some ways these traditions are of especial interest to feminists since part of their history is an opposition to seventeenth- and eighteenth-century versions of the Enlightenment and the mechanistic, scientific, atomistic picture of the universe. These are concerns shared by substantial numbers of feminists. However, it is clear from these three papers that the Continental traditions themselves need to be subjected to feminist scrutiny. These traditions are, in theory, more hospitable than the analytic one to the idea of different points of view, but in practice their point of view has been overwhelmingly male.

The feminist criticism of this volume is the more powerful because its contributors come from a variety of philosophical traditions. No doubt it will very quickly become apparent to the reader that there are differences in their philosophical assumptions that may not be reconcilable. Nor do they share any body of feminist dogma. It would be odd if they did, since feminists, like philosophers, do not speak with a single voice. We think it would be a mistake to try and establish any 'consensual' version of feminism or of feminist philosophy because we are committed to exploration of the beliefs and views we hold, even the ones which at present seem indisputable.

At this point the question may well arise: since there are such profound differences among the contributors, how could these different views be said to constitute a perspective? And given the diversity both of contemporary philosophy and of contemporary feminism (Delmar, 1986), how could a feminist perspective in philosophy be recognised?

One suggestion is that feminist philosophy could be identified by its content. This is not a suggestion we agree with, but it is a popular one, especially in North America where a number of closely related discussions have emerged recently about the content of feminist philosophy, or the form a feminist critique of philosophy should take (Flax, 1983; Hartsock, 1983; Jaggar, 1983; and see also Ruth, 1981). They include substantive conclusions about what would be different in philosophy if it were influenced by feminine rather than by masculine assumptions. For instance, Flax argues that certain preoccupations are typical of masculine philosophy, and arise out of dilemmas deeply rooted in the masculine unconscious, resulting from childrearing practices:

ɔparently insoluble dilemmas within philosophy are not the

product of the immanent structure of the human mind and/or nature but rather reflect distorted or frozen social relations.

(p. 248)

Philosophy reflects the fundamental division of the world according to gender and a fear and devaluation of women characteristic of patriarchal attitudes. (p. 268)

The apparently irresolvable dualisms of subject-object, mind-body, inner-outer, reason-sense, reflect this dilemma.

(pp. 269–70)

Hartsock (1983) argues that for men but not for women:

The core experience to be understood is that of discontinuity and its consequences. As a consequence of this experience of discontinuity and aloneness, penetration of ego-boundaries, or fusion with another is experienced as violent. Thus, the desire for fusion with another can take the form of domination of the other.

(pp. 299–300)

She argues that this perception of discontinuity and dominance has consequences for the way experience finds expression in the work of male philosophers. For women, in contrast, discontinuity is not the core experience, and relationships are not perceived as violent. Jaggar (1983) sums up the position as follows: 'The standpoint of women generates an ontology of relations and of continual process' (p 376).

There are serious problems with this kind of content-based assertion, as Grimshaw (1986) points out in her discussion of 'the maleness of philosophy'. Firstly, it ignores those male, often misogynist, philosophers who have emphasised relations and continual processes. She cites Hegel and Bradley as examples. We would also point out that prior to the seventeenth-century scientific revolution the universe was seen, by European men, as a great chain of being, connected rather than atomistic, necessarily related to humanity, rather than being a 'neutral domain of facts, of contingently correlated elements, the tracing of whose correlations will enable greater and greater manipulation and control of the world' (Taylor, 1985, p. 134). Secondly, it distorts the history of philosophy by assuming that it has been unchanging in its preoccupations and conceptualisations, which it clearly has not. However, as Lloyd (1984) shows in her tracing of changing ideas of reason, while ideas may change, their gender inflection may remain. Throughout the history of Western philosophy women have been thought inferior or less than fully human, though some philosophers, like Kant and Rousseau, have found them charming and necessary to men's well-being, as long as they keep in their place. Thirdly, it has a tendency to a rather static and essentialist picture of both 'men' and 'women', in this way ignoring the important and real differences between women themselves.

We do not think that any particular content in philosophy can be identified as female. Where we agree with the suggestions of the feminist philosophers we have just quoted is in their insistence that philosophical theory comes out of experience, so that philosophy formulated exclusively by men will reflect the experience of men. But we also want to emphasise that neither the experiences men have nor their ideas about masculinity have remained constant. They have varied over history and they still vary today with race, culture and class. But however much they vary, the symbolic division of the world by gender appears to be a constant and fundamental way of articulating experience. Therefore, the experience of women will vary systematically over time, place and circumstance, in step with, but different from, the experience of men. As several of the contributors point out, one should be wary of reducing women's experiences (plural) to women's experience (singular). But the division of the world by gender continues to underlie these changes.

Gender is defined by opposition. To be masculine is not to be feminine. Feminine is what is not masculine. What appears on either side of the male–female divide is extremely variable. For instance, whether males tend to be warlike, bookish, competitive, cooperative, individualist or role-oriented is specific to time and place. But where masculinity is associated with any one of these, femininity will be associated with the opposite, and, where women are oppressed, taken to be inferior. Philosophy, in so far as it is the articulation of the concepts, dilemmas, explanations and abstractions of a culture, will only be half the story unless both genders contribute equally. As far as our own history is concerned, feminist criticism shows that Western philosophy has been consistently masculine in orientation even while it has changed its preoccupations and methods. But the other half of the story cannot be simply added on. Grimshaw (1986) suggests:

> The trouble with [a view that what is needed is a re-evaluation of the feminine] is that it still leaves uncriticised the whole association of particular qualities with the masculine and others with the feminine . . . A response to the gender inflection or masculinism of philosophical theories should involve, I think, neither merely the assertion that women too should be seen as included under or capable of whatever norms are suggested by the theory, nor merely the assertion that what is seen as feminine should be valued too, or given equal status with what is male. Rather, what is needed is a critique of the polarisation of masculine and feminine qualities, and in particular a critique of the way in which such qualities may be interpreted or clustered.
> (pp. 47–8)

Grimshaw emphasises that femininity or masculinity are not fixed, nor are they independent of each other. We would add that to suggest giving equal status to what is currently thought to be feminine or masculine is to ignore the way in which one is defined by the other. In our culture to give equal status is a contradiction in terms, so long as gender is an expression of power relations and the male continues to be the superior term.

We are saying, in short, that a feminist perspective in philosophy is necessarily critical. Like any other philosophy it is specific to its circumstances. It will depend on the characteristic experiences of women and men at the time of its formulation, and on the way they have entered into philosophical discourse. Feminist criticisms and contributions need to expose and redress distortions where they are found. Thus, if maleness is especially associated with individualism, feminists may need to point to connectedness, but if connectedness is part of the male view, emphasising it won't be feminist. Intuition is now said to be 'feminine', and is opposed to logic (which is thereby 'masculine'). But intuition used to be the favoured type of knowledge, and St Thomas Aquinas, for example, would never have allowed intuition to constitute a specifically feminine attribute, because it would have meant admitting that women were nearer God.[3]

Since the feminist perspective is necessarily critical, feminist philosophy is not a way of articulating women's experience in parallel with men's: it is not a form of relativism. This is a particularly important point. That which a feminist perspective enables us to perceive is valid for everyone. However, since we have argued that content is not the defining criterion of feminist perspectives, we are not claiming a new objectivity or neutrality. We are not claiming that women on their own (or feminists on their own) have the truth, but rather that men on their own do not. Therefore, here again we have reservations about the position articulated by Alison Jaggar (1983) at the end of an excellent discussion of political philosophy from a feminist perspective:

> Women's subordinate status means that, unlike men, women do not have an interest in mystifying reality and so are likely to develop a clearer and more trustworthy understanding of the world. A representation of reality from the standpoint of women is more objective and unbiased than the prevailing representations that reflect the standpoint of men.
>
> The concept of women's standpoint also provides an interpretation of what it is for a theory to be comprehensive. It asserts that women's social position offers them access to aspects or areas of reality that are not easily accessible to men . . . The standpoint of women reveals more of the universe, human or non-human, than the standpoint of men.   (pp. 384–5)

Though appealing and heroic, such a vision seems to claim too much. But although we are not arguing that women or feminists have privileged access to the truth about reality, we agree with Jaggar that the standpoint of women offers an opportunity to see what is wrong with current male-defined theories and to correct them.

It could be objected at this point that all philosophy is critical, that all philosophical theory attempts to question, correct or overturn current orthodoxy and so that feminist philosophy is just philosophy, and there is nothing specifically feminist about it. The difference is, of course, that feminist criticism arises from the experience of feminism and from taking feminist theories seriously. This would be true whatever the particular circumstances which produced the feminist response.

The experience of becoming feminist inevitably leads to changes in one's view of oneself, and in one's view of the rest of the world. It is never an intellectual exercise which leaves everything the same. It is a discovery that changing concepts is a political activity: that it is not value-free, but is tied to the adoption of a particular interpretation of the world. The result is a re-evaluation of one's personal life, a re-evaluation which is often surprising and usually difficult. Things which were previously seen as obviously true come to be seen as obviously false. The tensions generated by this process (and by the kinds of activity, personal and political, which accompany it) have philosophical consequences, both concerning *which concepts* seem problematic, and also *what is problematic* about them. The articles in this book explore some of these consequences.

A preoccupation common to all the papers in the book springs directly from the difficulties involved in reassessing how the 'facts' of one's experience correspond to the descriptions of them offered by others. It could be summarised by the feminist slogans, 'the personal is political' or 'the politics of experience'. Whatever the problems with these rather global and unanalytic formulations, none the less they do encapsulate one indispensable and basic argument of feminism, the argument that women's experience has been left out: one of the central themes of feminism has been the importance of women's experience, and one of its central enterprises has been to show how a great deal of male theorising about women has tended to deny, invalidate, or be unable to account for this experience. This is not to say that women's experience, perceptions, feelings and emotions are self-validating and constitute in themselves an epistemological standpoint, or even to say that they are always correctly identified and described, but it is to suggest that philosophy would look rather different if women's experience had the same rights of entry as that of men. Most of the contributors draw attention to this point in one way or another. For example, Morwenna Griffiths refers to the feminist emphasis on generating abstractions on the basis of concrete, personal experience (rather than assuming that inherited abstractions adequately explain experience). One of the strengths of this approach is that it becomes much more immediately apparent why certain issues are felt to be important. The experience of trying to force one's perceptions into preconceived categories, and the pain and distortion that this has often led to, is now used as a basis by feminist theorists for the argument that to see feeling as 'contaminating' objective, scientific knowledge points to a distortion of conceptualisation. As Jaggar (1983) points out, this is not a simple process of incorporating the neglected experience: 'a theory may require that we revise even the description of the world on which the theory itself is based' (p. 381). The contributors are not making the easy assumption that to validate their experience women do not have to put themselves into question; on the contrary, it must be recognised that to be a feminist theorist may involve some painful and hard-won putting into question of the beliefs and commitments that are the point of departure. But the contributors all agree on the importance of that experience. In these papers, all kinds of non- and extra-philosophical activities become the basis for philosophical reflection, for instance menstruation and childbirth (Brenda Almond's paper); a gut reaction to pornography (Alison Assiter's paper); the fantasies that disturb because of their apparently unfeminist nature (Jean Grimshaw's paper); and non-violent demonstrations against missile bases (Anne Seller's paper); the point in each case being that these experiences are the starting point, because their importance did not seem to be recognised within the theoretical categories already provided, and so urgently impel the theorist to work out categories that are more adequate.

A second preoccupation evident in these papers is responsibility, and what could roughly be described as the ethical dimension of conceptualisation. Several contributors explicitly criticise the social atomist conception of human beings, defined by Mary Midgley in this volume as follows:

> This is the idea, implied by all Social Contract myths, that an individual is essentially a solitary unit, a free chooser, a being intrinsically without social ties.

As she goes on to argue, 'The pronoun "he" is an essential part of this description.' Because the life-experience of women is normally so different from that of men, they are likely to conceptualise freedom, equality, rights, responsibility and autonomy, to give but a few examples, in a rather different way from men. Thus Brenda Almond suggests that the ways in which women's lives differ from those of men are morally significant. In our culture women typically conceptualise themselves *in relation to* others; discussion of the implications of this can be found in several of the papers (Alison Assiter, Lorraine Code, Jean Grimshaw and Judith Hughes). The result of seeing the difference in women's experiences in positive rather than negative terms – seeing women as having something to offer philosophy rather than seeing them as inferior or aberrant versions of a male norm – is that the contours of familiar conceptual landscapes begin to change. Judith Hughes, for example, puts forward a way of seeing autonomy (and adulthood) based primarily on the notion of responsibility rather than that of rationality, thus giving an ethical dimension to autonomy. Lorraine Code argues that epistemology should not be divorced from ethics; one should be a responsible knower. Alison Assiter extends the notion of autonomy into the private realm where the tradition cautiously refrains from setting foot, and suggests that how we treat and are treated by other people in private has a direct bearing on our autonomy in the public sphere. The ideal of an unrelated self is shown to be an ideal developed by people who have never been in the position of having primary responsibility for the care of children or the old. This position, actual or potential for all women, leads to a version of the self which is more likely to be *defined in relationship* and which therefore implies certain commitments or responsibilities which can hardly be denied.

Where standard discussions of autonomy place it in the context of rights, freedom and equality, paternalism and rationality, here it is discussed in conjunction with questions of fantasy, how we treat others, social and personal relations, and responsibilities. Where standard discussions of the self talk about memory and unity, brain transplants, the rational agent acting on his beliefs and desires, or the self in its public aspect as citizen, here the self is looked at in the context of the past history of a person, unconscious or fantasy relationships with others, the importance of feelings, or the body.

This is not simply an alternative or complementary perspective, since it raises directly the issue that what counts as a philosophical problem is itself an issue for critical inquiry. We have been arguing that changing concepts is a political activity; that it is not value-free, but arises out of a particular ethical or political interpretation of the word, and that one of the aims of the dialogue between feminism and philosophy should precisely be to reconceptualise the world that is offered by philosophy as it is at present. Some feminists would expand this argument to suggest that the political and/or ethical discussion should be made an explicit part of the methodology of philosophy. Harding (1986) argues that since scientific knowledge (the epistemological paradigm) is in any case used for social ends, social aims should determine the formulation of scientific or epistemological problems. Along the same lines,

Anne Seller in this volume argues for a more democratic epistemology. From this perspective, ethics in the broad sense (the question of relations with and responsibilities towards other people or a community) is not just a branch of philosophy but informs the conception of what philosophy is or might be.

Contributors to this volume were given no more precise brief than the provisional subtitle 'explorations in philosophy from a feminist perspective', and they are working within quite different philosophical traditions and on different sorts of issues. However, the papers are unified by a common factor: they all draw on a body of writing and thinking – with admittedly elastic boundaries – which is not taken seriously by the mainstream as having anything to offer philosophy. Providing an outline of each paper in the second part of the introduction, below, we draw attention to the feminist debates which are the source for each contributor's point of departure. In the third and final section we give a brief survey of the most well-known publications in the area of philosophy from a feminist perspective. We hope this will be of value to both feminists and philosophers approaching these questions for the first time.

* * *

The opening paper, by Mary Midgley, discusses the central issue of the possibility and necessity of a women's point of view. She addresses the tensions generated by two related dilemmas in feminist thinking, and points out why they have a wider relevance in philosophical and political thought. The first of these tensions is about the degree of attention that needs to be paid to natural (i.e. genetically given) sex differences and similarities. The second, related one is about the reasons for treating all people as if they were the same, regardless of their individual peculiarities of sex and gender. She relates these concerns to the philosophical projects of finding universals of human nature, of morality and of political being, and in particular, to the project of achieving equality between individuals of varying class, race, age and cultural background. The questions are both political and controversial. As Midgley makes clear, discussions of natural sex differences can never be simply a *neutral* issue, even if it is an *empirical* one, since one still has to consider what consequences should follow from the differences one has discovered. Feminists began by arguing that sex differences are artificial and insignificant, for the very good reason that the idea of natural differences had so often been used to justify discriminatory treatment against women. Midgley argues that it is time to move on from this position. She sees natural sex differences as providing the basis for a critique of certain philosophical conceptions which exclude women, and in that way is enlisting them on the side of feminism.

The view that philosophical conceptions may be not so much 'universal' as 'male' is discussed further in the next paper. Brenda Almond draws on recent feminist arguments that women's distinctive perspective and experience lead them to view morality in a different light from men. This distinctive perspective is derived from a focus on the concrete, as opposed to the abstract, and is characterised by an emphasis on responsibility rather than on rights. Almond suggests a number of ways in which the ancient idea that the two sexes have – or should have – different moral outlooks can be given new life in the context of modern feminism. She considers whether it is true to claim that there is a sex-related divergence of views, and the possible reasons for any such divergence, and goes on to suggest that there are areas in which women's views may typically differ from those of men. In particular, Almond questions the notion of autonomy as it has been developed since Kant, arguing that this notion is of limited value to women, since 'the "masculine" goal of moral autonomy has in practice almost always been outside a woman's grasp'. She suggests that women's distinctive experience leads them to form a moral sensibility that is closer to aesthetic response than to the legalism implicit in much principle-based morality. Almond argues, like Midgley, that women's experience adds a positive and complementary contribution to our ethical conceptions.

An ethical perspective is also present in Alison Assiter's paper, in which she argues that the Kantian or Hegelian notion of autonomy should apply to sexual relations as much as to the public world of social contract. She suggests that persons and their autonomy should be respected in all private and personal activities, including erotic fantasy. The argument should be seen in the context of feminist debates about pornography and its significance. One of the clearest discussions of these debates can be found in Elizabeth Wilson's book *What Is to Be Done about Violence against Women?* (1983). She points out that what feminist thought has done is to take pornography out of its usual position in the argument between conservatives and liberals over censorship, and to put it into a completely different framework (p. 137). For feminists, there is another context which gives the phenomenon of pornography a different meaning: the social context of violence against women.

Pornography is seen as one manifestation among others of the way in which women are controlled by male power or violence (other manifestations are rape, or the fear of rape, wife-battering, prostitution, child-abuse, etc.). (For further discussion see Brownmiller, 1975; Lederer, 1980; Dworkin, 1981; Griffin, 1981; and Kappeler, 1986 which are directly concerned with pornography, and Snitow *et al.*, 1984; and Vance, 1984 on sexuality.) Like these writers, Assiter makes a consideration of pornography central to a consideration of women's social situation. She enters the feminist debate here, arguing that some feminists have misunderstood the significance of pornography, taking it to be a major cause of the oppression of women, rather than a symptom of it, albeit a symptom which itself then contributes to that oppression.

It is now beginning to be argued by feminists that in order to deal with pornography and what the phenomenon reveals, we have first to *understand* it, understand, that is, the meaning and function of fantasy for both men and women, and what effects it has on the rest of one's life (see Wilson, 1983 for a summary of this discussion, and also Carter, 1979; Linden *et al.*, 1982; Midgley and Hughes, 1983). For Assiter, fantasy is not just a harmless and essentially solitary activity in which everyone engages to a greater or lesser extent, but is something which also has an effect on the way people behave towards others, and on the way they may feel they can justifiably treat each other, particularly women. There is thus a connection between people's private fantasies and their status as autonomous individuals.

Drawing on a notion of autonomy which originates with Kant, and which is developed in the writings of Hegel and Marx, Assiter extends this notion and criticises the way in which it has been confined to the public sphere. In arguing for the relevance of the notion of autonomy in private life, she brings into question the demarcation point between private and public life which is assumed by most of the philosophical tradition she is working in. It has been pointed out by feminists that the tradition which depends upon this demarcation line fails to give a satisfactory account of conflicts that arise in the private sphere. Thus two apparently unrelated discussions: the notion of autonomy in relation to the public–private distinction, and pornography, are shown here to be intimately related.[4]

The notion of autonomy is discussed in a different context by Judith Hughes in the next paper which, like Assiter's, illuminates the concept from a new angle and, like Almond's, emphasises the importance of responsibility. Underlying Hughes's paper are questions about how children figure in political debate, what problems the considerations about children bring to light, whether these problems have any special significance for women, and whether women's new awareness of their own political situation can be used effectively in thinking about children. Thinking about these questions produces the conclusions that are the starting point for Hughes's paper: that the philosopher's child invariably turns out to be male and that autonomy seems to be for men only. These conclusions lead her to argue that rationality has been falsely assumed to be the criterion of political adulthood, and that rationality does not entail autonomy. Thus, analysing the attempt by political philosophers to justify the exclusion of women from public life on the grounds of their defective capacities (either rational, moral or cognitive), she suggests that there is a hidden argument which takes the exclusion of women to be unquestionable and attempts to justify the status quo by seeking an explanation in the defective capacities that women must then be assumed to have. She argues that autonomy should not be seen as a psychological capacity, but as a social one, depending on public acknowledgement, and that this acknowledgement arises from the recognition of responsibility rather than of rationality.[5]

A fourth paper discussing the notion of autonomy indicates the importance of the concept for women, for whom the experience of dependence and powerlessness is often a central feature of their lives. Jean Grimshaw looks at some of the ways in which feminists have tried to conceptualise what it is for a woman to be autonomous, and the relationship between these conceptions and philosophical ways of thinking about the human self. She locates her argument within both feminism and philosophical thought. She considers the idea, implicit in much feminist theory, of an authentic self which is said to be socially conditioned by patriarchal power, and argues that this idea owes much to a tradition in Western philosophy which dates back to the Aristotelian distinction between actions that are voluntary and actions which are coerced, a tradition that can be traced through Descartes to the present time. Grimshaw argues that feminists' appeal to this humanistic conception of the self as a unitary, atomistic, conscious and rational core is quite inadequate to conceptualise experiences such as self-deception or obsessional delusions, or the contradictions which feminists have described between their rationally held views and political convictions on the one hand, and their emotions and desires on the other. In order to account for women's lack of autonomy it is not sufficient to think merely in terms of removing a veil, or stripping away the outer layers. The concrete experiences of women (and men) are here used as the basis for a critique of a particular conception of the self.[6]

Grimshaw suggests that Freud and psychoanalysis might offer an explanatory account of the self of considerable value. Both feminists and contemporary philosophers in England and America have had an uneasy relationship with psychoanalytic theory. Philosophers have been primarily preoccupied with the scientific status of psychoanalysis and whether its therapeutic claims can be substantiated. They have, on the whole, ignored it as a theory of mind, though a few (such as Richard Wollheim) have been deeply influenced. Feminists have been antagonistic to psychoanalysis, seeing it as a means for the social control of women, although over the last few years, the mood has shifted, and psychoanalysis is being re-examined for its possible value to feminists (see Sayers (1986) for an overview).

In France, psychoanalysis has been taken more seriously by both feminists and philosophers, and the psychoanalytic model used as a basis for the reconceptualisation of a number of philosophical issues. The paper by Margaret Whitford shows how the feminist philosopher and psychoanalyst, Luce Irigaray, uses psychoanalytic theory to provide a critique of Western rationality and the traditional symbolism, which symbolises rationality as 'male' (see Lloyd, 1984). Foregrounding the theme of sexual difference, Irigaray locates male–female symbolism as one of the fundamental underlying polarities of Western thought. Placing Irigaray's work in the context of Freudian and post-Freudian theory, Whitford suggests that Irigaray's apparently very traditional and essentialist use of symbolism has a strategic function, like that of Derrida's analyses, designed to draw attention to the underpinnings of Western metaphysics, in order to undermine them. Feminists have approached the work of Irigaray eagerly, looking for a theory which would help to understand and change the situation of women, but have been divided in their interpretations of her writing. Some see a romantic celebration of difference, a static, essentialising, ahistorical view of women, others find her work politically equivocal. Whitford's view is that Irigaray's work has been read out of context, and that we need to give much more careful attention to the psychoanalytic dimension of her thought. Her argument is that Irigaray, as a psychoanalyst, sees psychoanalysis as a process of change rather than as a scientific theory: Irigaray's work suggests ways in which psychoanalysis could be seen as a model for feminists seeking fundamental social change, in particular by proposing an alternative model for the relation between the rational and the non-rational which would be more satisfactory than the dominant paradigm.

In the next paper Morwenna Griffiths also addresses the question of the relation between the rational and the non-rational. Drawing on the re-evaluation of emotion characteristic of contemporary feminist theory and practice, she argues that feminist conceptions of emotion constitute a critique of dualist conceptions of mind found in much Western philosophy in the English-speaking world and elsewhere. She refers, in particular, to radical feminists who turn on its head the criticism that women are more emotional than men, and claim that not only are women more emotional, but that this is their strength, and that in comparison, men are enfeebled, deadened and impoverished creatures. As Griffiths points out, there are problems with this position, but she argues that, despite its flaws, its passionate impetus to reconceptualisation is invaluable. Griffiths suggests that the legacy of Descartes to the philosophical understanding of emotions has been to subsume them into one of two categories, mind or body, and to make them rational or non-rational. She proposes an alternative model of mind in which feelings are paid sufficient attention, and in which, through language, they are seen to be intelligent rather than rational, non-rational or irrational. She argues that one's feelings are a source of knowledge as well as being a result of understanding, and that for both social and biological reasons they are gender-related. Thus she concludes that being male or female gives one a distinctive viewpoint which should be included in any theory of human beings. She also endorses the radical feminist view that the well-being of private and public life depends on a better understanding of feeling.

The legacy of Descartes comes in for further scrutiny in Joanna Hodge's paper, which examines the concept of 'the subject' which philosophy has inherited from Descartes. This concept, she suggests, has been both valuable and limiting for women. Valuable, in that, by providing a conception of an autonomous, rational and apparently neutral subject, it made it possible for Enlightenment liberalism (in particular Mary Wollstonecraft) to question the exclusion of women from public life. Limiting, in that it conceals a covert gender specificity which operates to justify women's continued exclusion – whether from public life or philosophy. Now, however, contemporary critiques of the notion of the subject (see, for example, Heideggerian phenomenology, structuralism, psychoanalysis or Derrida's deconstruction) have begun to dismantle the assumptions concealed in the notion of subjectivity.

In her densely argued and complex paper, Hodge points out that one can distinguish between the *subject*, a notion with ontological and metaphysical commitments, and *subjectivity*, an empiricist notion (developed, for example, by Hume) which retains its epistemological function while abandoning its ontological links. Descartes, effecting a split between rational consciousness and sensual embodiment, offered an account of the mind–body relationship which accepted the traditional hierarchy according to which reason governs the body or the senses. He saw the body in functionalist terms, but failed to make a distinction between the different functions of the male and female bodies. Subsequent empiricist versions avoid the Cartesian problem of the relation between mind and body by focusing instead on the epistemological processes of *subjectivity*, but in this way obscure even further the nature of the body attached to these processes. However, feminism brings back to the centre of the debate the ontological issue of the different kinds of body to which the rational processes may be 'attached'. Feminist analysis has shown in detail that women's bodies bear cultural meanings that are quite different from those ascribed to men's bodies. This difference is particularly visible in the phenomenon of pornography which serves to foreground the issue of the nature of the body, an issue not discussed by Descartes and completely absent from subsequent post-Cartesian philosophy. Hodge argues therefore that women's epistemological position cannot be exactly the same as men's. Like Assiter, then, Hodge suggests a link between the issue of pornography and the notion of an autonomous and rational subject. Her paper argues for the importance of standpoint to be taken into account in discussion of fundamentals such as epistemology and ontology, but also suggests that feminist political theories which assume that a conception of the subject is already available need to be complemented by more radical feminist theories (such as those of Daly or Irigaray) which criticise and take apart the metaphysical implications inherent in philosophical conceptions of the subject.

The epistemological issue is discussed in more detail in the following two papers. Firstly, Anne Seller's paper argues that the view of knowledge as a correct description of the world has only limited application. The epistemological model of truth and falsity which applies to formal statements of propositions turns out to be difficult to apply in the context of social and political life. Like Hodge, Seller takes the view that women who uncritically adopt philosophical conceptions of knowledge may find themselves saddled with consequences that are at odds with their perceptions of the world and their politics. She discusses this in relation to epistemological stances of realism and relativism. 'Realism' and 'relativism' are not exact terms. They are each used here to gesture at a range of philosophical positions. Realists are impressed by the constraints imposed by the 'external world' on what we know and can know. Seller takes realism as the view that 'there is an objective order of reality which can be known by the human observer'. She discusses this in relation to the view held by some feminists that 'every woman's experience of the world is valid, not false, illusory or mistaken, and that all views of the world are equally valid'. She considers the strengths and weaknesses of both positions and shows how the epistemological and political questions are intertwined with each other. She argues that the main task is that of deciding what to do, and that the best way of deciding is through a genuinely democratic epistemology. Once this is achieved, she suggests, the dichotomy between realism and relativism becomes irrelevant; both will proceed in the same way in trying to sort out what is going on and what to do.

Lorraine Code's paper arises out of a concern on the one hand with the epistemological status of experiences, and on the other, with the importance of recognising the ethical dimensions of knowing: what she terms 'knowing well' or 'taking epistemic responsibility'. She elucidates her concept of epistemic responsibility by focusing on the practice of stereotyping, and in particular, the stereotyping of women by men. The philosophical tradition she is working within is Kantian: she emphasises that human cognition is an 'active process of *taking* and *structuring* experience', and therefore, she argues, a process that entails freedom and responsibility and the associated ethical virtues of honesty, humility and courage. This active process is hindered for everyone if they use stereotypes. It is rendered particularly difficult for women who have been stereotyped, because the stereotype of women is one which precludes the exercise of active responsibility. The other central theme of Code's paper is the relation between experience and knowledge. She argues against the Kantian tradition of seeking a pure, clear objectivity in knowledge which will leave personal experience behind. A concept of knowing well which rejects stereotyping cannot move very far from the experience which generates the knowledge. She defines the area of feminist epistemology as that of developing theoretical accounts of knowledge which retain continuity with women's experiences. In a critical discussion of Carol Gilligan's work in moral development (Gilligan, 1982), she notes that Gilligan's methodological principles, in particular the aim of listening responsively with receptiveness and humility, supply an example of the kind of approach that might fulfil this aim.

The concluding paper, by Paula Boddington, returns to the issue of a women's point of view and what difference this might make to philosophy, leaving the reader with a kind of map of the basic issues to be explored: 'an opening up of complexities'. Situating herself within the Anglo-Saxon analytic tradition, she looks at different conceptions of philosophy, its content and methods. Readers unfamiliar with philosophy will find her discussion of the nature of philosophy illuminating; they should be warned, though, that philosophers are likely to find it contentious. Including a review of material already published about women and philosophy, she distinguishes between female, feminine and feminist points of view, and then, focusing on the first of these, she considers how philosophy could or would be affected by the inclusion of more women in its institutional structures. She looks first at how the present conceptions and practices of philosophy might admit of different points of view at all. She then goes on to consider what might be changed by the inclusion of more women. Finally she returns to her original distinction between female, feminine and feminist, and suggests how the relation between them might have implications for possible developments in the practice of philosophy. She concludes that women's views need to be considered and then synthesised with men's to 'find a human whole'.

* * *

What is now known as 'second-wave' feminism emerged in the late sixties and seventies. By the early seventies, articles that saw themselves as explicitly feminist were beginning to appear in

philosophy journals (e.g. *The Monist*, special issue, 1973). As
women began to cast a critical eye over the discipline of philosophy,
a number of different types of work appeared. These can be divided,
very broadly, into the following categories (although the categories
clearly overlap both chronologically and conceptually). Firstly,
there were discussions of issues thought to be of particular interest
or relevance to women, such as abortion or equality. Many of these
discussions are to be found in the early collections (see, for example,
Gould and Wartofsky, 1976; English, 1977; Vetterling-Braggin,
Elliston and English, 1977). An extended discussion of this kind can
be found in *The Sceptical Feminist* by Janet Radcliffe Richards (1980).
These discussions are characterised by an increasing scope and
depth as the issues are accorded greater philosophical seriousness.
Thematic collections on issues of particular concern to women
continue to appear, for example *The Family in Political Thought*
(Elshtain, ed., 1982) or *Mothering* (Trebilcot, ed., 1984). A couple of
recent collections which bring together a range of articles on a
variety of topics are *'Femininity', 'Masculinity' and 'Androgny': A
Modern Philosophical Analysis*, edited by Mary Vetterling-Braggin
(1982b) and the special issue of *Radical Philosophy* (1983) on 'Women,
Gender and Philosophy'.

Secondly there was the re-examination and reinterpretation of the
history of philosophy, looking at philosophers through 'the prism of
sex' to see what they had to say about women. In practice, since
philosophy often proceeds by paying attention to past philosophers
and their ideas, the two categories overlapped to some extent with
each other, and with a third category, political philosophy, which
looks at the political philosophers in the light of the practice and
experiences of feminist politics (see Okin, 1980; Elshtain, 1981;
O'Brien, 1981). As the often misogynistic views of philosophers
were exposed, two lines of approach were adopted. Either one
could discard what the philosopher had said about women and keep
the rest – which in fact often meant accepting conceptions of human
nature that took the male as paradigm, and trying to demonstrate
that women were as fully human as men, or one could argue that the
philosopher's thought formed a system within which the attitude
towards women formed an inseparable part (see Elshtain's (1981)
discussion of the private–public distinction or Grimshaw (1986) for
the examples of Aristotle and Kant), so that it was impossible just to
take certain parts and leave the rest. The second of these choices was
the one that most feminists adopted, and as a result the next decade

was marked by an increasing self-confidence on the part of feminists about their place in philosophy. This led to a fourth type of work which discussed the nature and limits of philosophy itself and whether there was any place for women in it, and considered whether the basic assumptions of philosophy included or excluded women. Here we would just like to mention briefly some of the studies that came out between 1980 and 1986, which attempt to develop accounts that would be either specifically feminist or draw upon a women's point of view.

Under the heading of political philosophy, feminist philosophers begin by arguing with the tradition, trying to reconcile feminist insights with already existing systems of thought such as liberalism or Marxism, and go on to attempt to define a new perspective in philosophy. In *The Politics of Reproduction* (1981), Mary O'Brien rereads traditional political theory's preoccupation with the family and reproduction, and uses a revised version of dialectial materialism with a view to developing a feminist theory. She argues for the view that there is such a thing as a 'feminist perspective' and criticises feminist theorists (de Beauvoir, Millett, Firestone and Reed) who depend too heavily on existing (male) theories. Jean Bethke Elshtain, in *Public Man, Private Woman. Women in Social and Political Thought* (1981), looks at the way political thought has conceptualised the public–private distinction and its bearing on attitudes towards women, and critically examines contemporary feminist versions of that same distinction. Alison Jaggar, in *Feminist Politics and Human Nature* (1983), looks at the relation between feminist theory and political philosophy, arguing that different feminist theories – liberal feminism, radical feminism, Marxist feminism and socialist feminism – imply different conceptions of human nature and have different implications for practice. A collection of essays edited by Ellen Kennedy and Susan Mendus, *Women in Western Political Philosophy* (1987), presents a feminist perspective on questions that have been central to political philosophy and raises questions about the philosophical underpinning of political theory.

In ethics, there have been attempts to incorporate or develop a women's point of view, perceived as missing from mainstream theory. Carol Gilligan, in *In a Different Voice: Psychological Theory and Women's Development* (1982), examines psychological theories concerning human moral development, and suggests that a male model has been developed which does not fit the experiences of most women's lives. Criticising a rights-based ethics, she suggests that an alternative view of morality is needed which would include a typically feminine way of conceptualising the relationship between self and other. Nel Noddings describes her book, *Caring: A Feminine Approach to Ethics and Moral Education* (1984), as 'an essay in practical ethics from the feminine view' and attempts to evolve a specifically feminine form of ethics. A recent collection, *Women and Morality*, edited by Eva Kittay and Diana Meyers (1986) widens the discussion by bringing together different viewpoints on the issues raised by Gilligan.

A variety of work has appeared addressing issues relating to reason, rationality and emotion. Carol McMillan, in *Women, Reason and Nature* (1982), argues that feminism makes the same mistake as anti-feminism in its excessive belief in rationality and empiricism, and consequently undervalues emotion, intuition and the private sphere. Genevieve Lloyd, in *The Man of Reason: 'Male' and 'Female' in Western Philosophy* (1984), looks at the way in which Western philosophy has conceptualised reason, and shows that throughout its history ideals of reason have incorporated an exclusion of the feminine, which creates both practical and conceptual problems for women who may experience conflicts between reason and femininity. (This study contains a useful bibliographical essay on women and philosophy, going up to 1983.) Mary Daly, in *Pure Lust* (1984), a polemical book subtitled 'Elemental Feminist Philosophy' which explicitly and insistently refuses to fit the usual categories of what philosophy is supposed to consist of, argues that the passions and their relation to reason must be renamed, and thus reunderstood by women if they wish to free themselves from the constrictions inherent in the male naming of them.

In the areas of language and epistemology, there is a collection of essays edited by Mary Vetterling-Braggin, *Sexist Language: A Modern Philosophical Analysis* (1982a), which usefully brings together a wide range of articles by a variety of contributors. Another collection, edited by Sandra Harding and Merrill Hintikka, *Discovering Reality* (1983), a wide-ranging and challenging selection of essays in epistemology, metaphysics, methodology and philosophy of science, argues that it is not just content but also methodological assumptions and epistemology which show male bias. This book draws extensively on the work of Nancy Chodorow (1978) and object-relations theory in psychoanalysis concerning the construction of male and female personality. A recent book by

Sandra Harding, *The Science Question in Feminism* (1986), develops the work in epistemology and philosophy of science, and examines the work of feminist theorists in this area. Harding shows the obstacles to, and the far-reaching consequences of, trying to construct a theory of gender as an analytic category that is relevant to the natural sciences.

Most recent work is often concerned with philosophical issues within feminism itself. Mary Midgely and Judith Hughes, in *Women's Choices* (1983), discuss the philosophical issues facing feminism. They locate the various strands in feminist thinking, and show the conceptual problems involved in combining them. The collection edited by Carol Gould, *Beyond Domination: New Perspectives on Women and Philosophy* (1983), discusses some of the philosophical problems raised by feminism. Jean Grimshaw, in *Feminist Philosophers: New Perspectives on Philosophical Traditions* (1986), explores tensions in feminist thought and examines some of the philosophical problems underlying them.

The work of French women theorists is also beginning to be translated and discussed in this country, although for French theorists, the boundaries between philosophy, literary theory and psychoanalytic theory are often fluid, so that their work does not always fall clearly into the familiar categories of philosophy. However, the work of Christine Delphy, Luce Irigaray, Julia Kristeva and Michèle Le Doeuff (to name the most well known) is currently being discussed by feminists working in the area of philosophy or feminist theory.[7] An impressive overview of the context in which contemporary French theory is being thought is offered by Alice Jardine in *Gynesis: Configurations of Women and Modernity* (1985). Jane Gallop's book, *Feminism and Psychoanalysis* (1982), is an excellent introduction to the range and implications of French feminist theory. A more accessible introduction can be found in Claire Duchen, whose book *Feminism in France: From May '68 to Mitterrand* (1986) contains a couple of chapters discussing the central theoretical issues.

NOTES

1. *Some* philosophical writing has had these characteristics, for instance, the work of Wittgenstein and Nietzsche – but it is far from being the norm.
2. We use 'they' rather than 'we' for philosophers and feminists because we want to avoid ambiguity, and because we do not claim to speak for others. So 'we' means Morwenna Griffiths and Margaret Whitford, not 'we feminists', 'we philosophers', 'we women', 'we human beings' or even 'we contributors'. It means 'we editors'.
3. With thanks to Michèle Le Doeuff who used this example in a discussion at the Royal Institute of Philosophy, October 1986.
4. These problems are discussed more fully in Alison Assiter's book, *Sexuality, Fantasy and Personhood* (forthcoming) in which she develops the radical feminist critique of pornography, and argues that pulp romantic fiction is a form of pornography.
5. Judith Hughes' argument arises out of contemporary and feminist debates on childhood (see Midgley and Hughes, 1983, ch. 3 for further discussion).
6. For further discussion around the argument of Jean Grimshaw's paper, see Grimshaw, 1986, chs 5 and 6.
7. Translations are available as follows: Delphy, 1984; Irigaray, 1981, 1985a, 1985b, 1986, 1987; Kristeva, 1978, 1981a, 1981b, 1982, 1984a, 1984b, 1986; Le Doeuff, 1977, 1981–2). See also the anthology edited by Toril Moi (1987), *French Feminist Thought*, which includes excerpts from a number of less well-known theorists.

REFERENCES

ASSITER, Alison (forthcoming), *Sexuality, Fantasy and Personhood*.
BROWNMILLER, Susan (1975), *Against Our Will: Men, Women and Rape* (London: Secker & Warburg).
CARTER, Angela (1979), *The Sadeian Women* (London: Virago).
CHODOROW, Nancy (1978), *The Reproduction of Mothering: Psychoanalysis and the Sociology of Gender* (Berkeley: University of California Press).
DALY, Mary (1984), *Pure Lust: Elemental Feminist Philosophy* (London: The Women's Press).
DELMAR, Rosalind (1986), 'What is Feminism?' in Juliet Mitchell and Ann Oakley (eds), *What is Feminism?* (Oxford: Blackwell), pp. 8–33.
DELPHY, Christine (1984), *Close to Home: A Materialist Analysis of Women's Oppression*, trans. Diana Leonard (London: Hutchinson).
DUCHEN, Claire (1986), *Feminism in France: From May '68 to Mitterrand* (London: Routledge & Kegan Paul).
DWORKIN, Andrea (1981), *Pornography: Men Possessing Women* (London: The Women's Press).
ELSHTAIN, Jean Bethke (1981), *Public Man, Private Woman: Women in Social and Political Thought* (Oxford: Martin Robertson).

ELSHTAIN, Jean Bethke (ed.) (1982), *The Family in Political Thought* (Brighton: Harvester).

ENGLISH, Jane (ed.) (1977), *Sex Equality* (Englewood Cliffs, NJ: Prentice-Hall).

FLAX, Jane (1983), 'Political Philosophy and the Patriarchal Unconscious: A Psychoanalytic Perspective on Epistemology and Metaphysics', in S. HARDING and M. HINTIKKA (eds), pp. 245–82.

GALLOP, Jane (1982), *Feminism and Psychoanalysis: The Daughter's Seduction* (London: Macmillan).

GILLIGAN, Carol (1982), *In a Different Voice: Psychological Theory and Women's Development* (Cambridge, Mass: Harvard University Press).

GOULD, Carol C. and WARTOFSKY, Marx M. (eds) (1976), *Women and Philosophy: Toward a Theory of Liberation* (New York: Perigee Books).

GOULD, Carol C. (ed.) (1983), *Beyond Domination: New Perspectives on Women and Philosophy* (Totowa, NJ: Littlefield Adams).

GRIFFIN, Susan (1981), *Pornography and Silence: Culture's Revenge against Nature* (London: The Women's Press).

GRIMSHAW, Jean (1986), *Feminist Philosophers: Women's Perspectives on Philosophical Traditions* (Brighton: Wheatsheaf).

HARDING, Sandra and HINTIKKA, Merrill B. (eds), (1983), *Discovering Reality: Feminist Perspectives on Epistemology, Metaphysics, Methodology, and Philosophy of Science* (Dordrecht: Reidel).

HARDING, Sandra (1986), *The Science Question in Feminism* (Milton Keynes: Open University Press).

HARTSOCK, Nancy (1983), 'The Feminist Standpoint: Developing the Ground for a Specifically Feminist Historical Materialism', in S. HARDING and M. HINTIKKA (eds), pp. 283–310.

IRIGARAY, Luce (1981), 'And the One Doesn't Stir Without the Other', trans. Hélène Vivienne Wenzel, *Signs*, vol. 7, no. 1, pp. 60–7.

IRIGARAY, Luce (1985a), *Speculum of the Other Woman*, trans. Gillian C. Gill (Ithaca and New York: Cornell University Press).

IRIGARAY, Luce (1985b), *This Sex Which Is Not One*, trans. Catherine Porter with Carolyn Burke (Ithaca and New York: Cornell University Press).

IRIGARAY, Luce (1986), 'Women, the sacred and money', trans. Diana Knight and Margaret Whitford, *Paragraph*, vol. 8, pp. 6–18.

IRIGARAY, Luce (1987), 'Sexual Difference', in T. MOI (ed.).

JAGGAR, Alison M. (1983), *Feminist Politics and Human Nature* (Brighton: Harvester).

JARDINE, Alice A. (1985), *Gynesis: Configurations of Woman and Modernity* (Ithaca and London: Cornell University Press).

KAPPELER, Susanne (1986), *The Pornography of Representation* (Cambridge: Polity Press).

KENNEDY, Ellen and MENDUS, Susan (1987), *Women in Western Political Philosophy* (Brighton: Wheatsheaf).

KITTAY, Eva and MEYERS, Diana (eds) (1986), *Women and Morality* (Totowa, NJ: Rowman & Allanheld).

KRISTEVA, Julia (1978), *About Chinese Women*, trans. A. Barrows (London: Marion Boyars).

KRISTEVA, Julia (1981a), 'Oscillation between Power and Denial', trans.

Marilyn A. August, in E. MARKS and I. de COURTIVRON (eds), pp. 165–7.

KRISTEVA, Julia (1981b), 'Woman Can Never Be Defined', trans. Marilyn A. August, in E. MARKS and I. de COURTIVRON (eds), pp. 137–41.

KRISTEVA, Julia (1982), *Desire in Language: A Semiotic Approach to Literature and Art*, ed. Leon S. Roudiez, trans. T. Gora *et al.* (Oxford: Blackwell).

KRISTEVA, Julia (1984a), *The Revolution in Poetic Language*, trans. Margaret Waller (New York: Columbia University Press).

KRISTEVA, Julia (1984b), *Powers of Horror*, trans. Leon S. Roudiez (New York: Columbia University Press).

KRISTEVA, Julia (1986), see T. MOI (ed).

LE DOEUFF, Michèle (1977), 'Women and Philosophy', trans. Debbie Pope, *Radical Philosophy*, vol. 17, pp. 2–11.

LE DOEUFF, Michèle (1981/2), 'Pierre Roussel's Chiasmas: From Imaginary Knowledge to the Learned Imagination', trans. Colin Gordon, *Ideology and Consciousness*, vol. 9, pp. 39–70.

LEDERER, Laura (ed.) (1980), *Take Back the Night: Women on Pornography* (New York: William Morrow).

LINDEN, Robin Ruth, PAGANO, Darlene R., RUSSELL, Diana E. H. and STAR, Susan Leigh (eds) (1982), *Against Sadomasochism: A Radical Feminist Analysis* (East Palo Alto, Cal.: Frog in the Well).

LLOYD, Genevieve (1984), *The Man of Reason: 'Male' and 'Female' in Western Philosophy* (London: Methuen).

MARKS, Elaine and COURTIVRON, Isabelle de (1981), *New French Feminisms: An Anthology* (Brighton: Harvester).

McMILLAN, Carol (1982), *Women, Reason and Nature* (Oxford: Blackwell).

MIDGLEY, Mary and HUGHES, Judith (1983), *Women's Choices: Philosophical Problems Facing Feminism* (London: Weidenfeld & Nicolson).

MOI, Toril (ed.) (1986), *The Kristeva Reader* (Oxford: Blackwell).

MOI, Toril (ed.) (1987), *French Feminist Thought* (Oxford: Blackwell).

THE MONIST (1973), Special issue on 'Women's Liberation: Ethical, Social and Political Issues', *The Monist*, vol. 57, no. 1.

MONTEFIORE Alan and ISHIGURO Hide (1979) see C. TAYLOR.

NODDINGS, Nel (1984), *Caring: A Feminine Approach to Ethics and Moral Education* (Berkeley: University of California Press).

O'BRIEN, Mary (1981), *The Politics of Reproduction* (London: Routledge & Kegan Paul).

OKIN, Susan Möller (1980), *Women in Western Political Thought* (London: Virago).

RADICAL PHILOSOPHY (1983), Special issue on 'Women, Gender and Philosophy', *Radical Philosophy*, vol. 34.

RICHARDS, Janet Radcliffe (1980), *The Sceptical Feminist: A Philosophical Enquiry* (London: Routledge & Kegan Paul).

RUTH, Sheila (1981), 'Methodocracy, Misogyny and Bad Faith: The Response of Philosophy', in Dale Spender (ed.), *Men's Studies Modified: The Impact of Feminism on the Academic Disciplines* (Oxford: The Pergamon Press), pp. 43–53.

SAYERS, Janet (1986), *Sexual Contradictions: Psychology, Psychoanalysis, and Feminism* (London: Tavistock).

SNITOW, Ann, STANSELL, Christine and THOMPSON, Sharon (1984), *Desire: The Politics of Sexuality* (London: Virago).

TAYLOR, Charles (1979), *Hegel and Modern Society*, edited and with an introduction by Alan Montefiore and Hide Ishiguro (Cambridge: Cambridge University Press).

TAYLOR, Charles (1985), *Human Agency and Language* (Cambridge: Cambridge University Press).

TREBILCOT, Joyce (ed.) (1984), *Mothering: Essays in Feminist Theory* (Totowa, NJ: Rowman and Allanheld).

VANCE, Carole S. (ed.) (1984), *Pleasure and Danger: Exploring Female Sexuality* (London: Routledge & Kegan Paul).

VETTERLING-BRAGGIN, Mary, ELLISTON, Frederick A. and ENGLISH, Jane (eds) (1977), *Feminism and Philosophy* (Totowa, NJ: Littlefield Adams).

VETTERLING-BRAGGIN, Mary (ed.) (1982a), *Sexist Language: A Modern Philosophical Analysis* (Totowa, NJ: Littlefield Adams).

VETTERLING-BRAGGIN, Mary (ed.) (1982b), *'Femininity', 'Masculinity' and 'Androgyny': A Modern Philosophical Discussion* (Totowa, NJ: Littlefield Adams).

WILSON, Elizabeth (1983), *What Is to Be Done about Violence against Women?* (Harmondsworth: Penguin).

2

On Not Being Afraid of Natural Sex Differences

Mary Midgley

THE LURE OF THE UNIVERSAL

The long-standing philosophical controversy into which this topic most obviously fits is the political one about equality. It concerns the degree to which human beings are standardised items. How far are we all essentially the same? My main point will be that this is not a simple, package-deal question. There are angles from which it is important to emphasise similarities, and others from which – for equally strong moral reasons – it is important to emphasise differences.

In the last century or two, the similarities have had more emphasis from philosophers. This has happened partly for good political reasons because there was need to demand a more equal society. But it has also happened for formal reasons which are not good ones at all. There is a notion that philosophy ought only to deal with matters which are absolutely universal. Now it is true that all very wide questions have a philosophical aspect. Philosophy, therefore, often does deal with these questions. But this does not mean that it is fitted only to be used on matters at the extreme end of the spectrum of abstraction – that it can, for instance, discuss people only in so far as they are rational beings, or sets of behaviour-patterns, or immortal souls. Philosophy deals with conceptual difficulties, and these arise in the working out of quite detailed and specific ideas, as well as of wider ones. Indeed, since we actually live in particular contexts and often have difficulty in understanding them, many of our mistakes arise at that level, before more abstract speculation begins at all. The hasty flight to apparently universal rules often gives philosophical notions only a specious air of universality. It is notorious that ambitious ideas claiming to mirror the whole human condition have often turned out to describe

29

chiefly the condition of the group doing the theorising. When a different set of people takes up the questions, this becomes obvious.

Of course, errors of this kind will always be made. We cannot jump off our own shadows. But after so many of these experiences, we ought to be becoming increasingly aware of the danger. Though we cannot look at things from all points of view at once, we can at least learn not to pretend that we are doing so. We speak with relative confidence about our own group. But to see what limitations this brings, we absolutely need to have a more lively sense of its differences from at least the groups which neighbour it. A gradient of dissimilarity leads away from each of us. Yet in spite of this, we all need to communicate and to get some general understanding of each other and of the world we live in. Total scepticism about this project is not an option for us. We therefore continually try to correct one philosophical perspective about it against another.

Among these corrections, feminist ones have by now resoundingly made good their place. Earlier generations had already noticed the odd consequences which followed from Aristotle's having seen the human condition as unquestionably that of an Athenian gentleman, and Kant's having seen it as that of a Prussian bourgeois. But until lately very few people had managed to make themselves heard when they pointed out the dramatic effect of all previous philosophers having seen it as that of a man – that is, of course, not an exact reflection of what men are like, but an image of how they tend to see themselves when they contrast themselves with women. How much does this particular limitation matter? Till lately, respectable intellectual opinion has held that it hardly mattered at all. From the ancient hierarchical point of view (unchanged from Aristotle to Kant and beyond) it could not matter because women themselves did not really matter. They were in effect an inferior kind of man, with no distinctive character of their own. They thus shared in the human condition to the extent that inferior men did, and needed no special comment. On the other hand, those who abandoned the hierarchical position and held, not only that all men were equal but that all people were so, lost interest in sex differences for the opposite reason. For them, women were as good as men because they were no different from men. They were effectively men but no longer inferior ones. The move is that which Aristotle or Kant would have made if they had promoted all outsiders (such as women and non-European peoples) to the status of honorary Athenian or Prussian men.

Now from certain points of view – mainly political ones – this is an admirable move. For the purpose of asking whether a given set of people may be enslaved, or deprived of their property, or denied access to the law courts, or the like, decency is best served by remembering that these are beings as conscious and valuable as ourselves, sharing our vulnerabilities and sensibilities. So we call them equal. But there is a whole range of other situations where the opposite move is needed, where we need to stress that people can differ from us, for instance over proposals to give all children the same kind of education or to make everybody live in the same kind of house. Notoriously, long and gruelling work is needed to make the notion of political equality fit both these kinds of demand.

To date, feminism has contributed a good deal of fuel to both sides of this dialectic, because the case of women is a peculiar one, and introduces even more complications into an already troublesome argument. The main need, however, is to bring the two sides somehow together, since all of us at one time or another need help from both of them. I think feminists have not seen this need clearly enough. They have been too ready to use one or other of the clashing theses as occasion served, without troubling to bring them into intelligible relation. This has happened naturally enough, because it reflects the habits of those with whom they were disputing. Reformers attacking the subordinate status of women have naturally appealed to the idea of equality, because it was already recognised as a proper and powerful tool of reform. But in other situations – for instance in asserting a mother's special right not to be deprived of her children, or in offering characteristically female insights to correct a narrowly male view of life – they have equally naturally appealed to the idea of a distinct female nature. Quite sharp conflicts continually develop between these two approaches, and will continue to do so until their relation is thought out properly. Is *all* difference eventually to be abolished? Should the dialectic process ideally lead to a simple merging, so that the views of men and women on any matter will normally be indistinguishable? Or is the position more like that of the interaction between two separate cultures – or indeed two individuals – where each can indeed gain a great deal from the other, but will always retain its own distinct identity?

AUTONOMY, SOLITUDE AND EGOISM

An interesting and crucial example of this difficulty concerns the 'social atomism' typical of Enlightenment thinking. This is the idea, implied by all Social Contract myths, than an individual is essentially a solitary unit, a free chooser, a being intrinsically without social ties. This unit can become bound to others only by his own free choice, and his choice is rational only in so far as he can safely expect it to serve his own interests. The pronoun 'he' is an essential part of this description. If 'she' is substituted, the ludicrous unreality of the picture at once becomes plain. The great Social-Contract theorists of the Enlightenment therefore explicitly excluded women from their systems. Each woman remained attached to some male contractor, according to the older organic and hierarchical pattern.[1] The resulting brand of individualism thus contains a radical anomaly, affecting half of those present – an anomaly which, however, does not seem to have been visible until light was specially directed on to it by feminists. (This little bit of extra enlightenment is a key move in the creation of modern feminism.)

There are two possible ways of curing the anomaly. One is to go the whole atomist hog and turn women too into full-time contracting egoists, no less exploitative and solitary than the males. Rousseau (1755), in his early accounts of the state of nature, attempted this heroic move, and he has recently been echoed from the feminist side by Shulamith Firestone in *The Dialectic of Sex* (1971). As a response to the brutal competitive individualism which is fashionable today, this proposal is understandable. If the rest of us cannot beat the gangsters, we may well be tempted to join them. But efforts to work out this atomistic society in detail are not very plausible. In particular, the situation of children both in Rousseau's world and in Shulamith Firestone's is a more or less impossible one. This is not just a matter of children's physical dependence; it concerns the emotional constitution of human beings generally. The asocial attitude which these pictures call for is not one normal to human beings of either sex. The only situation in which it tends to look so is the transient one of adolescents leaving home and protesting against their parents. Even Nietzsche expected his future Supermen to form a community. Why then has the atomistic image been so powerful? Why has it been extended so far beyond the large-scale political contexts where it was needed, to permeate modern ideas about choice and freedom? Why, when we all know that loneliness is a paralysing form of human misery, do we go on as if we thought that the deepest need of rational individuals was to be independent of one another?

Traditional thinking answered these questions by saying simply that such was the true nature of man. And it often explicitly contrasted that nature with that of woman. It is no accident that both the Greek and Latin words for 'virtue' originally meant 'maleness'. Much morality, and thereby much metaphysics, has been distorted by serving a polemical purpose in a clash of ideals seen as dividing the two sexes. Theorists have constantly and explicitly used antitheses such as active/passive, reason/emotion, form/matter, mind/body, autonomy/dependence as weapons in this supposed war, recommending their own ideals by directly claiming that the contrary ones were typical of women. The call to 'be a man' has regularly been seen as a self-explanatory moral exhortation. In this way, grossly oversimple notions about sex differences have affected philosophy far beyond the obvious context of egalitarian theory from which we started. False claims to universality have been used to cover a persistent warping in our notions of what it is to be an individual.

Once we have seen it, can we get rid of this distortion quite easily? We can certainly make some progress towards doing so by peeling away the gender-drama from the conflicts of ideals in which it has often figured, and trying to see those conflicts in sex-neutral terms. Freedom, we now notice, is not always a higher ideal than those with which it competes, nor is rationality necessarily just a matter of self-interest. Certain social bonds are essential for the highest activities that we are capable of, so that the antithesis 'bond or free' was always a tendentious one. And so on. Can we then go on from there to a new unbiased universality? Have we reached down to the true bedrock of human life, at which sex differences are revealed as artificial and insignificant, so that we no longer need a tribal division?

On this point, feminist thinking is – as I have mentioned – highly ambivalent. The egalitarian strand of it says yes, and dismisses all suggestions of genuine, irreducible sex differences as 'sexist'. Another and at least equally powerful strand says no, because it wants to emphasise the distinctive value of women's insights, and also the special bond of sisterhood which is seen as binding women together, rather than letting them be absorbed and assimilated into the wider human group. For both these purposes, it is inconvenient to regard the existing distinctive qualities of women – whatever these may be – as simply deformations produced by oppression, which could be expected to evaporate when that artificial pressure is removed. Those who stress sisterhood rather than equality value a great deal in women's distinctive approach as it now is (and has been in societies much less egalitarian than ours) and do not want it lost in the melting-pot of assimilation.[2]

Deeper thinking can no doubt resolve this clash. But until it does, constant confusion arises from trying to combine the two approaches. This (again) is not just a problem for feminism. It indicates much wider unfinished business in our long task of digesting Enlightenment ideas – of working out the proper relations between such large concepts as nature, freedom, equality, justice, individuality and the human affections. By ceasing to ignore the awkward case of women – as most of the traditional theorists did – we can often see what has gone wrong with our thinking in other, apparently more straightforward cases.

THE USELESSNESS OF STANDARDISING

One point which should help us to start here is already familiar from existing discussions of equality. Political equality does not call for standardisation. Political equals do not have to be indistinguisable in any respect. They do not even have to be alike at all beyond some minimum range of conditions which puts them into the same political category. This range varies for different purposes, but the aim is always to make it as wide as possible. Thus, for basic civic rights like not being enslaved or imprisoned without trial, people should need only to be people. For slightly more demanding purposes like voting or serving on juries, they need also some minimum level of maturity and sanity, because here their actions affect the interests of others, so they need to understand what they are doing. For more demanding purposes still more is required, and it is often hard to decide just where to fix the borderline. But what the ideal of equality never demands is likeness in any respect above this minimum. In spite of its quantitative sound, political equality never means having an equal amount of any chosen characteristic. It does indeed enshrine a quantitative metaphor, because it exists to counter an older picture which used one. This was the archaic picture of a king ten times as large as a noble, a noble ten times as large as a merchant – and so on down to the almost imperceptible peasant woman. Against this notion, the reformers contended that, in Bentham's words, 'each should count for one and nobody for more than one'. But there does not seem to be any useful way of developing this idea by seeing people as containing equal quantities of any special substance, or equal degrees of any property.

Imaginatively, however, negative moves of this kind have to be completed by devising new pictures to replace the old ones. To replace hierarchal pictures, the Enlightenment used many such images, and they often did tend to suggest some deeper kind of standardisation as the basis of equality. Thus when Burns wrote:

> The rank is but the guinea stamp,
> The man's the gold for a' that

he vigorously used an ancient notion of personal worth as resting in an original standard substance, and variation as introduced by society. How ancient this thought is we can see by noticing that it is just the figure Plato used in *The Republic* to supply his political myth justifying political *inequality* (Bk. III, 414–15). The hereditary caste of Guardians must (Plato says) be believed to be originally golden while the other castes are of various baser metals, and the various metals ought not to be mixed together. Therefore – except for an occasional mutated child which turns out to be plainly of the wrong metal for its caste – ranks must remain separate. Burns triumphantly hijacks this image by extending the golden substance to the borders of manhood – 'a man's a man for a' that', so that one could properly ask for 'one man, one vote'. Women, however, were still perceived as being made of a different metal and, in spite of Mill, their voting remained an absurd and scandalous project for many decades after 'manhood suffrage' became a reality. And indeed the otherwise democratic Swiss are still of Burns's mind in this matter; their women do not vote.

People who are denied political privileges like this on the ground that they are not standard items naturally tend to reply that the charge is false – to claim that they are actually just as standard as everybody else. When political conflicts rage, it is far harder to take on the awkward task of asking why this particular standard was set up in the first place. In class warfare, for instance, oppressed people easily find themselves claiming to be just as noble or gentlemanly as their supposed betters, without properly criticising existing ideas of nobility or gentility. (Burns avoided this move, which is what gives his protest its particular dignity.) Aspiring castes can easily be led in this way to inherit actual faults from their predecessors. More subtly and widely, they can be led to waste effort in imitating traits which had a point in the situations which gave rise to them, but become empty and even harmful when transplanted. The Victorian middle class seems to have become entangled in a good deal of bad faith of this kind by its attempts to imitate an aristocratic life which it did not fully understand. The pursuit of standardisation – the failure to value a difference – here goes beyond a mere passing mistake and becomes actively pernicious.

There will be similar trouble over the gender difference if indeed – as I am suggesting – it is true that ideas about the meaning of maleness have distorted moral thinking in our culture quite deeply, so as to affect the whole concept of individuality, and thereby condition the way in which some central metaphysical issues are seen. (If this is right at all, it is, of course, right to some extent for other cultures too, but that must be left aside for now.) If, therefore, women want to storm the citadel and share its existing treasures, they have to decide what to do about these autonomy-centred ways of thinking. Are they satisfactory, genuinely universal conceptual systems, which everybody in the new, gender-free intellectual cosmos can use with perfect comfort? Or are they biased, faulty and badly in need of revision?

The first option is Shulamith Firestone's. It is, I think, the logical conclusion of the line in Enlightenment thought which has run from Rousseau through Nietzsche and Sartre – the strand of truly anarchic individualist thinking which avoids the vulgar Nozickian 'libertarian' path of concentrating on the freedom of certain selected institutions such as commercial companies, and genuinely exalts only the freedom of the individual. Anyone who finds that this entire detachment from personal ties really is their highest ideal will be happy with this kind of utopia. Shulamith Firestone undoubtedly did everyone a great service by vigorously extending this notion to women, and pointing out the absurdity of men's viewing themselves as totally detached individuals in relation to the rest of society, while still expecting to go home to a wife who would always have their dinner hot for them in the evening. But once this absurdity is made clear, many of us today will probably find that extreme individualism, when thus exposed in its full aridity, is not a heritage that we want to claim. And that leaves us with the second alternative. We have to do the more general piece of work involved in clearing one more bias from our morality. We have to look at the range of ideals which are somehow clustered together to guide us, arrayed as they are in some sort of a rough priority system, and take out of its slot the unquestioned ideal 'be a man'. We must examine it to see what sense it can yield us in the case of those who, as it happens, are not men in the first place, and in what way, once this is done, it will have changed its meaning for those who, by no special fault or merit of their own, actually are so.

DIFFERENCE IS NOT INFERIORITY

As the title of this paper shows, I am sure that we cannot hope to do this rethinking while still clinging to the currently orthodox view that there are no natural, genetically determined sex differences. This orthodox view does not really rest on factual evidence, though such evidence is sometimes brought in to back it.[3] (There is no hypothesis which cannot find some facts to support it.) It is held because people believe the acceptance of natural sex differences to be dangerous. The danger has been a real one, but it has flowed entirely from distorted views about what the differences are, not from acceptance of difference as such. Different does not mean worse or better, it means different. And in fact the greater the difference is, the less easy does it become to dismiss one of the differing parties as a mere inadequate version of the other. This is clearly enough seen in the case of differing individuals, and also in that of differing cultures. And the case of the sexes is on the same footing.

The main reason why difference is harmless has already been mentioned. Equality does not mean standardisation. One can be 'as good as' somebody else in all kinds of ways while still being very different from them. This may sound obvious, but it is extremely hard to remember. Life is constantly astonishing us by confronting us with new kinds of character, and thereby with different kinds of goodness. Thus Anne Elliott in *Persuasion*, astonished at her friend Mrs Smith's cheerful acceptance of misfortune and hardship,

watched – observed – reflected and finally determined that this was not a case of fortitude and resignation only. – A submissive spirit might be patient, a strong understanding would supply resolution, but here was something more; here was that elasticity of mind, that disposition to be comforted, that power of turning readily from evil to good, and of finding employment which carried her out of herself, which was from Nature alone. It was the choicest gift of Heaven.   (*Persuasion* vol. 2, ch. 5)

Failure to be ready for this kind of thing is the main cause of our dismissing whole squadrons of our fellow-creatures as uninteresting or inferior. This was Aristotle's mistake over women. Judging them by the standard which he used for men, in a society where their roles were totally different, he naturally did not think much of them.

So far, what I say may not sound too shocking. Moral pluralism, the notion that there are different kinds of goodness, is quite acceptable to modern thought. What worries people is the idea that these differences, however valuable, are in any way naturally determined and therefore out of the control of the individual. In the case of personal differences, how much does that matter? It is true that I cannot become you, you cannot become me and Blake could not be Beethoven. But this is not an infringement of our freedom. As theologians have noticed, it is not clear that even God could become somebody other than himself. The power to become absolutely anybody goes beyond any normal notion of omnipotence; why should it be a necessary part of freedom? The idea of freedom which lies behind this kind of demand is confused in the same way as the idea of equality which calls for standardisation. Both universalise prematurely, hardening and expanding one aspect of the moral situation to cover ground that goes far beyond its relevance.

Does this point lose its edge if we think of the differences as socially rather than naturally produced? This too is a strange idea. Of course, it is true that much of the individuality which people show has been the result of their upbringing. Nobody who brings forward biological causes supposes that they replace social causes. They merely supplement them, as the original qualities of food supplement the effects of cooking in accounting for the properties of the finished dish. But this fact cannot save the inflated concept of freedom just mentioned, because people's upbringing is normally just as far out of their control as their genetic constitution is. What is called 'biological determinism' is not more of an attack on freedom than the social determinism (or economic determinism) which is accepted without moral qualms throughout the social sciences. What is injurious is not determinism but fatalism – that is, the pretence that bad things which are in fact within our control lie outside it and are incurable.

On any view of causes, a great deal in the life of each of us is completely out of our power, and our freedom must consist in the way we handle that small but crucial area which does actually come before us for choice. This situation is far more benign than people obsessed with freedom make it sound, because what comes to us by no choice of our own is a gift – a whole world which we could not possibly have made and at which, in spite of all its horrors, we can on the whole only bow our heads in wonder. Moralists able only to think of autonomy, of the active imposition of the will on what is round us, miss the essential values of receptivity, of contemplation, of openness to the splendours of what is not oneself. Our inheritance, both social and natural, is not a shocking intrusion on our privacy and freedom, but a realm for us to live in. Morally speaking, one of the worst aspects of the autonomy-centred Enlightenment attitude has been to denigrate the receptive virtues, to make us so obsessed with giving that we do not know how to receive. As usual, one of these aspects of life does not make much sense without the other.

About individual differences, much of what I am saying here may not sound too bad, but many people will want to treat sex differences quite otherwise. Here, the history of the various disputes has been important. Modern educational theory has strongly promoted the idea that individual differences are intrinsic and must not be ironed out. We have been told for several centuries now that every child is naturally different and it is therefore wrong to impose on one the mould which has been prepared for others unlike it. This important thought has been constantly at odds with the equally influential notion that we are all blank paper at birth, ready to be entirely formed by our society. This last wild exaggeration has also been popular with educators at times when they wanted to stress the importance of their task and the need to get it right. But the quite opposed notion of innate individuality has also maintained its strength, no doubt because there is so much in the experience of anybody who actually works with children to support it. If the little creatures were really blank paper at birth, nobody would ever have the slightest difficulty in writing on them whatever their particular culture required, and it would be impossible for them ever to surprise their elders by unexpected conduct. This is so far from the truth that on the whole, for those really attending to education, the notion of innate given individuality has remained the stronger.

Sex differences, however, have been put into a different box. By bad luck, the question of women's emancipation has been most often seen as parallel to that of non-European races. And race difference is, among all the differences which have been used to justify oppression, probably the most trivial. Where it does not coincide with cultural frontiers, it is insignificant. In this case, therefore, Burns's idea of treating differences of status built on it as idle and artificial is just as appropriate as it is in the case of class.

It cannot follow, however, that this is true of all other differences. Burns's image of the gold is, we should notice, bound to the Blank Paper theory of human difference. Gold can be made into all sorts of other things besides guineas. Is the gingerbread which is currently stamped into men equally capable of being stamped into standard unisex persons? If we are tempted to assume so, it may be worth while looking at yet another parallel to balance the highly peculiar one of race. How about age? This certainly has a biological basis as well as a social one. The physiological states of growing organisms – including human beings – vary greatly from one stage to another. Typical behaviour patterns also change. Play, sleep, sexual behaviour and other proceedings are differently distributed – typically – at different ages, in a way that broadly holds across cultural barriers. What reason would there be to deny the obvious causal connections with changing physique? 'Ageism' is objectionable, not because it means admitting these connections, but because it means treating old people – or children – badly. There is nothing fishy about simply admitting the reality of the difference, or that of the physical causes which – alongside cultural ones – help to produce it. To insist on denying the reality of such causes is to draw a bizarrely hard line between the physical and the mental aspects of a human being – a line which does seem sometimes to be drawn in the social sciences, and may prove handy in academic feuds between them and biology, but which seems very badly suited to the realistic description of our lives.

I have carefully said nothing here about the details of particular natural sex differences. The general point about the innocuousness of natural difference as such needs to be grasped on its own. Once seen, it gives us back a legitimate access to a great wealth of traditional human experience on the matter, which must of course be critically used, but which certainly does not leave us utterly puzzled, as we might be in starting to observe a strange species. Feminists have already made good use of this tradition. I think, however, that their use of it is still often confused and inhibited by mistaken ideas about what equality demands, and that the senseless ideal of standardisation still produces a waste of effort on this topic, as on many others. This is the sort of muddle which often causes good ideas to run out into the sand. I particularly do not want this to happen to feminism; hence my choice of subject for this essay.

NOTES

1. Well documented by Susan Möller Okin (1980), in *Women in Western Political Thought*.
2. This clash of ideals is a central theme in *Women's Choices: Philosophical Problems Facing Feminism* (Midgley and Hughes, 1983).
3. For those who want the factual arguments, the anthropologist Melvin Konner has an admirable, and extremely sympathetic, summary of them in his book, *The Tangled Wing* (1982), ch. 6. His conclusion – drawn with real reluctance – is that the case for innately caused behavioural differences is overwhelming.

REFERENCES

FIRESTONE, Shulamith (1971), *The Dialectic of Sex: The Case for Feminist Revolution* (London: Jonathan Cape).

KONNER, Melvin (1982), *The Tangled Wing: Biological Constraints on the Human Spirit* (London: Heinemann).

MIDGLEY, Mary and HUGHES, Judith (1983), *Women's Choices: Philosophical Problems Facing Feminism* (London: Weidenfeld & Nicolson).

OKIN, Susan Möller (1980), *Women in Western Political Thought* (London: Virago).

ROUSSEAU, Jean-Jacques (1755), *Discours de l'origine de l'inégalité*. English trans. by Maurice Cranston, *Discourse on the Origins of Inequality* (Harmondsworth: Penguin, 1984).

3

Women's Right: Reflections on Ethics and Gender

Brenda Almond

There is a view that is as old, probably, as the human race, and certainly as old as Homer and the ancient Greeks, that there is one ethical structure that represents right for men: a composite of manly virtues, such as courage, endurance, physical stamina, wiliness and political judgement, and a corresponding but complementary conception of what is right for women, womanly virtue being seen as a mixture of timidity, tenderness, compliance, docility, softness, innocence and domestic competence.

Views about the exact composition of virtue, male and female, have changed over time, and they may vary, too, with differing social and geographical contexts, but the underlying theme is constant: the theme, that is, of difference. It is recognisable even when it appears in feminist dress, as it does, for example, in these remarks of Hester Eisenstein (1984): 'I argue that feminist theory has moved from an emphasis on the elimination of gender difference to a celebration of that difference as a source of moral values. A woman-centered analysis presupposes the centrality, normality, and value of women's experience and women's culture' (p. xviii).

Clearly, a distinctively feminist conception of women's moral values will differ significantly from traditional stereotypes. But it is worth asking, nevertheless, whether the old and the new might not be rooted in the same set of facts. Any discussion of ethics and gender, then, must involve some reference to facts. But the primary question is not one about facts at all. It is about moral ideals. Should we – women and men – be aiming at a common ethical conception, a shared moral perspective? Or should we – women alone – be working to rewrite the map of morality to promote a separate moral perspective? Must we, in other words, accept an ultimate sexual apartheid as far as ethical values are concerned?

The larger question, then, is not about what *is*, but about what *ought* to be. But since answering this question involves reference to some matters of fact, it is necessary to say something about those facts. Essentially, they are of two kinds. First, there are facts about what different people's moral ideals actually are. Here it is important to know (a) whether male and female ideals diverge: whether, that is, the moral outlook people have depends in some causally related way on whether they are male or female, and (b) whether the ideals themselves are gender-relative: that is to say, whether what is good in a woman or right for a woman might not be bad in a man, or wrong for a man, and vice versa. Secondly, there are facts about the lives of men and women and the systematic ways in which their lives differ, which it would be unwise to overlook. A systematic difference in the life-experience of women and men can have ethical implications both in *generating* a different moral ideal – making women *think* differently about morality from the way men think about it – and also in *justifying* a different moral ideal – justifying, that is, a genuinely alternative moral perspective.

These last points may seem to imply a flagrant disregard of the well-known difficulty, first pointed out by the philosopher David Hume in the *Treatise of Human Nature* (1739), of reasoning from 'is' to 'ought' (Selby-Bigge ed., 1952, pp. 469–70). But no transgression against Hume's stricture is involved in pointing out that people's *views* about what ought to be – their moral stance and outlook – may be directly related to certain distinctive features of their lives. And no transgression, either, is involved in accepting that moral views and ideals must take account of, and be responsive to, facts. Ideals are not formed in an aseptic vacuum, but in the chemical brew of interacting personal lives and events.

So let me begin by making some impressionistic guesses about the views women do in fact currently hold on morality. I can do this best by way of a personal anecdote, which might be called the Incident of the Taxman and the Philosopher.

Discussing the case of a headmaster who had reported his pupils to the police for criminal behaviour, the Philosopher, who was female, expressed the opinion that, since the headmaster is *in loco parentis*, he should have tried to avoid resort to law; he should have dealt with his pupils himself, privately and without publicity – as would, she suggested, a loving parent. The Taxman expressed moral outrage at such a suggestion, declared that this was not his conception of the implications of being *in loco parentis*, and said that he, as a parent and husband, would have no hesitation in reporting the criminal actions of his child or indeed his wife, particularly if he saw no sign of either remorse or an intention to reform. He added that apprentice-Taxmen are coached in the matter of the known duplicity of women and their willingness to lie to protect members of their family. At this point, the Taxman's wife expressed moral outrage at the discovery that her husband would, without compunction, report her misdeeds, or those of her daughter, to the authorities, and the Philosopher was left with a sense of having stumbled upon a set of basic moral presumptions which are held in common by one sex, and entirely inverted in the case of the other – a looking-glass reversal of priorities and values.

As it happens, of course, this conclusion conforms to the observations of Freud, who believed that women had less sense of justice than men and are more often influenced in their judgements by feelings of affection or hostility. It conforms, too, to some more recent observations of Piaget, Kohlberg and Gilligan.

Lawrence Kohlberg's empirical work on moral development follows, as far as its basic stance is concerned, the structure and assumptions of Jean Piaget, who has demonstrated apparently invariant sequences of change, not only in relation to moral development, but in other areas, too. The underlying assumption is that there is a necessary maturation of cognitive processes, just as there is of physical and motor processes. Just as every normal human child first learns to crawl, then to stand and then to walk – and the motivation and capacity to do these things comes from within the child, and is not artificially imposed from outside – so, the moral development theorists hold, there is a necessary sequence of stages of emerging moral judgement. Their empirical research is directed to establishing what these stages are, and to describing the circumstances surrounding the transitions.

Kohlberg's stages of moral development are usually described as a progression from lower to higher – itself an inbuilt and at first unrecognised value-judgement. The early or lower stages that he has identified are first, a stage in which children's thinking is rooted in obedience to adults, fear of punishment and acceptance of authority; then a stage of an essentially self-interested acceptance, for the sake of reciprocity, of a principle of fairness between peers; and then a further stage of seeking approval and desiring to be well thought of by one's community or group.

Later comes a stage of respect for justice: recognition of the importance of *rules* for community living, followed by an awareness of the *universality* of some of these rules and their embodiment in principles of individual human rights applying across varying cultures and societies. Kohlberg has speculated on the existence of a seventh stage in which the universal human perspective is replaced by a holistic cosmic perspective which might have a religious or even a pantheistic orientation.[1]

All this is framed in gender-neutral terms, but researchers have become aware of difficulties in finding women who can be placed by this classification in the 'higher stages' of moral development. Women's answers to the questionnaires by which assignments to 'stages' are made show them to be more heavily represented in the early stages of development rather than the later. Women desire to please. Women rebel against impersonal principles of morality which, when rigorously applied, ignore individual pleas for sympathetic concessions, for mercy rather than justice.

Carol Gilligan's research, which focused on the distinctively female moral dilemma of an abortion-decision, suggested that what was emerging here was not a moral *deficiency* of women but a 'different voice' on morality. The findings of the male researchers, she claims, are dogged by what she calls the problem of women 'whose sexuality remains more diffuse, whose perception of self is so much more tenaciously embedded in relationships with others and whose moral dilemmas hold them in a mode of judgment that is insistently contextual'.[2] While she concedes the broad outline of the developmental model – a model which proceeds from an egocentric through a societal to a universal perspective – she sees this development as taking place, in the case of women, within a special moral conception. The nature of this moral conception is recognised by a distinctive use of a particular vocabulary: a vocabulary of selfishness and responsibility; or morality as an obligation to exercise care and avoid hurt.

The particular sequence of moral development revealed by Gilligan's research is described by her in this way: first, as in Kohlberg's findings, a stage of focus on the self; then, a second level of development in which the notion of responsibility is used to balance the claims of self against the claims of other people; this stage brings a notion of the good as caring for others; it involves a protective care for the dependent and unequal. It is succeeded by a third stage at which the tension between conformity and care, selfishness and responsibility, is dissipated by a self which, in Gilligan's words 'becomes the arbiter of an independent judgment that now subsumes both conventions and individual needs under the moral principle of non-violence' (Gilligan, 1977, p. 492).

Gilligan sees this as a morality of responsibility that stands apart from the morality of rights underlying Kohlberg's conception. In it, a positive conception of caring contrasts with the purely negative policy of non-interference suggested by an emphasis on rights.

What is missing from the latter, and its omission is deliberate rather than accidental, is the detail and texture that comes with knowledge of particular people and particular circumstances. Kohlberg's research is based on questionnaires which demand a response to hypothetical and imaginary situations in which concrete detail is necessarily omitted. Gilligan points out that Kohlberg thus divests his moral actors of the history and psychology of their individual lives. Many women, confronted by Kohlbergian questionnaires, ask for, or contribute out of their own imagination, concrete detail which might help them resolve the moral dilemma with which they are presented. They are told that this sort of question or embellishment is inappropriate. Kohlberg's dilemmas are not about real people – they can't be if the aim of the research is to discover objective principles of justice.

Gilligan mentions here the anonymous woman whose non-legalistic thinking enabled Solomon to display his legendary wisdom. She contrasts that woman's sacrifice of self and principle for the life of her child with the willingness of Abraham to sacrifice his son for principle and personal integrity. What both of these examples demonstrate is the concreteness and particularity of real life situations.

It is interesting to compare Gilligan's criticisms of Kohlberg on this point with Robert Nozick's parallel and equally cogent criticisms of Rawls. John Rawls, in *A Theory of Justice*, seeks to arrive at abstract principles of justice by means of a device which strips the procedure of arriving at principles bare of all reference to the particular and concrete. His principles are chosen by people behind a hypothetical 'veil of ignorance', where they know nothing of their social position in society, their sex, race, abilities or conceptions of the good (Rawls, 1972, in particular pt. I, ch. 3). Nozick points out that the very nature of Rawls's thought-experiments guarantees the *type* of principles that will be chosen: that they will be impersonal and grounded in future-oriented principles of distribution, rather than being personal and grounded in current or past circumstances (Nozick, 1974, in particular pt. II, ch. 7). To accept Nozick's criticism is not to judge in favour of Nozick's conception of justice against Rawls, any more than acceptance of Gilligan's argument involves rejection of Kohlberg's abstract principles of justice. It is simply to recognise that the structure of the 'proof' in both cases, in Rawls's case an *a priori* proof, in Kohlberg's case an experimental one, actually presupposes what it sets out to establish. The outcome is guaranteed before the procedure, whether logical or empirical, is embarked upon.

But Gilligan does not, in fact, reject the notion of a rights-based morality. Instead, she argues that the feminine strand should *contribute* to an enlarged and revised universal conception of morality, in which the ideals of compassion and care are added to the more impersonal ideals of autonomous judgement and action. She believes, then, that a morality of rights can be integrated with a morality of responsibilities – that the two conceptions are essentially complementary. This coincides with the views of some other feminist writers who have been impressed by this distinctively 'female' contribution to morality. Hester Eisenstein, for example, looks forward to women transforming the world in the image of what she calls 'the woman-centered values at the core of feminism'. This means, she believes,

> associating feminism with the liberating traditions of Western thought, from Locke and Rousseau to Marx and Engels, tending in the direction of greater equality, shared decision-making and justice. But it means, too, transforming these traditions, by imbuing them with the woman-centered values of nurturance and intimacy, as necessary and legitimate goals of political life.
>
> (Eisenstein, 1984, pp. 144–5)

Reflecting on the same contrast, Carol McMillan refers to Hegel's view of the family as an inferior organisation to the state because it is based on love. She points out that much of a woman's life is based on a spontaneity of moral response that many philosophers, in particular Hegel and Kant, would say had no moral worth (McMillan, 1982). The idea that acts of love are inferior to principled acts is a deep-rooted philosophical tradition.

This area of love, care and spontaneous response which ignores, or deliberately flouts, principle and convention is one, then, where an initial impressionistic guess about male and female differences can be given an impressive weight of support. There is a second impressionist guess, however, which it is harder to document. This is the extent to which women's moral perceptions are tied to the aesthetic.

The link between awareness of beauty and recognition of the moral good was a fundamental aspect of Plato's ethical theory, but few writers since Plato have tied awareness of beauty in nature so closely to a deeper notion of the good. However, it is a striking observation that women's moral sensibilities are, more often than men's, triggered by an awareness which is essentially aesthetic. The following account is given by Helen Weinreich-Haste of a response to a question designed, not to explore this point, but simply to discover more about significant changing points in people's lives:

> I was driving on my way through beautiful scenery in Wales where I live and it suddenly occurred to me how this would all be altered in a nuclear war. And it just stopped me dead in my tracks. I couldn't keep driving. I had to stop and I felt really physically very unwell. And I was crying. I sat for about three quarters of an hour before I could continue the journey.
>
> (quoted in Weinreich-Haste, 1987)

The woman who gave this account thereafter changed her established way of life to become an activist in the Greenham Common protest against the siting there of cruise missiles.

To cite a personal response of a comparable nature, I find in myself an apparently irrational extra revulsion at the occurrence of bombings or murders that take place in beautiful places on beautiful days. It would be absurd to approve of such events taking place on grey, sunless days in dark, depressing places. Nevertheless, there is a sense of incongruity and inappropriateness about an ugly act which involves the destruction of what was, in some wider and more general sense, previously beautiful.

But this, even more than the previous example, is not, of course, an attitude *confined* to women. It must be something of the sentiment that inspired the war poets, enduring indescribable ugliness – the mutilation and destruction of people and places – amongst the fragile flowers that nature silently but abundantly proffered in the stench, decay and squalor of the trenches. The sentiment was expressed many times over, but it is succinctly put in the following lines by R. E. Vernède, who was killed in action in 1917:

The sun's a red ball in the oak
And all the grass is grey with dew,
A while ago a blackbird spoke –
He didn't know the world's askew. . .

Strange that this bird sits there and sings
While we must only sit and plan –
Who are so much the higher things –
The murder of our fellow man. . .[3]

Or, as Edmund Blunden put it:

Bold great daisies' golden lights,
Bubbling roses' pinks and whites –
Such a gay carpet! poppies by the million;
Such damask! such vermilion!
But if you ask me, mate, the choice of colour
Is scarcely right; this red should have been duller.[4]

The early war poems had promoted patriotism, justice and principle. It is striking that there was this shift from principle to aesthetic response as the war progressed. It might be that it was the incessant closeness to blood, death and suffering that brought out these sentiments in men who had, on the whole, been raised in an education system that rejected such responses as feminine and unmasculine, and that promoted an abstract conception of justice and a stern morality of obedience to rules. If so, it could be that the impact of that experience parallels in a sharpened and intensified form the impact on women of the experience of child-bearing – a potent, personal experience that, however sanitised, brings a woman face-to-face with these three realities.

Again, as in the previous case, if this aesthetic response is accepted as especially characteristic of women's moral awareness, it can be argued that it is an important element to *incorporate* in any full account of the moral. It should be encompassed within, rather than competing against, any universal conception of morality.

These are, then, two ways in which women may, and probably do, see morality in a different light from the way men typically see it. This means that the first set of questions about facts mentioned at the outset can now be answered. Male and female do appear to diverge in certain identifiable and significant ways. The moral outlook a person has may – though this is, of course, only a statistical or average truth – depend on whether that person is male or female. But these ideals are not *necessarily* gender-relative. And indeed, it is the potential complementarity of the views that is their most striking feature.

But before turning to the central question of what ideals men and women *should* adopt, it is worth speculating a little about what it is that causes these observable differences of moral outlook. Answering *this* question involves reference to the second group of facts which were mentioned at the beginning of this discussion – facts about the systematic differences in the life-experience of women and men. Two main types of explanation are offered as accounting in these terms for the distinctive ways in which women and men approach moral questions: these are, first, predominantly biological explanations, and, second, predominantly social or cultural explanations. Differences, it is assumed, must either be biologically based, or they must be culturally induced, the result of education, upbringing and social pressure.

One important aspect of attributing differences to biology as opposed to attributing them to culture is that the second type of explanation leaves room for views to change, while the former appears to rule this out. This contrast may be more apparent than real, however, for new technologies of birth and reproduction may alter the biologically given so as to make possible a changed perspective that would have been inconceivable in the past. Anti-patriarchal utopias in which male power, if not man himself, has been eliminated, and in which women have created a new social structure, are convincingly depicted in feminist science-fiction, and advocated as social policy by some radical feminist writers (see, for example Firestone, 1971).

Both biological and cultural explanations, however, have sceptical implications as far as morality is concerned. If moral scepticism is to be avoided, then, it is important to appreciate both the scope and the limits of these sorts of explanation.

The Biological Thesis

This, which may also be called the socio-biological or 'geneticist' thesis, asserts that innate biological factors determine a person's morality. Thus, in the case of the sexes, it sees different moral qualities as part of male or female 'nature' – qualities and contrasts such as aggressiveness or docility; kindness or cruelty; selfishness or unselfishness; conscientiousness or carelessness. The thesis is essentially deterministic: we cannot escape from what our genes make of us. And so it considerably curtails the scope for morality, for it leads to such questions as: Why, if it is genetic factors that make people what they are, praise or blame them for what they do? Why not simply accept the way they – men and women – behave?

The Sociological Thesis

This is the thesis that it is social or cultural factors that determine a person's moral view – factors such as environment, upbringing and social context. Coupled with this factual thesis is the full-blooded relativist view that there *are* only these different views; that to talk about morality is to make reference to them; and that there is no fact-of-the-matter; no independent concept of right and wrong; of good and bad; of duty or responsibility.

Within this second type of explanation, two very different theses may be distinguished:

(i) the view that dominating differences are related to non-gender-related contrasts: for example, social class, economic structure, and a broad range of cultural factors.

(ii) the view that the salient and overriding cultural phenomenon *is* gender. This view, then, may be distinguished from the 'orthodox' sociological view for separate consideration: it is the patriarchy thesis.

The Patriarchy Thesis

This is the thesis that women's morality, which in certain vital respects, particularly in relation to sexual behaviour, often differs from men's, has been imposed on them by centuries of conditioning by men. It differs from the standard sociological thesis in that it regards the gender difference as the most fundamental and most fully explanatory division in human society. It holds that across *all* cultures and forms of social arrangement women have been kept in subservience to men.

In so far as there is this domination, it must be acknowledged that men have been aided in their domination of women by women themselves – sometimes older women, whose own conditioning has matured in conformity with that of men. In other words, men's moral requirements may not be imposed *directly* on women, but indirectly through the filter of female complicity. Recognising this paradox lends weight to the patriarchy thesis, explaining away many apparent counter-examples. For instance, if clitorectomy – often known as female circumcision – is a 'moral' requirement to serve male interests, it is nevertheless women who carry out, maintain and insist upon the practice, and it is women who express their moral offence if it is not carried out. This may lead those who would otherwise oppose the practice to defend it on cultural grounds. Because of its far-reaching effects on individual women's lives, however, it is difficult not to see it as, on the contrary, a potent example of the weakness of an orthodox relativist view – a view, that is, which attempts, incoherently, to maintain the equal validity of all moral perspectives. For many feminists resist the relativist conclusion in this case to demand that both women and men shake themselves free of their conditioning. This reveals a fundamental contrast between either biological or sociological determinism and the patriarchy thesis. Characteristically, the patriarchy thesis generates a revolutionary ideology rather than a fatalistic acceptance of determinism and relativism. It rejects the tyranny of local culture and regards even biological 'necessity' as manipulable. It results in an appeal, a call, to women to throw off the bonds of conditioning, to take freedom to control their own lives.

But it must be asked how far such autonomy is a realistic possibility. If there are some brute facts, perhaps social, but founded in biological difference, which separate the lives and experience of women from those of men, may these not continue ineluctably to affect the moral ideals they may hold? Is there something about woman's experience as a biological and social being that gives her a common identity and differentiates her forever from the male? Or are differences only superficially cultural? Was Margaret Mead (1935) right to see woman as 'an infinitely malleable clay figure upon which mankind has draped ever varying period-costumes'? And was Simone de Beauvoir (1972) justified in believing that, because women 'live dispersed among the males, attached through residence, housework, economic condition, and social standing to certain men – fathers or husbands – more firmly than they are to other women', they can have no common identity or history?

I want to suggest that whatever anthropological and economic truths are embodied in these and similar statements, the fact is that there are indeed certain systematic differences in the lives of women and of men, and that this fundamental contrast in life-experience does indeed account for and to some extent also justify a difference in their moral outlook and assumptions.

This is not simply a matter of those aspects of women's sexual lives that are so often cited in evidence as disqualifying women from running the affairs of nations, or even from running a small business: menstruation and premenstrual tension; conception, pregnancy and childbirth; lactation and child-care. These are important, but they are surface phenomena, overtly physical. What they connect with is a much deeper and more significant fact. This central fact is the fact of change, together with the problems of identity and self-concept that this generates. For women characteristically experience change in their lives in a way which is only experienced by a man if he is unfortunate enough to be the victim of some mutilating accident or illness. The horror depicted in Kafka's *Metamorphosis*, in which a man awakens to discover that he has become a large insect, invites comparison with the norms of women's existence – her passages from childhood to puberty, from mature womanhood to menopause and old age; her experience of pregnancy. Kafka's *Metamorphosis* begins with the following passage:

As Gregor Samsa awoke one morning from uneasy dreams he found himself transformed in his bed into a gigantic insect. He was lying on his hard, as it were armour-plated, back and when he lifted his head a little he could see his domelike brown belly divided into stiff arched segments on top of which the bed quilt could hardly keep in position and was about to slide off completely. His numerous legs, which were pitifully thin compared to the rest of his bulk, waved helplessly before his eyes.

What has happened to me? he thought. It was no dream. His room, a regular human bedroom, only rather too small, lay quiet between the four familiar walls.[5]

It is interesting to compare this with Sylvia Plath's poem about her own experience of pregnancy and child-bearing:

I am a mountain now, among mountainy women.
The doctors move among us as if our bigness
Frightened the mind. They smile like fools.

> They are to blame for what I am, and they know it –
> They hug their flatness like a kind of health.
> And what if they found themselves surprised, as I did?
> They would go mad with it.[6]

Pregnancy, however, is a relatively brief and dramatic bodily change, succeeded by reversion to something like the former state. As Plath later continues:

> I am not ugly. I am even beautiful.
> The mirror gives back a woman without deformity.
> The nurses give back my clothes, and an identity.[7]

This contrasts with the two major irreversible shifts of a woman's life, first to puberty, then to menopause. These not only cause a change in *self*-concept – the way a woman sees herself – but, more important, a change in the way she is perceived by other people. In vain she may cry, as Gregor Samsa does to his parents, sister and employer, that the same person is there inside, looking out in the same way at the world. The world *sees* a woman, in a way it does not see a man, as old or young, sexual or non-sexual, defining her frequently by nothing other than her biological role: mother, spouse, grandmother, widow. It is not surprising, then, that both the phases of major transition, as well as the experience of pregnancy and childbirth can bring mental disturbance and breakdown in their wake. These are rightly described as pressure-points in the lives of women.[8]

It would not be surprising, either, if this flux and change in the self were to generate a more flexible response to morality, and one that is peculiarly sensitive to the aesthetic dimension. Women's experience continually forces them to react to situations in which *all* the parameters have shifted. If one adds to this one other incontrovertible fact – that the overwhelming majority of women have lived their lives without economic freedom or autonomy, but as dependants or chattels lacking control over the crucial fixed aspects of their own lives – then it becomes clear that the chameleon nature of women is their necessary self-protection. As in the case of that animal, their clothes must fit their habitat, changing in response to external change. In this respect, a famously offensive passage by Rousseau on the education of girls may be seen as, after all, no more than realistic for period and place: recommending that girls be taught to break off games they are enjoying to return to work without complaint, he writes:

> This habitual restraint produces a docility which woman requires all her life long, for she will always be in subjection to a man, or to man's judgment, and she will never be free to set her own opinion above his. What is most wanted in a woman is gentleness; formed to obey a creature so imperfect as man, a creature often vicious and always faulty, she should early learn to submit to injustice and to suffer the wrongs inflicted on her by her husband without complaint. (Rousseau, 1762, trans., p. 333)

The 'masculine' goal of moral autonomy, then, has been no more in woman's grasp than it was within the grasp of the Stoic slave of ancient times. And just as the ethical perspective of Stoicism was shaped by the slave-status of some of its principal proponents, so the ethical perspective of women has evolved within a framework of powerlessness to affect external events – even the lives of her own children within the family structure – and powerlessness to resist the inexorable internal cycle of obtrusive biological change, with the social and economic concomitants of that change that are absent in the case of the more modulated maturing and ageing processes of men.

The conclusion to be drawn from these reflections is, I believe, that the ways in which women's lives differ from those of men are indeed morally significant. It may be that the effects of those significant differences can be mitigated by social change, and by education for mutual understanding. But because the weight of explanation is preponderantly biological rather than cultural or social, it may be that women's moral perspective will continue to be one which reflects a distinctive range of values.

The feminist goal must be the interweaving of those values, which have a richness, complexity and spontaneity lacking in more abstract conceptions, with the universalistic goals of traditional moral theory. In practice, this may mean as little as insisting on modest changes in decision-making procedures and modes of academic debate; or it may mean as much as the sacrifice of a whole way of life for activism in some major political cause. But if there is to be a new morality – new values for the new situation resulting from technological and political change in the closing years of the twentieth century – then the creation of that new morality must in the end be a joint enterprise of both women and men.

NOTES

1. See Kohlberg (1981), vol. 1, chs 4 and 9. The six stages are set out in an Appendix, pp. 409–12.
2. Gilligan (1977), p. 482. A revised version of this paper was subsequently published in Gilligan (1982).
3. From 'A Listening Post' in Gardner (ed.) (1964), p. 33.
4. From 'Vlamertinghe' in Gardner (ed.) (1964), p. 125.
5. In Kafka (1983), p. 89 (translated by Willa and Edwin Muir).
6. From 'Three Women' in Plath (1971), p. 44.
7. Ibid., p. 48.
8. See, for example, the studies of individual women in Scarf (1981).

REFERENCES

BEAUVOIR, Simone de (1972), *The Second Sex*, trans. H. M. Parshley (Harmondsworth: Penguin).

EISENSTEIN, Hester (1984), *Contemporary Feminist Thought* (London: Allen & Unwin).

FIRESTONE, Shulamith (1971), *The Dialectic of Sex: The Case for Feminist Revolution* (London: Jonathan Cape).

GARDNER, Brian (ed.) (1964), *Up the Line to Death: The War Poets 1914–1918* (London: Methuen).

GILLIGAN, Carol (1977), 'In a Different Voice: Women's Conceptions of Self and of Morality', *Harvard Education Review*, vol. 47, pp. 481–517.

GILLIGAN, Carol (1982), *In a Different Voice: Psychological Theory and Women's Development* (Cambridge, Mass: Harvard University Press).

HUME, David (1739), *Treatise of Human Nature*, ed. L. A. Selby-Bigge (Oxford: Oxford University Press, 1952).

KAFKA, Franz (1983), *The Penguin Complete Short Stories of Franz Kafka*, ed. Nahum N. Glatzer (London: Allen Lane).

KOHLBERG, Lawrence (1981), *Essays on Moral Development*, vol. 1: *The Philosophy of Moral Development* (San Francisco: Harper & Row).

McMILLAN, Carol (1982), *Women, Reason and Nature* (Oxford: Blackwell).

MEAD, Margaret (1935), *Sex and Temperament in Three Primitive Societies* (New York: William Morrow).

NOZICK, Robert (1974), *Anarchy, State and Utopia* (Oxford: Blackwell).

PLATH, Sylvia (1971), *Winter Trees* (London: Faber).

RAWLS, John (1972), *A Theory of Justice* (Oxford: Oxford University Press).

ROUSSEAU, Jean-Jacques (1762), *Emile*. English trans. B. Foxley (London: Dent, 1974).

SCARF, Maggie (1981), *Unfinished Business: Pressure Points in the Lives of Women* (London: Fontana).

WEINREICH-HASTE, Helen (1987), 'Engagement and Commitment: The Role of Affect in Moral Reasoning and Moral Responsibilities', in Wolfgang Edelstein and Gertrud Nunner-Winkler (eds), *Zur Bestimmung der Moral* (Cologne: Suhrkamp).

4

Autonomy and Pornography

Alison Assiter

There is a notion of autonomy implicit in some philosophical writing and including the work of Rousseau, Kant, Hegel and Marx. According to this conception, a person is autonomous if he or she subscribes to principles that have been formed by his or her own moral scrutiny. Integral to at least some of the philosophers' thinking is the idea that the individual is part of a collective; a member of society. For me to be autonomous, it is not sufficient that you leave me alone; rather the way I am treated by you has a bearing on my autonomy, and reciprocally for you.

In this paper, I shall defend a qualified version of autonomy along Kantian lines. I shall then show, by reference to the work of Kant and Hegel, how autonomy has been excluded from the private realm. Even Hegel, who apparently extends the notion of autonomy to the private domain does not really do so. Indeed, ironically, the relation between lovers turns out, for him, to involve the most extreme possible violation of autonomy; in fact, the relation between lovers turns out to fit a relation Hegel argues must be transcended – that between Master and Slave.

Against the thinking of these philosophers, I propose to defend the view that the individual should be treated as a rational, autonomous being in perhaps the most private of all domains – that of love-making. I shall support the view by means of a criticism of pornographic eroticism. Pornographic eroticism, I will argue, is, therefore, to be condemned, but it does not function in quite the way some feminists have argued that it does. Andrea Dworkin, in her book *Pornography: Men Possessing Women* (1981), argues that porn lies at the heart of male supremacy, of the oppression of women. I believe that this view is too strong, that, although porn does reinforce certain attitudes towards women, in the main, it is rather a symptom, and not a major part of the cause, of power

58

relations that exist outside the pages of *Penthouse, Playboy*, etc., and outside the cinemas in Soho or Amsterdam (see Moye, 1985).

A DEFENCE OF AUTONOMY

An autonomous person is one who is self-legislating and self-determining. The most common sort of violation of autonomy is paternalism – where the person is coerced into giving up some or all of it. At its most extreme, someone's capacity to choose which course of action to perform is removed from them. Thus, if a person is given a drug which gets rid of any resistance he/she might have had to being taken into captivity, then, in a very strong sense, his/her autonomy has been violated. But, in a slightly weaker sense, someone may lose their autonomy if the opportunity for them to exercise their capacity to choose is removed. Thus, a person who becomes a slave loses this opportunity. A particular sort of slavery, what we might call moral slavery, occurs if a person is forced to act according to someone else's moral values.

All the above types of violation of a person's autonomy involve what Kant described as treating the person as a means to someone else's end, and not as an end in themselves. We ought, he said, to 'treat humanity whether in your own person, or in the person of any other, never simply as a means, but always at the same time as an end' (Kant, 1948, para. 429).

Intuitively, we would judge these violations of a person's autonomy as wrong. Why? Kant argued that no one could voluntarily relinquish their autonomy without giving up their personhood. It is logically impossible, he argued, to contract to give up all one's rights, since such a contract would deprive the person of the ability to make any agreements at all. This argument has been questioned. One person who has done so recently is Arthur Kulfik (1984). He says:

> the argument falters on a temporal equivocation. Up to the moment that the contract is made, or more accurately is to take effect, the agent retains both his status as a person and whatever rights this entails, including the right to make a contract. Only after the contract takes effect does the agent (putatively) 'cease to be a person'. (p. 283)

I agree with Kuflik that it is not actually impossible to contract to give up one's autonomy, but I do not think, however, that Kant's argument can be so easily disposed of. Who, in their right mind, would voluntarily relinquish something that has as a consequence the loss of their personhood? Who, if they recognised and understood the consequences of their actions, would choose such a course? Perhaps only those for whom life itself had ceased to be worth living. Of course, if they didn't recognise the consequences, they might choose to do it, but this illustrates Kant's point. Even if a person did not know the consequences of giving up their autonomy, it is in fact these consequences which make the relinquishing of autonomy wrong.

It has been argued recently, however, (see Graham, 1982) that it must be rational for a person to give up their autonomy sometimes. One case often cited is that, for instance, it is rational to take orders from a competent doctor in a course of treatment. Another is that two people may have conflicting beliefs about which course of action to perform. Since it may not be possible for both sets of belief to be realised in action, if the courses of action are incompatible, it may be rational for one person to give up his/her autonomy.

As far as the first case is concerned, I take it that part of the process of rational reflection on a set of moral principles and courses of action for myself would involve consulting others (the experts, if you like). Deferring to a doctor is not in itself being coerced into accepting a view against one's will, thus this need not involve the loss of autonomy. As for the second type of case, something that Kant had to say may again be relevant. He argued that I should treat other people's wants and needs as constraints upon the satisfaction of my own. In other words, the rational being who is autonomously evaluating the most appropriate courses of action for him/herself must consider the wants, needs and interests of others. The non-satisfaction of my wants, needs etc., therefore, is not always a violation of my autonomy. Autonomy involves the right and the capacity to exercise choice and to make reasoned judgements, and not the capacity to have those judgements invariably realised in action. The dictator (to look at one of Keith Graham's examples) who allowed everyone to decide for themselves what they wanted and then told them what they must do, is violating their autonomy not because their wants and needs are not realised in action, but because they have been coerced into doing something they do not want. Thus autonomy is lost or renounced either if someone is coerced into thinking/acting against their will, or if a person is treated – perhaps willingly – as a means to the satisfaction of someone else's desires or ends.

There may conceivably be cases where it is all right for someone willingly to allow themselves to be treated as a means. If, for instance, I volunteered to give up some of my bone marrow to save a person suffering from leukaemia, then, so long as my own health was not in danger, there would seem to be nothing wrong with my momentarily relinquishing my autonomy. Perhaps, therefore, a distinction should be drawn between allowing oneself voluntarily, and where there is no danger to oneself, to be treated as a means to the satisfaction of someone else's *needs*, and being treated as a means to the satisfaction of someone else's desires. Only in the former case could a violation of autonomy conceivably be justified. Again, it might be argued that there can be nothing wrong for a person voluntarily to allow themselves to be treated as a means to the satisfaction of somone else's desires. If Justine, in the work of the eighteenth-century 'pornographer', the Marquis de Sade, willingly submitted, what is wrong with her allowing herself to be treated in whatever fashion her persecutors wanted? I shall argue, later, that such treatment is wrong, not necessarily *per se*, but for other reasons.

HEGEL AND LOVE-MAKING

Most philosophers who have defended autonomy have exempted the private realm from the domain of its operation. Kant, for instance, quite explicitly did this. He reduced wives, children and servants to the status of 'things' so far as their relation to husband/father in the family is concerned. He argued that the husband/father has the right to the possession of wife/children as 'things'. In other words, wives, in their marital relation to their husbands, were quite specifically treated by Kant as not autonomous. In their role as wives and lovers, then, women, for Kant, were viewed as means to the satisfaction of the man's needs and wants.

Ostensibly Hegel's view is different. In *The Philosophy of Right* he argues, against Kant, and others, that the sphere of operation of contractual relations is limited. Family life lies quite outside its domain. Hegel is adamant than human beings cannot be reduced to the status of 'things'. He argues, against Kant, that no one has the right to alienate their entire 'person' through a contract. He claims that rights arising from contract are never rights over a person, but only rights over something external to the person – for instance, that person's body. Kant, according to Hegel, forgets that there are some aspects of personality that cannot be alienated: for instance, 'my universal freedom of will, my ethical life, my religion' (para. 66). In marriage, Hegel argues, neither husband nor wife treats the other as his/her property.

Family members are linked through love. Morality, at this level, appears as something natural. Through love, the individual renounces his/her egoistic standpoint, and becomes united with the loved one. Individuals, through love, become real social beings, each identifying with and loving through the other. The love between man and wife, therefore, apparently presupposes man and wife treating one another as equal, autonomous beings. Each has to find him/herself partly through the other. In love, men and women are 'living subjects who are alike in power and thus in one another's eyes' (para. 62).

Apparently, then, Hegel is extending a notion of full autonomy to the sphere of love-making. Yet, on the other hand, and in tension with the foregoing, Hegel argues that, although the male does not 'own' wife or children, he is in control of family property. For legal purposes, the family is represented by its head: the father/husband. Moreover, it is also the father/husband's role in modern industrial society to go 'out' to work in the world outside. It is only the man who enters civil society (the 'public' sphere) and, in that world, he represents the other family members. Daughters and wives, by contrast, are expected to remain, throughout their lives, in the family network. Their activities have no direct economic significance.

Thus, although ostensibly the relation between husband and wife in love-making is a relation between equals, in fact it is not. The power of the father is not quite like that of the 'patriarch' in Filmer's *Patriarcha* (1680), yet his activities outside the home invest him with an importance which the wife does not have.

These powers will limit the extent to which men and women can be autonomous and equal in love-making. Moreover, Hegel explicitly distinguishes the 'natures' of the two sexes. Man is a creature of 'reason', woman is intuitive; man is 'powerful and active', woman passive and subjective (para. 166). In other words,

Hegel elevates some of the traits which characterise men as powerful masculine beings, women as feminine, to the status of differences in their natures.

Therefore, the appearance that the relation between husband and wife in love-making is one between equal autonomous partners, is an appearance only. In losing themselves in their partners, men and women are renouncing unequal qualities. The man has to give up some of his power; the woman must gain some. But this suggests that it is actually impossible for Hegel to realise what appears to be an ideal notion of the relationship between lovers. Losing oneself in the other when one party is more powerful than the other can only mean the one submitting to the other. Two wills becoming one, when the two wills were initially unequal can surely only mean the one will subordinating itself to the other. Thus, in the end, it looks as though Hegel's view of the relation between husband and wife in marriage is not very different from Kant's.

Indeed, although Hegel does not admit quite what I am now suggesting, he effectively concedes that, given the difference between the sexes, unity between them is impossible. 'Man has his "substantive life" in the State, in learning and so forth, whereas the "substantive destiny" of woman lies in the family' (para. 166 again).

In addition, Hegel restricts his discussion of love to that between husband and wife in marriage. It is only inside what is, in the end, a contractual relation, that 'love' can prevail. 'Love' therefore between a non-married man and woman, or between two men or two women would be impossible.

Rather than describing a relation between equals, Hegel's picture of love-making is very like his account of the relation between Master and Slave, in the Master–Slave dialectic, described in his *Phenomenology of Spirit*. This relation in fact, for Hegel, represents a stage to be overcome, in the evolution of spirit towards rational self-awareness.

Indeed, Kant and Hegel's accounts of the relation between man and wife in love-making are actually not far removed from a description of pornographic eroticism. The Master–Slave dialectic is an apt metaphor for the latter. Let us have a look at the passage to see how this might be.

THE MASTER–SLAVE RELATION

In this passage Hegel is asking the question: How do I become aware of myself as a self? He believes that 'desires' are important to the consciousness of our own existence. As people act on things because they want them – the child wants a teddy bear, or wants something to eat – they begin to gain a sense of themselves as distinct from those objects. Hegel, however, argues that we cannot be fully aware of ourselves, as selves, unless we are conscious of other people. Here he is on the importance of the view of 'the other' to one's sense of self: 'Self consciousness exists in and for itself, when, and by the fact that, it so exists for another; that is, it exists only in being acknowledged' (Hegel, 1979, p. 111).

Hegel suggests that we all aim to be recognised by others – wanting to be noticed by others, to be deemed worthy by others are traits we all have. Sometimes, indeed, we identify *with* another; instead of seeing ourselves as independent autonomous subjects, we identify with Lady Diana, our headmistress or somebody at work. But, says Hegel, if *my* identity lies outside myself – in my head of department, in my father – it is outside my control. Therefore, Hegel suggests, I – the jealous one – may set out to destroy the person in whom my 'self-hood' resides. Of course, few of us *really* set out to destroy someone of whom we are jealous; none the less Hegel is describing an extreme form of such a feeling. Taking it as far as it can be taken, Hegel suggests that the conflict between myself and the person in whom my identity resides will become a struggle between life and death, because, he says, it is only by risking one's life that one becomes fully aware of oneself as a free, autonomous individual. It is only when I realise how fragile my life as a human being is, by becoming aware of its limits, that I can become a fully free person. However, we must remember what we earlier quoted Hegel as saying: that the other person's attitude towards me is important for my sense of self-identity. So I must neither die myself, nor must I destroy the individual in whom my identity resides. Since we cannot go on struggling with one another indefinitely, Hegel says that one must submit to the other. The one who submits he calls the 'slave' and the one to whom that person submits him/herself becomes the 'master'. Thus we get Dependence and Independence of Self Consciousness: Master and Slave. Hegel believes that the 'Master–Slave dialectic' is a phase in the development of world history – in the progression towards freedom of the 'Spirit' that controls historical change. In fact, the relation is disadvantageous both for the slave and for the master. Indeed, he thinks that whereas the master fails to gain a proper sense of himself from the slave, because the slave merely carries out his (the master's) will, the slave *does* gain a certain degree of self-consciousness by means of the work he performs for the master.

It seems to me that this passage describes the way loving relationships turn out to be for Hegel. Ostensibly, the relation between man and wife, where they are linked by love, and that between Master and Slave, are very different. Yet, as I argued earlier, giving up one's identity to another who is more powerful can only mean submitting oneself to the other. In the end, the role of the wife in marriage is very like that of the Slave.

But the Master–Slave dialectic seems to capture the relation between people in pornographic eroticism. In much pornography, people, usually women, become objects for another. The philosopher Sartre believed that, in the act of love-making, the lover becomes at once subject and object – for she sees herself partly as the body desired by the lover. But then her identity is partly outside her control, so she tries to turn her lover into an object as well (Sartre, 1957, pt. III, ch. 3). In the case of pornography, what happens is that the one person becomes a body desired by the other, but this is not reciprocated. In much porn, the woman becomes the 'object' of male desire. She either involuntarily submits in this role (as does the woman on the pages of *Penthouse*) or she does it voluntarily, like de Sade's Justine or 'O' in the pornographic novel by Pauline Réage, *The Story of O*. In that story women are taken to a castle, where they are abused and tormented by men. 'O' is enslaved by her lover René, yet she voluntarily submits; she is represented as desiring subordination. Since the identity of the lover – the woman – becomes submerged in the other lover's desire for her/his body, one of the two may become afraid and want to kill the other. In a recent hard-core pornographic film from Denmark, the woman ends up killing the man. Throughout the film, it has been the man, the dominant male, who got the woman to act out his wishes and fantasies. The woman's killing the man seems metaphorical only, but it fits the present idea – that the one whose identity becomes submerged may want to kill the other. But sometimes, in porn, it is the dominant man who takes his domination to the extreme and kills the woman: in Norman Mailer's *The American Dream*, the woman – the slave – dies. De Sade said that if one wants to know about death one should look at sexual excitement. And Sigmund Freud, in *Beyond the Pleasure Principle*, described the 'drive to inorganicism' as 'the most radical form of the pleasure principle'. Sexuality affords us the opportunity of transgressing the barrier separating life from death.

But mostly, even in porn, the taboo against killing is upheld. Instead we have the Master–Slave relation: one person partly being seen as the body desired by the other, but where this is not reciprocated. Unlike Hegel's slave, however, who loses his subjectivity to the Master, the 'slave' in porn must retain some subjectivity or she will cease being desirable to the master. The subjectivity she has is as a subject who desires to be object – a subject who wants only to satisfy the wants of the Master.

Things ought not to be this way, in love-making, however. People ought to treat one another as people, as autonomous beings, in love-making, as elsewhere. One of the things wrong with porn, therefore, is that someone's – usually the woman's – autonomy is violated.

PORN AND FANTASY

Porn, however, involves fantasy. Often, in pornographic eroticism, there is no real love-making between people. One writer claims that the use to which the most heavily read porn[1] – *Penthouse*, *Playboy*, *Men Only* and *Mayfair* – is likely to be put, is as material for masturbatory fantasies (Moye, 1985, p. 53). What can be wrong with this?

Let us imagine ourselves as a reader of *Penthouse* in order to answer this question. In one picture in the centre pages of a copy of the magazine, a woman is smiling, relaxed; she stares erotically at her viewer. The viewer can lay aside, in his fantasy relation to this woman, the difficult, complex emotions he will experience in any actual relationship with a real woman, and concentrate upon his own desire. He can picture the woman to whom he is relating, as uncomplicatedly wanting him, her desire being to satisfy his. Thus to use the contemporary philosopher Richard Wollheim's (1985) analogy of the mind as a theatre, he is, in his fantasy, an actor in a play that he has written, and she – the woman on the page – is in it too, as his adoring lover, his woman who is totally fixated upon him. The woman represented on the pages of *Penthouse* is depicted, as I have said, as a subject who desires to be object: she appears to want just to satisfy the desire of the man who gazes at her as he masturbates. What can be wrong, however, with fantasising, treating a woman as an object, if there is no connection between the fantasy and real life and if she is depicted as wanting to be treated this way?

Wollheim, as I have mentioned, depicts the mind as a theatre. In the theatre, he argues, there is (a) an internal dramatist – who makes up the characters and their actions; (b) an internal actor – who represents to the reader for his benefit the actions he has made up as dramatist; and, finally, (c) an internal audience. After the fantasy performance, we, the individuals doing the fantasising, are left with some reactions to our fantasy. The first type of link between the fantasy representation and the world outside is that the fantasy materials – the characters in the play and their actions – are drawn from real life. Even novels which appear to be furthest removed from the lives of those who wrote them – the work of Kafka, of Lewis Carroll, of the contemporary feminist writer Marge Piercy – have drawn on the real life surroundings of their authors. And there is a particularly close connection in the case we are considering. The fantasy relation between reader and text, in the case of a man reading *Playboy*, is more like the relation between consumer and a realist novel than it is like that between reader and the text of Kafka.

But this is obviously not sufficient reason for us to condemn the porn. The fantasy had by the reader of *Penthouse* may not involve any beliefs that real women behave as he imagines the woman on the page does. So what grounds are there for condemning the porn?

Part of the grounds are the following. The evidence for a causal connection between reading pornographic material and committing violent acts against women is inconclusive (Williams, 1979). But even if there is not *this* causal connection, the fantasy does have *a* causal effect. Returning to Wollheim's analogy: when the reader of the porn performs, as internal actor, his fantasy, he is left, as internal audience, in a state that simulates the state he would be in if he had *actually* had a relationship with a woman like the imagined one. The reader of *Penthouse* is left feeling pleasure. And this, as once again Wollheim argues, though it may not lead to action like that in the representation, acts as a lure to the formation of fresh dispositions to act – of fresh desires. In other words, the representation of the desire as pleasurably satisfied, reinforces the desire. Thus pornographic representations are to be condemned because they reinforce the desires to treat people, and it is usually *women*, in the way I have been arguing they are treated. The fantasy desire on the part of a man, to have a woman adoring him, and to have her interested only in satisfying his desires, reinforces such desires in him. And such desires, as I have argued, involve treating women as means, and not as ends in themselves. Such desires may involve coercing the woman into behaving in the way the man wants her to. Even if the desire is *never* satisfied in any but the fantasy way, the man who constantly has such desires is to be condemned, for he is gaining satisfaction from a person whom he has divested of personhood and turned into a slave. Because he is constantly having desires for these partial relationships satisfied, he is less likely to seek out non-distorting, non-partial relationships in the rest of his life.

Thus a full description of what is wrong with pornography is that it reinforces desires on the part of men to treat women as objects, as means, and thus, indirectly, it reinforces male power. Though the woman depicted on the pages of the magazines may be represented as wanting to be treated as a means, this type of depiction of women is commonplace, and is one of the major expressions of women's oppression. Thus, no one should be treated purely as a means anyway. But, additionally in the case of porn, treating women this way has the consequence of reinforcing male power. Not treating women as autonomous, in pornographic love-making, has the consequence of reinforcing women's subordination.

Pornography is not, as Dworkin (1981) suggests it is, the main causal agent of women's subordination, because it is merely one case of a phenomenon that is commonplace: women have been treated as objects throughout history. In much Greek thought, women were represented as being closer to nature than men; their role in reproduction connected them to nature's fertility. Being closer to nature, they are more like objects than human beings. In the courtly love tradition, the woman was put on a pedestal – objectified. Such a conception of women has continued down the centuries.

If fantasy depictions of others are likely to have consequences for one's behaviour outside the fantasy, then so are *real* ways of treating the other in love-making. Thus, a man's not treating a woman as autonomous in love-making is likely to have consequences for the way he treats her elsewhere.

Before concluding, I would like to raise a couple of objections to the view I am advocating.

SOME OBJECTIONS CONSIDERED

First of all, it might be argued that there is no reason why the man should treat the woman, in fantasy, in the way that I've described. Why should he not view her as a fully rounded subject, with wants and desires of her own? Part of the answer is surely just the way in which the woman on the page is presented. She appears, somehow, just as a woman whose main desire is to satisfy the wants of the one who gazes at her. But, additionally, pornographic magazines are bought and sold. In other words, once the magazine has come into his possession, the man as it were acquires the right to treat the images on its pages in whichever way he chooses. Thus he is able to treat the woman as infinitely desirous of sex, as wanting nothing so much as to satisfy his desires.

A second objection that will be brought is that it is odd to treat another as a rational being, in the Kantian sense, in erotic relations, of all places. It will be objected that love-making necessarily includes an irrational, a Dionysian, element that is obscured by what I am saying at the moment. I would argue, however, that love-making ought not to be treated as drawing only on the irrational side of a person's nature. Part of the process of treating another well, in love-making, is attempting to satisfy her/his desires, and this, of necessity, involves the ability to recognise them. In turn, this presupposes treating the other as a person, as, at least partly, a rational being. So, although there is an irrational element to eroticism, it ought, I am arguing, not to be so irrational a process as to violate the other's autonomy.

Thirdly, the criticism might be made that the distinction I earlier drew (in the section on 'Autonomy') – between someone voluntarily being treated as a means to the satisfaction of another's needs, and their being treated as a means to the satisfaction of another's desires – is not adequate here. The man reading *Playboy* will argue that he has a need for it. This suggests, I think, that I must refine my earlier criterion in the following way: it is wrong for a person to be treated as a means to the satisfaction of another's desire, and only allowable for them to be treated, with their consent, as a means to the satisfaction of another's needs, if no other means for their satisfaction can be made available. The need to read *Playboy* is of a different order from the need for my bone marrow – in the latter case, it is assumed, at the present level of development of medicine, that no alternative is possible while, in the former, it is much easier to produce alternative means (including other sorts of magazines). Indeed the former is a matter of life and death, while the latter is not.

CONCLUSION

In this paper, I have argued that, contrary to the thinking of some of the major representatives of the tradition which distinguishes the public world from the private one, the notion of autonomy ought to be extended to the private sphere. Part of what is wrong with pornographic eroticism, where people are not treated as autonomous, is that it reinforces men's desires to treat women as means, as objects, in areas of their lives other than the erotic. By excluding love-making from the sphere of operation of the notion of autonomy, Kant and Hegel were limiting its scope in the 'public' realm. What goes on inside the family, even in the most private of all relations between human beings, has effects outside the family.

NOTE

1. See Williams (1979).

REFERENCES

CARTER, Angela (1979), *The Sadeian Woman* (London: Virago).
DWORKIN, Andrea (1981), *Pornography: Men Possessing Women* (London: The Women's Press).
GRAHAM, Keith (1982), 'Democracy and the Autonomous Moral Agent', in Keith Graham (ed.), *Contemporary Political Philosophy* (Cambridge: Cambridge University Press), pp. 113–37.
GRIFFIN, Susan (1981), *Pornography and Silence: Culture's Revenge against Nature* (London: The Women's Press).
HEGEL, G. F. W. (1967), *The Philosophy of Right*, trans. T. M. Knox (Oxford: Oxford University Press).
HEGEL, G. F. W. (1979), *The Phenomenology of Spirit*, trans. A. V. Miller (Oxford: Oxford University Press).
KANT, Immanuel (1948) see H. J. PATON.

KULFIK, Arthur (1984), 'The Independence of Autonomy', *Philosophy and Public Affairs*, vol. 13, no. 4, pp. 271–99.

LLOYD, Genevieve (1984), *The Man of Reason: 'Male' and 'Female' in Western Philosophy* (London: Methuen).

MARX, Karl (1970), *Economic and Philosophic Manuscripts of 1844*, ed. Dirk J. Struik, trans. Martin Milligan (London: Lawrence & Wishart).

MARX, Karl and ENGELS, Friedrich (1965), *The German Ideology*, trans. C. Dutt *et al.* (London: Lawrence & Wishart).

MOYE, Andy (1985), 'Pornography', in Andy Metcalfe and Martin Humphries (eds), *The Sexuality of Men* (London: Pluto Press), pp. 44–70.

PATON, H. J. (ed. and trans.) (1948), *The Moral Law: Kant's Groundwork of the Metaphysic of Morals* (London: Hutchinson).

ROUSSEAU, Jean-Jacques (1969), *The Social Contract*, trans. Maurice Cranston (Harmondsworth: Penguin).

SARTRE, Jean-Paul (1957), *Being and Nothingness: An Essay on Phenomenological Ontology*, trans. Hazel E. Barnes (London: Methuen).

WILLIAMS, Bernard (1979), *Report of the Committee on Obscenity and Film Censorship* (The Williams Report), Cmnd 7772 (London: HMSO).

WOLLHEIM, Richard (1985), *The Thread of Life* (Cambridge: Cambridge University Press).

5

The Philosopher's Child

Judith Hughes

SOME OF OUR CHILDREN ARE MISSING

Children have served philosophy very well. That is the first thing which anyone surveying the literature would notice. Along with a selection from a list including women, animals, madmen, foreigners, slaves, patients and imbeciles, children have served in that great class of beings, the 'not-men', in contrast with which male philosophers have defined and valued themselves. Unlike the others who appear and disappear as fashion and progress dictate, children occupy a permanent place in the list partly because of their continuing presence as a potential sub-class, partly because they have never protested and mainly because it is assumed that in favourable circumstances they will become men and therefore require attention. They have received it in the shape of detailed educational theory carefully worked out to see them through the maturation process from infancy to adulthood. Generations of philosophers have documented this process. Perhaps the best known version is Shakespeare's seven ages of man which is a poetic statement of what had already been received wisdom for centuries and was to remain so for centuries to come. Education was to guide the infant through the transition to manhood including such stages as childhood, boyhood and youth. That is the second thing to notice; the philosopher's children are boys. The fact that at least half of the world's children would not actually go through this process beyond the first two stages is conveniently forgotten or ignored and, no doubt, the reasons for this were largely social. But the neglect of girl children through the centuries of theorising is more than a social injustice, though many might think this real and bad enough.

Education has an end. Although it is fashionable to talk about its value 'for its own sake', what prompts the theorising is the strong and well-founded belief that the experiences of childhood affect the kind of adult which the child turns out to be. Where the end is

72

person- rather than role-oriented – that is, where the end is the development of the human mind and spirit rather than the production of, say, information technologists – then education is valued in relation to some conception of worthwhile human existence which it is meant to serve. Such an ideal does not stand isolated from the practices which strive towards it but interacts with those practices, helps to construct them, and is in turn constructed by them.

The great philosophers have always produced such a person-oriented account at least for those whose education was thought to matter. Education has been directed at the production of the rational, the free, the independent of mind, the dignified, in short, the autonomous human being. Yet because the philosopher's adult has traditionally been male, his children boy children, and his educational programmes designed to facilitate the transition between them, the ideal of the fully human person has been masculinised to the point where otherwise thoughtful and sometimes good and wise men have unashamedly admitted that this defining ideal is not applicable to half the species. Rationality turns into narrow intellectualism, freedom into licence, independence into isolationism, dignity into selfish pride; the autonomous human being turns out to be no more than a social atom after all.

The degeneration occurs, not because men are congenitally or even incorrigibly narrow, libertine, isolated or selfish, but because in defining themselves as autonomous beings in opposition to other human beings they have had to seek what separates them as a group from others. It is a curiously paradoxical foundation upon which to build a theory of autonomy. Moral autonomy is concerned with individuals not with groups; a conception of autonomy which depends upon group membership displays its own contradiction.

This paper is partly about the rejection of certain accounts of autonomy though not with the rejection of the ideal of autonomy itself. It is also about children.

WOMEN PHILOSOPHERS AND GIRL CHILDREN

Why should women in general and women philosophers in particular be specially interested in the nature and status of children? There are, of course, the familiar and obvious reasons connected with women's traditional role in child-rearing but there are less obvious reasons too. When philosophers dismiss women as 'not-men' they frequently do more than simply lump them together with children or lunatics. Explicitly or implicitly the suggestion is that women *are* children or lunatics or whichever other company they keep. It would be well to know just what this entails. Schopenhauer said that women remain big children all their lives; it would be interesting to know what he thought children were like. A common result of this is that when the philosophers deny autonomy to women, they do so for the same sorts of reason that they deny it to children and cite lack of rationality, capriciousness and vulnerability among their characteristics. We can do more than to reject such descriptions of ourselves; we can ask further questions: are children like this? is this why children are not autonomous?

Again, women well know what it is like to be treated as children and they find it offensive. It would therefore be reasonable to consider whether children find it offensive to be treated like children. Is being treated as a child an intrinsically humiliating and self-denying experience? What is it to be treated as a child? Women philosophers are in a special position to consider such questions for in the image of the philosopher's child they see themselves. It is no accident that the liberation of women, such as it is, should form part of a wider movement of liberation in general; liberation for one part of the 'not-men' is bound to have a knock-on effect when your fellow groups are sometimes quite literally identified with you.

The assumption that all groups in the 'not-men' class are identical with each other is so firmly rooted that, as we shall see in the fourth section, it is readily assumed even by modern libertarian thinkers that showing that, for example, some ground for distinguishing between men and women is false or irrelevant, immediately commits us to the view that the same ground is irrelevant in distinguishing men from children. 'That's what they used to say about women' is not a proof that saying it about a child is false. But it should make us very suspicious. That when women are given the vote it follows that children should be given it too is no argument at all, but a version of it occurs in modern debates over the justice or injustice of Mill's famous disclaimer in his essay *On Liberty*. Having denied that we may ever legitimately interfere with the liberty of another except on the grounds of self-protection, Mill (1910) asserts:

this principle is meant to apply only to human beings in the maturity of their faculties. We are not speaking of children or of young persons below the age which the law may fix as that of manhood or womanhood. Those who are still in a state to require being taken care of by others must be protected against their own actions as well as against external injury. (p. 73)

This view, as we shall see, has been attacked on the grounds that it rests on the false assumption that the distinction between adults and children is identical with the distinction between rational and non-rational beings. The attacks are based on empirical observation; most women and older children are actually quite as rational as most men while some men are actually less rational. If we agree that in that case women should be embraced by the liberty principle then so should children. I shall suggest that this does not follow because rationality is not in fact the grounds for the distinction in the first place.

Partly to redress the balance and partly because talking about 'children' covers such a wide range of potential images, I shall try to keep before my mind an ordinary 10-year-old of our society. She is the child of this paper unless I indicate otherwise. Throughout we should ask ourselves, does *this* (whatever is being said) apply to *her*? First of all, let us remind ourselves of the traditional picture of children drawn for us by some great philosophers of the past. One thing they are all quite sure about is that children are not like adults; in particular they agree that children lack some capacity for rational thought which adults have.

NOW WE ARE 6 – OR 10 – OR 18 . . .

the slave has absolutely no deliberative faculty; the woman has but its authority is imperfect; so has the child, but in this case it is immature. (Aristotle, 1959, 1260A)

Children . . . are not endued with Reason at all, till they have attained the use of speech but are called Reasonable Creatures for the possibility apparent of having the use of Reason in time to come. (Hobbes, 1914, p. 21)

[Children] . . . love to be treated as Rational Creatures sooner than is imagined . . . [by which] . . . I mean, that you should

make them sensible by the Mildness of your carriage, and the
composure even in your correction of them, that what you do is
reasonable in you and useful and necessary for them.

(Locke, 1968, p. 181)

In training for youth, the child must be given reasons; in the
training of the infant for childhood this cannot be done. Young
children ought merely to have things shown to them as they are,
or they get puzzled and ask question after question. But as we
approach the age of youth reason appears. At what age ought the
education for youth to begin? Roughly at the age of ten years,
when by nature the child enters the stage of youth and begins
to reflect . . . The youth . . . is capable of having principles; his
religious and moral ideas can be cultivated, and he is able to
attend to his own refinement.   (Kant, 1930, pp. 250–1)

If a society lets any considerable number of its members grow up
mere children, incapable of being acted on by rational
consideration of distant motives, society has itself to blame for the
consequences.   (Mill, 1910, p. 139)

What are the philosophers' children like? They have an
'immature' deliberative faculty (Aristotle), are not 'endued with
Reason' (Hobbes), until roughly the age of 10 (Kant) and are
'incapable of being acted upon by rational consideration of distant
motives' (Mill). But they are not completely lost causes. The
immature deliberative faculty will mature; children have the
'possibility apparent' of turning into rational beings (Hobbes); they
love to be treated as though they were rational though they are not
so yet (Locke); you can give the prerational child reasons for acting
in certain ways and he will turn into the youth who is capable of
having principles (Kant). Until the time when these things happen
then Mill's disclaimer comes into operation. Children must be taken
care of by others and protected from external injury and against
their own actions.

The traditional view is encapsulated in the claim that children are
not autonomous; that is, on a standard interpretation, they lack the
capacity to act rationally in pursuit of their own self-chosen goals. It
is then a matter of preference whether you say that they cannot
choose the goals or that they cannot form strategies to achieve them
or both. In either case, the political implication is that denying rights

to children is entirely justified, and there the matter rests. In all this, there are perhaps a couple of things which look plausible when we compare the philosopher's child with our mental picture; Aristotle's observation that children are immature and Mill's suggestion that they might need protection. Beyond that, the similarities seem remote.

There is obviously something wrong with a portrayal of children as totally lacking in reason until they leap out of bed on their tenth birthday announcing that they are now able to act on principle. Apart from being false, such an account leaves no room in our thinking about children for things like teaching and learning, or development in understanding and character and all those other concepts which refer to processes and not to states. The tension between these theoretical views of children as non-rational, non-autonomous beings and the practical knowledge of real children is evident in those quotations from Hobbes and Locke and Kant and Mill.

Children, according to Hobbes, have the 'possibility apparent' of becoming reasonable. In what does the possibility consist? Hobbes is not using an inductive argument here; the 'possibility apparent' is not an inductive argument from observations about past children but is meant to refer to some discernible feature of present ones. But what? Hobbes does not tell us, but whatever it is it had better be something which a monkey does not have. It is not language since Hobbes is here talking about the prelinguistic child. Perhaps it consists in the ability to respond intelligently to the language of others. But then, either Hobbes has failed to distinguish the child from at least the higher and domesticated animals or the force of 'intelligently' must be explained in such a way as to exclude animals. In any case, if such a qualification is called for it is hard to see how a creature with no rationality at all could possess it.

Locke's remarks are just as puzzling. Children are definitely not rational but love to be treated as if they were. How is this possible? Apparently they like having things explained to them without understanding either the explanation or even what an explanation is. Perhaps he just means that they like the sound of my voice? Well, maybe they do, but making any old noises is clearly not sufficient to enter the rationality stakes; I must at least *say* something. Is it just that I talk to them that they love? Maybe, but I can also, if I like, talk to my car, but yelling at it in the approved Basil Fawlty manner is hardly treating it as rational. Lockean children have the added amazing ability to recognise reason in you without possessing any themselves, while Kantian kids, two stages back from rationality, have the disconcerting habit of getting puzzled and asking questions.

Mill's minors are a little more complicated. Part of the time he sees them in the familiar way as creatures who lack rationality to at least some degree. But in the disclaimer his children need above all to be protected from the ghastly consequences of their own actions. Their problem seems to be not one of the inability to choose goals or to form strategies for achieving them, but an incorrigible propensity to choose the wrong ones and an awesome efficiency in achieving them unless adults intervene.

All in all, it is a pretty unconvincing picture. If you say that children are completely non-rational then you have to account for the fact that they become rational, and to do that it appears from these examples that you have to assume that they already are. If, on the other hand, you allow rationality to children, then you cannot use their lack of it as a criterion to distinguish them from adults. Hobbes *et al.* are not aware of the unreality of their original pictures which is why, often in the same sentence, they produce these contradictions. The one thing they do not do is to re-examine the original for the tell-tale signs of forgery.

ILLEGITIMATE INFERENCES

The recognition that children cannot simply be written off in the rationality stakes and cannot therefore be denied autonomy on this account has led some writers to conclude that they cannot, therefore, be denied it on any account. We should notice that this view is not just a flight of fancy from the loony left, the pederast lobby or children themselves. It is also to be found in stronger or weaker versions of more cautious academic thought.

In *Escape from Childhood* (1974), John Holt notes that children are, in fact, capable of a great deal more than modern society allows them to be. He sees childhood as a fairly modern invention designed to fit adult rather than children's needs, and an oppressive invention at that. He suggests that children should be given a comprehensive range of civil and legal rights including the right to vote, to manage their own financial affairs, to direct and manage their own education and to control their own sex lives and to make and enter into, on a basis of mutual consent, quasi-familial relationships outside one's immediate family – i.e. the right to seek and choose guardians other than one's own parents and to be legally dependent on them. (Holt, 1974, p. 16)

This is also the view put forward by John Harris, though in less specific terms. Like Holt, Harris believes that the so-called incompetence of children is an adult invention imposed on children for adults' convenience. He makes a firm proposal that the age of majority should be gradually reduced to 10 years, and remarks:

We must remember that to deny someone control of their own lives is to offer them a most profound insult, not to mention the injury which the frustration of their wishes and the setting at naught of their own plans for themselves will add. Perhaps we should conduct annual examinations from an early age to be sure that we do as little of this sort of damage as possible?
(Harris, 1982, p. 49)

Now Holt and Harris both have many wise, enlightened and humane observations to make about some of the injustices which we inflict upon children, but as these remarks show, putting them right without inflicting equally grave injustice is no easy matter. Both of them appear to suffer from a form of mental myopia in imagining the consequences of such proposals, and I am not here referring only to Mill-type consequences of harm brought about by unwise decisions.

What, we may ask Holt, happens to the child who, dissatisfied at home, seeks in vain for guardians who would suit him? What if no one wants him? Our papers are currently full of 'hard-to-place' children in local authority care advertising for foster or adoptive parents. In such a situation the skilled care of social workers is crucial to ensuring that an unwanted by-product of success for some children is not the total destruction of self-esteem for others. What, we may ask Harris, happens to the child who repeatedly fails his annual examination? To impose such a test on children would be a particularly invidious way of discriminating against them, unless Harris has in mind that we should all undergo such examination. He might then be open to bitter objections from many adults. These two suggestions, far from being enlightened liberation of all children, are actually oppression of a deeply damaging kind to at least some, and Harris's suggestion contains a capacity criterion in disguise.

In any case, it would be dishonest to pretend that Mill-type consequences are not relevant here. Suppose Holt's 6-year-old does opt out of school? What happens to her then? What happens if her father is unwilling or unable to stay at home with her? Is it any better to oblige her to go abseiling or butterfly-catching instead? However much she may enjoy such pursuits, there will be times when she would actually rather wander the streets unaccompanied. Given that Holt is presumably not volunteering himself to take care of her, who will? His view that letting children run in and out of busy airports smartly avoiding the traffic is perfectly reasonable depends upon a conception of a child which is far narrower than even the sex divide. Holt's child is actually the Artful Dodger; mercifully, not all children are.

There are other difficulties too. It is not clear whether or not Harris thinks that children of 10 should be obliged to take on full political status whether or not they want to, but Holt clearly does not. He proposes that 'the rights, privileges, duties, responsibilities of adult citizens be made *available* to any young person, of whatever age, who wants to make use of them' (Holt, 1974, p. 15). If Holt thinks that this proposal would remove an arbitrary boundary line between adults and children, then he is mistaken.

The point about an adult citizen is that he has these rights, privileges, duties and responsibilities whether or not he wants them. He may not exercise his rights or he may shirk his duties, but he cannot forgo them. They are not just *available* to him, they are his. That is what being a citizen involves. Rights and privileges do not pose any particular problems in the case of children. Holt can and does believe that children should have them as adults do, and then leaves it up to the child to decide whether or not to exercise them. But the same cannot be said for duties and responsibilities. Failure to exercise one's rights may be morally neutral; failure to carry out one's duties is not. It would be perfectly possible to give the rights to children without imposing the duties on them, the one does not entail the other, but we would then still be distinguishing between adults and children as citizens. Children still would not have full political status. Duties and responsibilities are not merely *available* to a citizen; they are an integral part of being a citizen. Holt does not want children to be obliged to take on any of these responsibilities and he manages to make his point by concentrating solely on the rights so that he can remark:

> I do not say, either, that these rights and duties should be tied into one package, that if a young person wants to assume any of them, he must assume them all. He should be able to pick and choose.
> (Holt, 1974, p. 16)

If he can 'pick and choose', I suggest, he is not a citizen, he does not have full political status and he is quite distinguishable on these grounds alone from the adults around him who do not have this option.

Holt and Harris both, in the end, face the same problem. They attack the status quo by pointing out that the reasons given for denying rights to children are *bad* reasons, and then explicitly or implicitly deny them duties for no reason at all. Whatever else such a strategy may achieve, it certainly does not manage to produce a situation in which children are politically indistinguishable from adults and it rests on premises which, unless they can be defended, gain nothing for any defence to the charge of arbitrariness.

WHEN IN DOUBT, GO BACK TO ARISTOTLE

The trouble with all the views which we have looked at is that they tie the notion of autonomy firmly and solely to that of knowledge interpreted in either a broad or narrow sense.[1] That it is firmly tied must be correct; the inhabitants of Brave New World are not autonomous precisely because they are denied access to relevant information. Relevant knowledge is a precondition of autonomy but it is not synonymous with it.[2]

Aristotle said something very interesting in that extract from the *Politics* which I quoted earlier; he said that women have a deliberative faculty but that it lacks full authority. What did he mean?

What he did not mean is that women lack rationality; they can and do deliberate. At first sight what he seems to be saying is simply that no one is going to take any notice of the conclusions which a rational woman reaches after deliberation. On further reflection, I think this is exactly what he is saying, and its significance is immense. His

view is that the judgements which women make have no standing.
Keeping to the domestic front for the moment, what this means is
that the conclusions which women reach, no matter how carefully
and intelligently they are worked out, can never have the status of
decisions. You cannot decide, though you may desire, to divorce
your husband if the law does not allow; you cannot order the wine if
only his signature makes the order legitimate. And your inability to
decide or to order has nothing to do with your mental powers. But
Aristotle is not just making a sociological point about what is and is
not permitted to women in his society. His remark goes deeper than
that. It refers not to power but to authority, and what I think he
means is that although a woman can make good and wise
judgements, she cannot be the arbiter of that goodness or wisdom.
For that she needs the ratification of men, and that is enough to
conclude that her judgements lack authority. Now that is quite
different from saying that women always make *bad* judgements,
that is to say, that they suffer from some deficiency of rationality.
Aristotle only produces spurious suggestions about a woman's
incapacity to think or to stick to principles when he is obliged to say
something about *why* their judgements lack authority. It then looks
as though the argument runs:

> (1) Women lack some moral or cognitive capacity
therefore (2) Women (must) lack authority.

In truth this version is the argument on its head; its real form is:

> (1) Women lack authority
therefore (2) Women (must) lack some moral or cognitive capacity.

The important point here is that Aristotle's women are not
autonomous, not because they lack abilities or capacities but
because they lack authority; that is, their right to make decisions, to
speak for themselves is not acknowledged. This acknowledgement
is absolutely essential, for without it no mental act which they
perform, however well, will count as a decision at all.

The point I am making here is based on an observation by Stanley
Cavell (1979, p. 460) and repeated by him in many contexts: 'a
human being could not fail to know, confronting me, that I am a
human being'. Why not? Because to see someone is to see them as a
human being and to see them as a human being is to acknowledge
them as such. This acknowledgement is not derived from a prior
knowledge of facts, rather it is a precondition of there being any

facts. We do not, on the Cavell model, first discover certain truths about an object and then conclude that it is a person; we first acknowledge the person and only inquire into facts later if necessary. The point was put graphically by my colleague, Ian Ground. Faced with a row of objects we do not, he said, lampooning Wittgenstein, perform appropriately by pointing to one after the other saying that's a tree, that's a tree, that's a man, that's a tree. Rather we will say (pointing) that's a tree, (pointing) that's a tree, (waving) hello! (pointing) that's a tree. What makes us *greet* the man is not an albeit swift chain of inference, it is his presence which commands the acknowledgement while the presence of the tree does no such thing. Of course, if the man is clearly carved from stone then pointing is in order, and if we subsequently discover that 'he' is an inflatable rubber doll we are suitably embarrassed. But we are embarrassed because we got it wrong when usually we do not. In our viewing of the other we see ourselves being viewed; the recognition is mutual.

How then is it possible to withhold acknowledgement? Cavell's answer is that it is not. There is no way of seeing another human being except as another human being. In a poignant discussion of the hypothesis that Southern slave owners did not see their slaves as human beings he disagrees:

> When he wants to be served at table by a black hand, he would not be satisfied to be served by a black paw . . . Everything in his relation to his slaves shows that he treats them as more or less human – his humiliations of them, his disappointments, his jealousies, his fears, his punishments, his attachments.
>
> (Cavell, 1979, p. 376)

Treating people as if they were not people is not a possibility; to try to do so requires all the resources of evil which the human mind can muster, but it always breaks down.

What is possible is to treat people as more or less human. We can withhold acknowledgement from them on limited or selective fronts. This may not be downright evil, but in the absence of potential disbarments (like possibly being a rubber doll) it requires a considerable amount of bad faith. It is very *hard* to do. This is what Aristotle appears to do to his women. They are human, and are acknowledged to be, they can think but they are not to be acknowledged as authoritative, and if their presence demands such acknowledgement, they are bad women who should have been taught to hide or repress such demands. Rousseau's blueprint for the education of Sophie is directed at this end, and if it is truly successful, she will internalise the lesson until neither her behaviour nor her demeanour will demand the acknowledgement. Then she has been infantilised and she is no longer autonomous. But Rousseau's blueprint contains its own contradiction. If you need to teach people or compel them in some other way to repress their natural demand for acknowledgement as rational, competent, authoritative human beings then you have no answer to the charge of some malefaction between bad faith and dreadful wickedness.

Is this unfair to children? When we deny autonomy to our 10-year-old, are we too guilty of bad faith? What reason could we produce to allow that she may have the capacity to act autonomously while denying her the capacity-to-act-autonomously? Whatever it is we should first notice that while the capacity to act autonomously is construed as a psychological capacity, the capacity-to-act-autonomously is not. It is a social capacity which depends upon the acknowledgement of others. What we need to do is to show that withholding this acknowledgement is neither arbitrary nor unjust; we have to ask, does her being demand it.

CARRYING THE CAN

To do this we need to consider another element in the picture of autonomy which was so meticulously side-stepped by Holt. That is, the matter of responsibility. In *Freedom and Resentment* (1974, p. 19) Strawson talks not of a child's emerging autonomy but of 'the progressive emergence of the child as a responsible being'. Responsibility is an aspect of autonomy to which lip-service is commonly paid but which takes a back seat in most discussions about children. I believe it to be central.

In his essay, 'In Defense of Anarchism' (1970), R. P. Wolff does give responsibility a central place in his brief analysis of autonomy. He argues that freedom of choice makes a man responsible for his actions while the capacity to reason about those choices places him under a continuing obligation to *take* responsibility for those actions. To *take* responsibility is to accept the duty of deciding for oneself what is right. A man, Wolff argues, can forfeit his autonomy by not *taking* the responsibility on himself; by, for example, obeying commands blindly; but he cannot abnegate the responsibility which the possibility of choice confers upon him. Since being autonomous includes both freedom of choice and the capacity to reason about those choices, the impairment of either is a bar to autonomy.

Against this background he makes two remarks about children:

> It is quite appropriate that moral philosophers should group together children and madmen as beings not fully responsible for their actions, for as madmen are thought to lack freedom of choice, so children do not yet possess the power of reason in a developed form. It is even just that we should assign a greater degree of responsibility to children, for madmen, by virtue of their lack of free will, are completely without responsibility, while children, insofar as they possess reason in a partially developed form, can be held responsible (i.e. can be required to take responsibility) to a corresponding degree.
>
> (Wolff, 1970, pp. 12–13)

> All men refuse to take responsibility for their actions at some time or other during their lives, and some men so consistently shirk their duty that they present more the appearance of overgrown children than of adults.   (Ibid., p. 14)

There is a striking similarity between Wolff's way of talking about children and the views we saw put forward by Hobbes, Locke and Kant. Wolff begins with the assurance that children are not rational and then immediately back-pedals to say that actually they are, partially at least. Four paragraphs later where the second quotation appears, the child is not unable to take responsibility but is refusing to take it. She is not an incompetent but a degenerate. Having denied that she is incompetent, I am certainly not going to concede that the only alternative is to make her a degenerate; there must be another choice available.

What is missing from Wolff's analysis, though it is present in his terminology, is the recognition of the public face, the mutuality of responsibility. He talks of *assigning* responsibility to children, *holding* them responsible, *requiring* them to take responsibility and these are natural ways of speaking. What they do is to introduce a new element into the concept of responsibility which involves more than free will and reason; now a third party is present and is an active participant in the language game in which responsibility has a role. People are not only responsible *for* something, they are responsible *to* God, other individuals, society or themselves, and this latter Kantian notion is derived from the primary social context in which it makes sense for the concept of responsibility to be invoked. This is just what I was claiming for authority. To say either that someone acts authoritatively or that someone is responsible for his actions may depend upon the possibility of ascribing mental states or capacities but neither is merely a shorthand way of ascribing them. In the case of the fully autonomous person, authority and responsibility go hand in hand. The capacity-to-act-autonomously *is* the coming together of the two. If both or either is impaired then so is this capacity, and both depend upon the psychological capacities of the agent *plus* the recognition of other members of the moral and political community. This raises a difficulty.

PASSING THE BUCK

The problem here seems to be this: am I saying that a child is responsible if and only if we declare her to be so, given that she knows what she is doing? This view has some historical clout. Given the knowledge it is always possible to hold someone responsible for their actions. Children were still being imprisoned and deported when Mill wrote that disclaimer. Is it then just a matter of fashion, of the times in which we live? Not entirely; to begin with we might take a pragmatic line in the light of new knowledge about the long-term effects of such treatment on a child's subsequent development. We might argue that while we *can* hold her responsible, the consequences of so doing turn out to be unacceptable. But the horror which writers such as Dickens expressed at the cruelty of his times was prompted by no such knowledge. Dickensian child victims grow into upright citizens if they grow up at all. What Dickens saw was what most of us see, the *inhumanity* of treating a child in certain ways. In what does the inhumanity consist? Not just in harsh action; increased concern about children is almost always part of a larger concern about people in general, but when horrible things are happening to people it is not unusual to focus on children and try special pleading on their behalf. This special pleading is, no doubt, partly emotional but it might very well include reference to children's lack of knowledge and understanding. Yet the inhumanity does not consist in the ascription of certain cognitive states either. We may be quite right to ascribe agency to a child for his acts. The inhumanity seems to lie in allowing the full weight of responsibility to fall on the child. Responsibility is not only about agency. 'When we say a person is responsible for what he does we mean not just that he was the agent . . . we also say that the act reflects (back) on the agent,' writes David Wood (1973, p. 191). How much reflecting goes on depends upon the reflective capabilities of the child and also on the strength and direction of the beam which we, the adults, determine.

Perhaps now we can take Mill's insight on board without opening ourselves to the charge of arbitrariness. Mill wanted to protect children against the harm which they might do themselves. The problem which was supposed to bring liberal theory crashing to the ground was that we do not wish to justify interfering with adult liberties on these grounds. It may be that what we are protecting children from is not so much the awful consequences of their ignorant decisions but of the burden of responsibility for those decisions which children are not yet ready to bear and which, for entirely non-political reasons, we cannot choose to impose upon them. If giving or withholding this responsibility were possible options in a one-person game, then this criterion would do nothing to counter the charge of arbitrariness but I have already argued that they are not and could not be. We can only *play* at ascribing responsibility outside this mutual interaction; making the horse a senator, blaming the toy which the child trips over are games which do not fool the horse or the toy.

Growing up, maturing, emerging into autonomy is the process of the child taking from the adult more and more of the responsibility for those actions which she does knowingly. Respect for the dignity and freedom of the child consists in the recognition that the burden of responsibility shifts from the adult to the child as she herself demands it. We leave unhappy teenagers who 'don't want to talk about it' alone; the tearful 5-year-old comes and dumps the problem in your lap. In between, we say, we 'play it by ear' and what we listen for is the child's own claim to have its decisions treated as authoritative and to be ready to bear the responsibility. This claim is not a conscious, spoken claim; if it gets to that stage, we have already left it too late. The claim is implicit in the child's own social interactions and unless we are blind or acting in chronic bad faith we can do no other than acknowledge it. But neither can we impose it. Holding a child responsible is not the same as making her responsible; we may succeed in the former, without her cooperation we can never succeed in the latter.

Now it can still be objected that this is also true of adults and that I have still, therefore, failed to distinguish them from children. However, there is a difference. With children, the presupposition is that we take the responsibility until they show us that they want it; with adults we assume that they take the responsibility unless they show us that they don't. (We are surprised when the 'man' turns out to be a robot.) That is what membership of the moral and political community is, and it is a serious business which deserves more attention than I can give here.[3] It is quite correct that children's application for membership should be taken seriously; once accepted there is no turning back, resignation is not an option.

To end, a word about voting. Voting is not just a matter of knowing how to put a cross on a piece of paper, nor of having a rough or even quite refined view of the policies of the major political parties. It also, in a democracy, involves being responsible to some degree for the society which we have. Maybe 'I didn't vote Tory', but even that does not enable me to opt out of that responsibility entirely. Why else would I buy the sticker?

Let us ask our 10-year-old's mother if her daughter is ready to take that responsibility. What would she say? Perhaps that, yes, her child is intelligent and thoughtful and even knowledgeable; yes, she would be as competent as many adults in coming to sensible conclusions. Also, perhaps, that sometimes at night, she finds her crying for the starving of Africa or unable to sleep with the terror of the possibility of nuclear war or desperately seeking a denial of the reality of the horror of the Holocaust. Perhaps she would be angry if, by trying to impose responsibility on her daughter by giving her the vote, we were also taking from her the only comfort which she has, namely that when she is older she will change all that. Or perhaps she would just tell us that her child is not yet ready; she would be right.

Denying the vote to children is not based on some false assumption about 10-year-olds' political knowledge, nor to deny that they have interests, nor to protect them from the harm their votes might do. It is to take responsibility to ourselves for the way the world is. And that really does belong to us.

NOTES

1. For accounts which include emphasis on experience and understanding see Scarre (1980) and Schrag (1977).
2. I am grateful to Michael Bavidge of the Department of Adult Education in the University of Newcastle for sharing his time and his ideas with me on the main point of this section.
3. Some interesting and illuminating remarks about what constitutes membership of a political society are to be found in Easton and Dennis (1969).

REFERENCES

ARISTOTLE (1959), *Politics*, Everyman series (London: Dent).
AXTELL, James L. (ed.) (1968), *The Educational Writings of John Locke* (Cambridge: Cambridge University Press).
CAVELL, Stanley (1979), *The Claim of Reason: Wittgenstein, Scepticism, Morality and Tragedy* (Oxford: Oxford University Press).
EASTON, David and DENNIS, Jack (1969), *Children in the Political System* (New York: McGraw-Hill).
HARRIS, John (1982), 'The Political Status of Children', in Keith Graham (ed.), *Contemporary Political Philosophy* (Cambridge: Cambridge University Press), pp. 35–55.
HOBBES, Thomas (1914), *Leviathan*, Everyman series (London: Dent).
HOLT, John (1974), *Escape from Childhood: The Needs and Rights of Children* (Harmondsworth: Penguin).
KANT, Immanuel (1930), *Lectures on Ethics*, trans. Louis Infield (London: Methuen).
LOCKE, John (1968), 'Some Thoughts Concerning Education', in J. AXTELL (ed.), pp. 111–325. (First published 1705).
MILL, John Stuart (1910), *On Liberty*, Everyman series (London: Dent).
SCARRE, Geoffrey (1980), 'Children and Paternalism', *Philosophy*, vol. 55, pp. 117–24.
SCHRAG, Francis (1977), 'The Child in the Moral Order', *Philosophy*, vol. 52, pp. 167–77.
STRAWSON, P. F. (1974), *Freedom and Resentment and Other Essays* (London: Methuen).
WOLFF, Robert Paul (1970), *In Defense of Anarchism* (New York: Harper Torchbooks).
WOOD, David (1973), 'Honesty', in Alan Montefiore (ed.), *Philosophy and Personal Relations* (London: Routledge & Kegan Paul), pp. 191–223.

6

Autonomy and Identity in Feminist Thinking

Jean Grimshaw

Issues about women's autonomy have been central to feminist thinking and action. Women have so often been in situations of powerlessness and dependence that any system of belief or programme of action that could count as 'feminist' must in some way see this as a central concern. But what is meant by 'autonomy' and under what conditions is it possible? This has been an important and contentious question in philosophy. But questions about autonomy, and related questions about self and identity have also been important to feminism, and within feminist thinking it is possible to find radically different ways of thinking about these things. In this paper, I want to look at one kind of way in which some feminists have tried to conceptualise what it is for a woman to be 'autonomous', and at the implications this has for ways of thinking about the human self. I shall argue that this conception is not only philosophically problematic, but also has an implicit politics which is potentially damaging. And I shall try to suggest some ways of beginning to think about 'autonomy' which seem to me to be more fruitful and adequate, and to draw on different traditions of thinking about the self which have become influential in some recent feminist thinking.

Feminist thinking does not, of course, exist in a vacuum, and in thinking about women's autonomy, feminists have drawn on different (and conflicting) approaches to questions about the human self, some of which have a long history. I want to begin by going back to an argument that Aristotle put forward in the *Ethics*, since I think that the point at which his argument breaks down can illuminate the nature of the problem some feminist thinking has faced.

Aristotle's argument concerns the question of what it is that makes an action 'voluntary', done of a person's own free will, and in order to answer this question, he distinguished between actions whose origin was 'inside' a person, and those whose origin was 'outside', which resulted from external influences or pressure or compulsion. He discussed at some length the problems that arise over trying to define ideas such as 'compulsion', and in estimating the degree of severity of pressure that could make an action not voluntary. But in this sort of model of autonomy, what defines an action as autonomous is seen as its point of *origin*; it must have an 'immaculate conception', as it were, from *within* the self.

Now ultimately I think that it is this definition of 'autonomy' in terms of origin, and the associated distinction between an 'inner' self which can in some way spontaneously generate its 'own' actions, and 'external' influences which are not 'part' of the self, that will need challenging. But I think it is possible to defend the Aristotelian version of autonomy up to a point, provided notions of 'inside' and 'outside' the self are defined in a certain way. If a person is prevented from doing what they would otherwise intend or desire to do, or if they are coerced into doing what they would *not* otherwise want or desire to do, they are not acting autonomously. Under this interpretation, actions which originate from 'inside' the self are those which are seen as in accordance with conscious desires or intentions, and those which originate from 'outside' the self are those which one would not do if one were not coerced. The pressure here is to consider the sorts of circumstances which do, in fact, coerce people in these sorts of ways. And, of course, a central concern of feminism has been to identify and fight against the kinds of coercion to which women have been subjected, including things like physical violence and economic dependence.

But it is at this point that an Aristotelian-type argument fails to be able to deal with the most difficult questions about autonomy. The Aristotelian view, as I have interpreted it, 'works' only to the extent that it is assumed that there is no problem about what I shall call 'the autonomy of desires'. Autonomy is defined as acting in accordance with desire (or intention). But what of the desires themselves? Are there *desires* (or intentions) which are not 'autonomous', which do not originate from 'within' the self, which are not authentic, not really 'one's own'?

Feminist writers have wanted, of course, to indict the various forms of brutality and coercion from which women have suffered. But this brutality and coercion has been seen not merely as a question of physical or 'external' coercion or constraint; the force of subjection has also been seen as a psychic one, invading women's very selves. The language of 'conditioning', 'brainwashing', 'indoctrination', and so forth, has been used to describe this force. The female self, under male domination, is riddled through and through with false or conditioned desires. But set against this conditioned, non-autonomous female self are various images of a female self that would be authentic, that would transcend or shatter this conditioning. I want now to look at some of these images of the female self in feminist discourse: my particular examples are from the work of Mary Daly, Marilyn Frye and Kate Millett.

Daly, Frye and Millett all stress the way in which women have been subject to the *power* of men. Much of Daly's book, *Gyn/Ecology* (1979), is an account of the barbarities inflicted on women such as suttee, clitorectomy, foot-binding and other forms of mutilation. Millett, in *Sexual Politics* (1977), sees patriarchal power as something so historically all-embracing that it has totally dominated women's lives. Frye, in *The Politics of Reality* (1983), uses the situation of a young girl sold into sexual slavery and then systematically brutalised and brainwashed into a life of service to her captors as an analogy for the situation of all women. And all three writers stress the way in which they see the female self as 'invaded' by patriarchal conditioning. Millett writes:

> When, in any group of persons, the ego is subjected to such invidious versions of itself through social beliefs, ideology and tradition, the effect is bound to be pernicious. This should make it no very special cause for surprise that women develop group characteristics common to those who suffer minority status and a marginal existence.   (Millett, 1977, p. 55)

Women, she argues, are deprived of all but the most trivial sources of dignity or self-respect. In her discussion of Lawrence's depiction of Connie in *Lady Chatterley's Lover*, what she sees Connie as relinquishing is 'self, ego, will, individuality' (p. 243); all those things which, Millett argues, women had but recently achieved, (and for which Lawrence had a profound distaste).

Mary Daly's picture of the way in which women's selves are invaded by patriarchal conditioning is even more striking. She describes women, for example, as 'moronised', 'robotised', 'lobotomised', as 'the puppets of Papa'. At times she seems to see women as so 'brainwashed' that they are scarcely human; thus she describes them as 'fembots', even as 'mutants'. In Millett, Daly and Frye, women are seen primarily as *victims*: the monolithic brutality and psychological pressures of male power have reduced women almost to the state of being 'non-persons'. And indeed, as Daly sees women as having become 'mutants' or 'fembots', so Millett sees them as not having been allowed to participate in fully 'human' activities (which she characterises as those that are most remote from the biological contingencies of life), and Frye sees them as simply 'broken' and then 'remade' in the way that suits their masters.

But behind this victimised female self, whose actions and desires are assumed to be not truly 'her own', since they derive from processes of force, conditioning or psychological manipulation, there is seen to be an authentic female self, whose recovery or discovery it is one of the aims of feminism to achieve. The spatial metaphor implicit in the word 'behind' is not accidental, since this model of self is premised on the possibility of making a distinction between an 'inner' and an 'outer' self. Ibsen's Peer Gynt compared his quest for identity to the process of peeling layers off an onion; but after shedding all the 'false selves', he found that there was nothing inside, no 'core'. The sort of spatial metaphor implicit in Peer Gynt's account of himself is also apt in the accounts of self given by Daly, Millett and Frye, except that there *is* assumed to be a 'core'. This is clearest in the work of Daly. In *Gyn/Ecology*, discovering or recovering one's own self is seen as akin to a process of salvation or religious rebirth, and Daly writes of what she calls the unveiling or unwinding of the 'shrouds' of patriarchy to reveal the authentic female Spirit-Self underneath. And this Self is seen as a unitary and harmonious one. Splits and barriers within the psyche, she argues, as well as those between Selves, are the result of patriarchal conditioning. In the unitary and harmonious female Spirit-Self there will be no such splits.

Millett's picture of the authentic female self is rather different from that of Daly. It does not draw, as Daly's does, on religious metaphors of salvation and rebirth. It derives, rather, from a picture of the self as fundamentally a unitary, conscious and rational thing, a picture which, in Western philosophy, can be traced back to Descartes. It emerges most clearly in her discussion of Freud. She describes Freud's theory of the Unconscious as a major contribution to human understanding, but her account of the self owes, in fact, scarcely anything to Freud. She is scathingly critical of Freud's theory of penis envy: Freud, she argued, 'did not accept his patient's symptoms as evidence of a justified dissatisfaction with the limiting circumstances imposed on them by society, but as symptomatic of an independent and universal feminine tendency' (Millett, 1977, p. 179). He made a major (and foolish) confusion between biology and culture. Girls, Millett argues, are fully cognisant of male supremacy long before they see their brother's penis; and what they envy is not the penis, but the things to which having a penis gives the boy access – power, status and rewards. Freud ignored the more likely 'social' hypothesis for feminine dissatisfaction, preferring to ascribe it to a biologically based female nature. What we should be studying, Millett argues, are the effects of male-supremacist culture on the female ego. And what will undo these effects, she writes in the Postscript, is altered consciousness, and a process of 'human growth and true re-education' (p. 363).

The 'social' factors of which Millett writes are here seen as pressures which are 'external' to the self, and which have the effect of thwarting the conscious and unitary rationality of female individuality, or the female ego. And the task is that of *removing* their influence. If, in *Lady Chatterley's Lover*, the scales were to fall from Connie's eyes and she were to see the worship of Mellor's phallus for what it is, a means of subordinating and oppressing women, she could free herself and develop her authentic will, ego and individuality.

The paradigm of coercion, writes Frye, is *not* the direct application of physical force. Rather, it is a situation in which choice and action *do* take place, and in which the victim acts under her own perception and judgement. Hence, what the exploiter needs is that

> the will and intelligence of the victim be disengaged from the projects of resistance and escape but that they not be simply broken or destroyed. Ideally, the disintegration and misintegration of the victim should accomplish the detachment of the victim's will and intelligence from the victim's own interests and their attachment to the interests of the exploiter. This will effect a displacement or dissolution of self-respect and will undermine the victim's intolerance of coercion. With that, the situation transcends the initial paradigmatic form or structure of coercion; for if people don't mind doing what you want them to do, you can't really be *making* them do it.   (Frye, 1983, p. 60)

And, she writes:

> The health and integrity of an organism is a matter of its being organised largely towards its own interests and welfare. *She* is healthy and 'working right' when her substance is organised primarily on principles which align it to *her* interests and welfare. Co-operation is essential of course, but it will not do that I arrange everything so that *you* get enough exercise: for me to be healthy, *I* must get enough exercise. My being adequately exercised is logically independent of your being so. (Ibid., p. 70)

Frye is writing here as if it were possible to distinguish the interests of one self sharply from those of another, and as if, were the effects of male domination to be undone, it would not be too much of a problem for the self to know what its interests were.[1]

In various ways then, underlying much of the work of these three writers is a set of assumptions about the self. First, that it is, at least potentially, a unitary, rational thing, aware of its interests. Second, that 'splits' within the psyche should be seen as resulting from the interference of patriarchal or male-dominated socialisation or conditioning. Third, that the task of undoing this conditioning is one that can be achieved solely by a rational process of learning to understand and fight against the social and institutional effects of male domination. And implicit in these assumptions about the self, I think, is a conception of autonomy. Frye writes that 'left to themselves' women would not want to serve men. Daly writes of unveiling or unwinding the 'shrouds' of patriarchy. Millett writes of the individuality and ego that women can discover in themselves once they recognise the effects of their patriarchal socialisation. And in all three, what is autonomous (or authentic) is what is seen as originating in some way from *within* the self; what is in some way *untainted* by the conditioning or manipulation to which a woman has previously been subjected.

Before I come to discuss the philosophical problems that are raised by this sort of account of self and autonomy, I want to look at what I have called its implicit politics; and what I mean by this primarily is its possible consequences for the way in which women might think about their relationships to each other, and the way in which they might think about themselves. The first consequence seems to me to be this. Any view which sees self-affirmation in terms of an 'authentic' inner self arising from the smashing of a socially conditioned 'false self', or which sees autonomy as a question of the origin of actions from 'inside' rather than 'outside', is almost bound to adopt, however implicitly, a derogatory attitude towards those who are not yet 'authentic'. The precise nature and tone of this attitude may vary. But Mary Daly, for example, in *Gyn/Ecology*, sometimes writes as if most women were really little more than the programmed, robotic puppets to which women were reduced in Ira Levin's novel *The Stepford Wives*; the language of 'fembots' and 'mutants' and 'puppets', whilst intended, I am sure, to enunciate a critique of women's oppressors, veers perilously near to sounding like contempt for those who are subject to that oppression. And this is related, for example, to Daly's scorn for 'tokenism' – for those women who participate in what are seen as patriarchal institutions. Kate Millett's language is less obviously extreme. But the picture she paints of women is nevertheless often a derogatory one. She describes them, for example, as 'infantilised'; she accepts without question research which purported to show that most women despised each other (Millett, 1977, p. 55); she sees women as having little 'self-respect', and as devoting almost all their time and attention to pleasing and flattering men.

This implicitly derogatory attitude to women is linked both to an overmonolithic account of male power, and to a failure to give much attention to the ways in which women have, in fact, often spent much of their lives, and to the activities which have been particularly theirs (such as the rearing of children, for example). Sometimes women are depicted almost as a caricature of a male stereotype of themselves – they *are* servile, weak, powerless etc. (Millett even suggests (p. 56) that the fact that women commit less 'crime' than men is due to their patriarchal conditioning in passivity.) Millett basically dismisses the activities which have tended to dominate women's lives as 'infantilising', because they restrict women to the level, she argues, of the merely biological, and do not allow them to enter upon the 'fully human' activities which have been the province of men. And it is interesting, as Toril Moi (1985) points out, that in her discussion of literature, Millett concentrates almost wholly on male authors, with the exception of Charlotte Brontë, of whose work she tends to be very dismissive. Furthermore, as Moi suggests, she seems to avoid much in the way of recognition or acknowledgement of feminist work prior to her own, or of the existence of female traditions and strengths which might have tended to challenge or subvert the supposedly monolithic nature of the male power which it is the main aim of her book to describe.

Mary Daly's indictment of male power and brutality similarly allows little space for a consideration of the patterns of women's lives, or the strengths and capacities that these might have enabled them to develop. Her female Spirit-Self simply seems to rise mysteriously like a phoenix from the ashes of patriarchal conditioning. And Frye is sceptical about the possibility of women looking to their foremothers as a source of inspiration; of seeing some women, at least, as having led lives that were not wholly male-mediated. Feminist vision or imagination has no real resource to turn to.

Now these kinds of accounts (or perhaps one might say *failures* to give an adequate account?) of women's lives are implicitly divisive and threatening. They are divisive because they have a tendency to divide women into two camps; those who have and those who have not shaken the dust of patriarchal conditioning from their feet. And they are threatening, because it is offensive and undermining to be told that the life one has led has merely been one of servility, that it has not been of truly 'human' value, that one has been a 'fembot' or a 'puppet'. I think that one important strand in the rejection of feminism by many women has been a feeling that feminists are saying that their lives have been of no value, and that their activities and concerns have been trivial.

But this image of autonomy and of the self can be threatening, too, to women who *do* have a strong allegiance to feminism; and the threat intersects with assumptions that have been made in some feminist discourse about who is or is not 'really' a feminist. The threat arises because this account of autonomy is in fact often a strongly *normative* one; it presents an image of what a 'feminist self' should be like. To be autonomous or authentic one should be strong, independent, rational, coherent or consistent, able to distinguish clearly those aspects of one's previous self which derive from male-dominated conditioning and reject them. If one is am-bivalent, conflicted, uncertain, confused, unwilling to make whole-sale rejections, one stands to be accused, whether by oneself or by others, of bad faith, of lack of courage, of 'selling out', of tokenism.

I am here giving an account of just one (influential) strand in feminist discourse. There are other strands which have rejected this account of self and autonomy.[2] As I have said before, a picture of the self as conscious, unitary and rational can be traced back, in Western philosophy, to Descartes. I do not have space here to discuss the various ways in which versions of this conception of self have been influential, in philosophy and psychology, for instance. But the major tradition which has queried this view of self has been that which derives from psychoanalysis. Feminism has had a complex relation to psychoanalysis. Freud's theories have been the target of a great deal of feminist criticism. In *Sexual Politics*, for example, Kate Millett sees Freud simply as the proponent of a biologistic theory of male supremacy, and as one of the arch-villains in the male plot of patriarchy. Other feminist writers, however, have tried to re-evaluate the significance of psychoanalytic theory for feminism. And they have argued that, whilst feminism should indeed always have a critical relationship to psychoanalytic theory, the latter has within it the potential for allowing a better understanding of the complexities of human desires and of the psychological construction of 'masculinity' and 'femininity'.

Now any adequate account of self needs to be able, I think, to encompass and try to make intelligible the ways in which women and men experience themselves. And the central reasons for rejecting the 'humanist' paradigm of the self – as I have outlined it above – are, firstly, that there may be aspects of the development of self which are not easily accessible to consciousness, and secondly, that there are conscious experiences which are not easy to make intelligible within the humanist paradigm.[3] I want now to look at some aspects of self-experience that I think should be central to any theory of self, and hence to any discussion of women's autonomy.

*   *   *

Fantasy

The dream (on which we may try hard to impose a narrative structure, to make sense of it) is unlike much fantasy in that it often doesn't, of itself, contain any such structure, and the 'story', if it tells one, may be deeply unintelligible to us. Much conscious fantasy is different; we may 'tell a story' to ourselves (or listen to a story and fantasise it as about ourselves); and sometimes we may attempt an imagined resolution, through fantasy, of some aspect of our social situation. One might, thus, fantasise the death of someone seen as a threat, or imagine oneself as possessing enormous fame or wealth. But fantasies, not always in the form of a coherent narrative, may irrupt or intervene; one can be plagued, dominated or obsessed by them. Freud wrote of the way in which fantasies or desires, often seen as evil or dangerous, could come to dominate a person's life. Fantasy may be a threat; it may be inexplicable, bizarre and intrusive. Discovering the fantasies of others, too, may be threatening; the discovery, for example, as Rosalind Coward (1984) suggests, that the 'mild' man one lives with is a secret addict of sadomasochistic pornography. Female sexual fantasies can be disturbing as well. Why do many women find *The Story of O* erotic, and why is there a 'split' between sexual fantasy and that which one might find pleasurable or erotic in real life?

Fantasy may be experienced both as pleasurable and as dangerous. But sometimes it can just be pleasurable. Coward discusses, for instance, the importance of the fact that one of the biggest growth areas in publishing in recent years has been women's romantic fiction. Unlike the 'modern' women's novel in which, usually after a series of disastrous sexual misadventures, the female heroine ends up (more or less) 'her own person', romantic fiction is stylised, formulaic and unrealistic. It offers women, Coward argues, the fantasised pleasure (and apotheosis of sexual desire) of finding security in the strong arms of the hard-bitten patriarchal hero, along with the pleasure of having 'tamed' him and domesticated his wild ways by the power one enjoys over him in being a woman.

We have to understand the pleasure there is for women in such fantasies. We have to understand what seems often to attract women more than men to soap operas, or to a passionate interest in the doings of the Royal Family. We need to understand how and why male fantasies may commonly differ from female ones, and why the sorts of fantasies I have mentioned, which may in some ways seem antithetical to feminism, may still have a strong appeal to women who have a feminist allegiance.

The 'Split' Between Reason and Desire

I will suggest, as a first example of this, a book by Suzanne Lowry, on Princess Diana, called *The Princess in the Mirror* (1985). The appearance of the book is at first glance like that of any other glossy book about the Royals. But it sets out, its author says, to deconstruct the image and appeal of the Princess. At the end of the book, Lowry states that the image of the Princess is conformist and reactionary, that it acts as a powerful form of social control, and that Diana is an unwitting agent of that. Yet the presentation of the book, and Lowry's text, often speak of a fascination with the Princess that is more than simply the fascination one can derive from the exercise of deconstructing an image. And this fascination is often in tension with the attempt to articulate a critique.

Or think about the Fonda phenomenon. The text of Fonda's book, *Women Coming of Age* (1984), exhorts women not to 'think thin', and its theme is mainly that of health. Yet the illustrations are nearly all of women who are pencil-thin enough not to be out of place on the catwalk in a Paris fashion show. The discourse of 'health' is almost inextricably intertwined, in the case of women, with discourse about youth and beauty and sexual attractiveness. The reasons women have for concern about fitness and health are often multiply overdetermined. Notions, for example, of *Ageless Ageing* (Kenton, 1986) *slide* between discussions of how to preserve a youthful skin and a young-looking body and how to stave off the ravages of *appearing* older, with discussions of mental vitality and energy, and so forth. A young-looking body is a *sign* of an alert mind.

There is a type of feminist criticism, both in literature and other media (and in fields such as education), which has been called 'Images of Women' criticism.[4] This has supposed that feminist effort should be devoted, first, to showing how the 'images' in question oppress or denigrate women, and second, to offering positive images of women to replace these. One problem with this kind of criticism is that the 'images' in question have often been misinterpreted, since they have been discussed without reference to the context or narrative structure in which they may appear. But there are two other problems with this type of criticism which I want to focus on here. First, what this approach often fails to recognise is the importance of understanding the *appeal* of the 'images' that are criticised; the relations they may have to women's pleasures, desires, fantasies, fears and conceptions of themselves. Second, it fails to recognise what is signally obvious in the experience of many women, myself of course included, namely that it is perfectly possible to agree 'in one's head' that certain images of women might be reactionary or damaging or oppressive, while remaining committed to them in emotion and desire. I suspect that this 'split' happens at times in all women, and perhaps particularly in those who have some commitment to feminism. And what it suggests is that structures of desire, emotion and fantasy have deep roots of some sort in the self which are not necessarily amenable in any simple way to processes of conscious rational argument. An adequate theory of subjectivity has to recognise and try to understand these roots.

Contradictions

I have already identified more than one type of contradiction; those that can exist between one's fantasies and what one would actually do or enjoy in real life, and those that can exist between one's understanding of the oppressive nature of some discourse or practice and one's continuing investment of desire and finding of pleasure in it.

In his *Introductory Lectures on Psychoanalysis* (1973), Freud discussed the way in which symptoms are experienced in certain forms of obsessional neurosis. He wrote:

> Obsessional neurosis is shown in the patient's being occupied with thoughts in which he is in fact not interested, in his being aware of impulses which appear very strange to him and his being led to actions the performance of which give him no enjoyment, but which it is quite impossible for him to omit. The thoughts (obsessions) may be senseless in themselves, or merely a matter of indifference to the subject; often they are completely silly, and invariably they are the starting-point of a strenuous mental activity, which exhausts the patient and to which he only surrenders himself most unwillingly. (p. 297)

Obsessional neurosis is characterised, Freud argued, by the fact that the symptoms are not only debilitating, but are experienced by the person as *alien*; they do not seem 'part' of him or her, and they seem discrepant with an everyday or normal sense of the self. In the case of many of Freud's patients the disruption and debilitation caused by the symptoms was so extreme that they were scarcely able to carry on their lives adequately at all. But Freud insisted that there was no sharp dividing line between 'normal' and 'neurotic' people, and would have argued that similar, though less extreme, obsessions and apparently inexplicable compulsions can be found in all of us. In these cases, the self is, as it were, split against itself, subject to desires and impulses that seem 'out of character'.

But one cannot assume that an everyday 'coherent' sense of self is readily available. One reason for this is that women (and men, of course) are often faced with the problem of negotiating contradictory or conflicting conceptions of themselves. Women may, for example, be required to be *both* sexually exciting and available, *and* modest and chaste. And gender relationships may be subject to the problems that can arise from conflicting discourses about femininity or masculinity. Men may, for example, *both* see themselves as 'stronger' than women and tend to see women as more weak and passive, but *also* see women as having a power over them that can seem to engulf the man in forms of emotional dependence by which he may feel threatened.[5] Discourse about femininity and masculinity is by no means a homogeneous or stable thing.

In the twentieth century, the advent of a 'consumer culture' and of mass communications has given questions about self and identity a peculiar intensity and difficulty in some respects. They have led, for example, to a focus on appearance and 'style', and the way in which these may 'express' one's individuality, that is historically novel. The clothes one wears, the 'room of one's own' in the Sunday Supplements: one may, apparently, now 'try on' identities as if they really were clothes. And women have often tended to be the main target of fashion and 'lifestyle' talk. For all the rejection of what was sometimes called 'woman garbage' by American feminists, the issue of appearance is something that no woman can wholly avoid. Feminists too, of course, have used style of dress and demeanour to express a sense of self and of political commitment. (Elizabeth Wilson recorded once realising that she was more than usually anxious about the question of what to wear when she was going to talk to a feminist group.)

Self-knowledge and Self-deception

The concept of self-deception is one that has constantly puzzled philosophers. How can one both know and yet not know something about oneself. I do not have space here to discuss the question of self-deception in detail. But an important thing to recognise at the outset is that knowing about oneself can never be a matter of 'mere information'. One cannot be distanced from or emotionally neutral about issues of self-knowledge. (Freud stressed this in his account of the transference in the analytic situation.) Herbert Fingarette (1959) uses the concept of 'avowal' to give an account of the concept of self-deception. We do not see everything that we think or do or fantasise or desire as equally 'central' to ourselves. It is quite common, in everyday discourse, to say things like 'I wasn't really myself' or 'It wasn't like *me* to do that'. Sometimes this process of rejection, of not avowing, is quite conscious. At other times it may be barely admitted to consciousness, if whatever it was is seen as threatening to the self. And sometimes it is, I think, not conscious at all. Psychoanalysts have talked, for example, about the process of 'projection', in which aspects of oneself of which one is fearful may be projected on to other people.[6] (A number of writers have seen 'projection' as involved in the problem of masculinity, and have suggested that men may sometimes project their own fears of such things as emotional intimacy on to women, who are then seen as 'bad' because they cause these problems.)

Self-knowledge can never be a matter of easy or immediate introspection. This is partly because aspects of oneself may be disavowed, sometimes unconsciously, and partly because the 'meaning' of the deliverances of introspection is always dependent on an interpretation. One may be *aware* of feelings, sexual ones for example, that one is not able to conceptualise *as* sexual at the time. Freud believed that at the root of all neuroses lay repressed sexual desires, but even if one does not follow him in this, it would be hard to resist the conclusion that this was true of some of his patients. Sometimes his patients lacked the kind of knowledge that would have enabled them to interpret the experience as 'sexual' at all. Sometimes they possessed knowledge about sex, but could not admit that *this* was sexual, or that *they* had those sorts of desires.

I have outlined above some of the experiences and the problems about subjectivity that any adequate theory of self must be able to encompass, in a way that the 'humanist' paradigm is, I think, unable to do. There are approaches to understanding and theorising self which depart radically from the humanist paradigm. I shall not attempt to enumerate them all here, nor do I think that feminism should accept any of them uncritically. What they share, despite their differences, is an insistence that there is no 'original' wholeness or unity in the self, nor a 'real self' which can be thought of as in some way *underlying* the self of everyday life. The self is *always* a more or less precarious and conflictual construction out of, and compromise between, conflicting and not always conscious desires and experiences, which are born out of the ambivalences and contradictions in human experience and relationships with others.

Accounts of the construction of the self vary, in the degree of stress, for example, that they lay on the period of infancy and early childhood, and on the importance given to sexuality. But it seems to me that the theories of Freud must be seen as centrally important. It is sometimes argued that Freud's theories must be accepted or rejected all of a piece, and that one cannot simply accept or reject 'bits' of them as one fancies. It is true, I think, that there is a certain sort of eclecticism, practised for example by some neo-Freudian writers such as Erich Fromm or by the American 'ego psychologists', which may undermine anything useful that Freudian theory really has to offer. But whatever we may take or reject from Freud, what I think we should not lose is the way in which he raises questions and problematises things which are sometimes taken for granted. Freud questions any easy (or utopian) idea or ideal of the unity of the self, he questions the idea that self-knowledge could ever be a matter of simple introspection, and he sees issues about desire and fantasy as central to subjectivity. He stresses the way in which the acquisition of a *gendered* subjectivity is necessarily conflictual and involves struggle. And above all, perhaps, he forces a radical questioning of the concepts of the 'individual' and the 'social'. Nothing could be further from the truth than Kate Millett's accusation that Freud believed that women's destiny was a simple outcome of their biology. In Freudian theory, there is a constant concern with the way in which entry into culture and human relationships, and the conflicts and struggle this causes, should be seen as *constitutive* of the human self.

Freud's particular view of human culture was problematic. He stressed that psychoanalysis was never concerned solely with desires seen as arising unmediated from the body, but always with psychic representations of these. But he also believed in a sort of Lamarckian view of the inheritance of a 'primal schema' of desires and fantasies which determined the form taken by the Oedipal situation. The French psychoanalyst, Jacques Lacan, argued that Freud himself (as well as virtually all the psychoanalysts who revised Freud's theories) never managed to escape fully from the assumption of an already existing gendered subjectivity which entered into the Oedipal situation. And Lacan argued that the human subject must be seen as constituted through language, through entry into the Symbolic Order. According to Lacan, the aim of psychoanalysis should be rigorously to deconstruct and expose the contradictions and radical fissues in which human subjectivity is born.[7]

Feminism, as I have said, needs to preserve a critical distance from all theories of self. But it needs also to engage with those theories which deconstruct the distinction between the 'individual' and the 'social', which recognise the power of desire and fantasy and the problems of supposing any 'original' unity in the self, while at the same time preserving its concern with lived experience and the practical and material struggles of women to achieve more autonomy and control over their lives.

The appeal of what I have called the 'humanist paradigm' lies, I think, in the way it can seem to conceptualise the need women have experienced for this greater degree of autonomy and control, for overcoming the fragmentation and contradictions in their lives, and for a capacity for self-definition. No theory of self should lose sight of these things. I have argued, however, that there are also aspects of women's experience which the humanist paradigm is unable to conceptualise adequately; hence the appeal of theories which attempt to 'deconstruct' the self in more radical ways. But the danger in some 'deconstructionist' theories, however, is that they seem to leave no space for the material struggles or ordinary aspirations of women. Thus it seems that Lacanian psychoanalysis, both in theory and practice, aims *merely* to show what a fragmented, decentred thing the human subject is, and Lacan has dismissed all talk of 'unity' or 'identity' as an illusion. It can be argued (though I do not have space to do it here), that there is an incoherence in a view of the subject which regards all notions of unity as an illusion. But there is also a practical and political problem, since it is difficult to see how such a theory could speak in any way to the practical or material concerns of women.

The problem, then, is not to be seen as one of whether we should continue to use concepts like 'identity' or 'autonomy' at all, or simply reject them out of hand. It is a problem, rather, of how to offer an interpretation of them which neither assumes the original unitary self of the humanist paradigm, nor ignores the needs of women. And Freud can again provide a useful starting point. It is true that Freudian theory questions any notion of the original unity of the self. But it is not true that Freudian theory has no space for ideas of unity or autonomy. The purpose of psychoanalytic therapy, according to Freud, was to remove the power of the symptom by making it intelligible, by showing the *sense* that it had. Psychoanalysis aimed to trace its roots in unconscious desires (though this was not a process merely of intellectual understanding). The unintelligible, alien quality of the symptom will be removed. But for this to happen, a person's conception of themselves must also be transformed. They must, for example, be able to think of themselves as 'the sort of person who *does* have incestuous sexual desires', is prepared to avow them as 'part' of the self, and ceases to be so threatened by them. Part of this process of change is a greater tolerance of certain aspects of oneself, and a lesser propensity for these to cause guilt or anxiety. But, paradoxically perhaps, this greater tolerance may result in *less* fragmentation, more coherence, and less subjection to the forms of anxiety or guilt or compulsive behaviour that may once have been so deeply disturbing or threatening.

It seems to me that there is a sort of dialectic we need to preserve when thinking about autonomy. There is no authentic or unified 'original' self which can simply be recovered or discovered as the source of 'autonomous' actions. But we are often faced with the experienced need to make 'sense' of our lives and our feelings and goals, to relate confused fragments of ourselves into something that seems more coherent and of which we feel more in control. We are often also faced, however, with the need to tolerate contradictions, not to strive for an illusory or impossible ideal, and to avoid self-punishing forms of anxiety, defence and guilt (and feminist guilt can be as punishing as any other kind). The dialectic of autonomy is one in which a constant (but never static or final) search for control and coherence needs balancing against a realism and tolerance born out of efforts to understand ourselves (and others) better.

NOTES

1. Further discussion of some of the philosophical traditions which have influenced this type of view, and of the problems with such a conception of 'interests', can be found in Jaggar (1983) and Grimshaw (1986).
2. Two in particular are important. First, there is the strand in feminist thinking which rejects what it sees as a typically male 'individualism'. (For discussion of this see Flax, 1983; and Grimshaw, 1986, ch. 6.) Second, there is the strand which sees psychoanalytic accounts of the self as having a great deal to offer to feminist analysis. A great deal has

been written about this, but for two influential accounts, see Mitchell (1975) and Mitchell and Rose (1982).
3. The words 'humanism' and 'humanist' have a complex history which I do not have space to go into in this paper. For a clear and interesting discussion of this, see Soper (1986).
4. There is an interesting discussion of 'Images of Women' literary criticism in Moi (1985).
5. Wendy Hollway discusses such contradictions in her article 'Gender Differences and the Production of Subjectivity', in Henriques *et al.* (1984).
6. Nancy Chodorow (1978), for example, discusses and uses the notion of 'projection'.
7. For accessible discussions of the work of Lacan and of his influence on French feminist thought, see Duchen (1986), Sayers (1986), and Soper (1986). See also Whitford (1986) for an interesting discussion of the work of the French feminist writer Luce Irigaray.

REFERENCES

CHODOROW, Nancy (1978), *The Reproduction of Mothering: Psychoanalysis and the Sociology of Gender* (Berkeley: University of California Press).
COWARD, Rosalind (1984), *Female Desire: Women's Sexuality Today* (London: Paladin).
DALY, Mary (1979), *Gyn/Ecology: The Metaethics of Radical Feminism* (London: The Women's Press).
DUCHEN, Claire (1986), *Feminism in France: From May '68 to Mitterrand* (London: Routledge & Kegan Paul).
FINGARETTE, Herbert (1959), *Self-deception* (London: Routledge & Kegan Paul).
FLAX, Jane (1983), 'Political Philosophy and the Patriarchal Unconscious: A Psychoanalytic Perspective on Epistemology and Metaphysics', in S. HARDING and M. HINTIKKA (eds), pp. 245–81.
FONDA, Jane (1984), *Women Coming of Age* (Harmondsworth: Penguin).
FREUD, Sigmund (1973), *Introductory Lectures on Psychoanalysis* (Harmondsworth: Penguin).
FRYE, Marilyn (1983), *The Politics of Reality: Essays in Feminist Theory* (Trumansburg, NY: Crossing Press).
GRIMSHAW, Jean (1986), *Feminist Philosophers: Women's Perspectives on Philosophical Traditions* (Brighton: Wheatsheaf).
HARDING, Sandra and HINTIKKA, Merrill B. (eds) (1983), *Discovering Reality: Feminist Perspectives on Epistemology, Metaphysics, Methodology, and Philosophy of Science* (Dordrecht: Reidel).
HENRIQUES, Julian, HOLLWAY, Wendy, URWIN, Cathy, VENN, Couze and WALKERDINE, Valerie (1984), *Changing the Subject: Psychology, Social Regulation and Subjectivity* (London: Methuen).
JAGGAR, Alison M. (1983), *Feminist Politics and Human Nature* (Brighton: Harvester).

KENTON, Leslie (1986), *Ageless Ageing* (London: Century Arrow).

LOWRY, Suzanne (1985), *The Princess in the Mirror* (London: Chatto & Windus).

MILLETT, Kate (1977), *Sexual Politics* (London: Virago).

MITCHELL, Juliet (1975), *Psychoanalysis and Feminism* (Harmondsworth: Penguin).

MITCHELL, Juliet and ROSE, Jacqueline (eds) (1982), *Feminine Sexuality: Jacques Lacan and the École Freudienne* (London: Macmillan).

MOI, Toril (1985), *Sexual/Textual Politics: Feminist Literary Theory* (London: Methuen).

SAYERS, Janet (1986), *Sexual Contradictions: Psychology, Psychoanalysis, and Feminism* (London: Tavistock).

SOPER, Kate (1986), *Humanism and Anti-Humanism* (London: Hutchinson).

WHITFORD, Margaret (1986), 'Speaking as a Woman: Luce Irigaray and the Female Imaginary', *Radical Philosophy*, vol. 43, pp. 3–8.

7

Luce Irigaray's Critique of Rationality

Margaret Whitford

This paper is about a feminist philosopher, Luce Irigaray, whose work raises particular difficulties for the Anglo-Saxon reader unfamiliar with the Continental tradition of philosophy.[1] In attempting to elucidate, with reference to its context, one of the strands of her critique of Western metaphysics, I hope to make her work more accessible for discussion to a wider readership. I must emphasise that this paper is only attempting to deal with one aspect of Irigaray's thought and will inevitably touch on issues that I won't have space to develop.

The work of Irigaray raises questions about the edifice of Western rationality. I would like here to approach these questions indirectly, to clarify their import by means of a detour through the concept of the imaginary. The term *imaginary* as a noun is current in French theoretical work, but not in English (except via Lacan, who gives the Imaginary, with a capital I, a major role in his theory). Like its English cognate, *imagination*, however, it is rich in connotations and operates differently in the different conceptual frameworks of the different authors who use it (authors as varied as Sartre, Bachelard, Barthes, Lacan, Castoriadis, Althusser). My view is that Anglo-American feminists have tended to assimilate, and then dismiss Irigaray's work too quickly, in part because the concept of the imaginary has not been closely examined. Either the imaginary has been ignored altogether, in which case Irigaray is mistakenly described as a biological essentialist (Sayers, 1982, p. 131; 1986, pp. 42–8), or else it has been interpreted as purely and simply a Lacanian concept, in which case the conclusion is that Irigaray has misunderstood or misread Lacan, and has not taken on board the implications of his theory (see Mitchell and Rose, 1982, pp. 54–6; Rose, 1985, pp. 136, 140; Ragland-Sullivan, 1986, pp. 273–80). In either case, the challenge to the Western conception of rationality has largely been ignored. I will suggest that the implications of this challenge cannot be clearly seen if one merely looks at Irigaray through a Lacanian window.

I will begin (first section) with a description of the difference between the male and the female imaginary as characterised by Irigaray, without at this point trying to say what exactly the imaginary is, or to explain or account for the elements in the description. I will then (second section) examine the evolution of the concept of the imaginary in Irigaray's work, and its origins in psychoanalytic theory. This section will clarify the initial description of the imaginary and show what is meant by the claim that rationality is imaginary. Finally, in the third section, I will return to the categories of male and female as applied to the imaginary, and argue that Irigaray does not see them primarily as empirical categories, but as reconceptualisations which might help us change and transform our society in a direction which is less inimical to women. Although Irigaray is not what is commonly thought of as a political philosopher, I would like to suggest that it might be useful to see her work as a contribution to political philosophy, in so far as she is dealing with the issue of *change*: how to alter women's status in Western society.[2] For as she writes in *This Sex Which Is Not One* (1985c), 'There is no simple manageable way to leap to the outside of phallogocentrism, *nor any possible way to situate oneself there, that would result from the simple fact of being a woman*' (p. 162). The problem with which she is dealing, then, is that of creating the conditions in which change can take place. Her aim, I believe, is not to formulate a programme, but to set a process in motion.

THE SYMBOLISM OF MALE AND FEMALE

There have been a number of discussions recently, which I shall not attempt to summarise here, about whether it makes sense to talk of the 'maleness' of philosophy (see Harding and Hintikka, 1983; Lloyd, 1984; Grimshaw, 1986, ch. 2). Very briefly, the argument concerns what it would mean to describe philosophy, or rationality, as male. Lloyd, for example, argues that 'our ideas of Reason have historically incorporated an exclusion of the feminine, and . . . femininity itself has been partly constituted through such processes of exclusion' (p. x). Grimshaw suggests that conceptions of masculinity are built into certain philosophical theories, arguing, for example, that Kant defines moral worth in such a way that women – as described by him elsewhere – are incapable of it (pp. 42–5). From the point of view that concerns me here, the problem is that conceptions of rationality seem to have been based upon exclusion models. Male–female symbolism has been used 'to express subordination relations between elements of a divided human nature' (Lloyd, p. 28) and reason, conceptualised as transcendence, in practice came to mean transcendence of the feminine, because of the symbolism used, despite the fact that 'it can of course be pointed out that mere bodily difference surely makes the female no more appropriate than the male to the symbolic representation of "lesser" intellectual functions' (Lloyd, p. 32).

Irigaray's work constitutes an attack upon such exclusion models, drawing for its symbolism on psychoanalysis, of which Irigaray is critical, but to which she is also indebted. There is a view in psychoanalytic theory, based on clinical evidence, that psychic health may be conceived of, unconsciously, as a state in which both parents, i.e. both the male and the female elements, are felt to be in creative intercourse within the psyche. Along these lines, then, Irigaray argues that for rationality to be fertile and creative, rather than infertile and sterile, it must not be conceived of as transcending or *exclusive of* the female element. The model is that of a creative (sexual) relationship in which the two elements in intercourse bring forth offspring, rather than a domination–subordination model in which one part of the self is repressing another part (as reason may be said to dominate the passions, for example). For Irigaray, the conceptualisation of rationality is inseparable from the conceptualisation of sexual difference; thus the imbalance in the symbolisation of sexual difference is a clue to other forms of imbalance that have far-reaching consequences: sexual difference is 'a problematic which might enable us to put in check the manifold forms of destruction of the world . . . Sexual difference could constitute the horizon of worlds of a fertility which we have not yet experienced' (Irigaray, 1984, p. 13). Ideas of fertility/sterility, creation/destruction, health/sickness (e.g. sclerosis) form part of her vocabulary, and reflect the ethical dimension of her analysis.

What is meant by male and female in this context? Although the terms are sometimes used to refer to biological males and females, it is much more common to find the pair being used as a kind of basic and fundamental symbolism (of which Genevieve Lloyd gives many examples in the history of philosophy and Alice Jardine (1985) in contemporary French thought). I shall keep the terms male and female (without inverted commas) for their symbolic use, and use the terms men and women to refer to social or biological categories.

Irigaray would argue that rationality in the Western tradition has always been conceptualised or symbolised as male. She adds a psychoanalytic dimension to this – which I will explain further in the second section – by making a connection between the morphology of the body and the morphology of different kinds of thought processes. It must not be assumed that the body here is the empirical body; symbolism (or representation) is selective;[3] and it is clear from *Speculum* (1985b) that Irigaray is talking about an 'ideal morphology' (p. 320), in which the relationship to anatomy is metaphorical, somewhat schematic, a 'symbolic interpretation of . . . anatomy' (Gallop, 1983, p. 79). Anticipating, one might say that it is an imaginary anatomy. So she can say that in the phallomorphic sexual metaphoricity (*Speculum*, p. 47) of Western rationality, there is 'no change in morphology, no detumescence ever' (ibid., p. 303). Western rationality, governed by the male imaginary, is characterised by: the principle of identity (also expressed in terms of quantity or ownership); the principle of non-contradiction (in which ambiguity, ambivalence or multivalence have been reduced to a minimum); and binarism (e.g. nature/reason, subject/object, matter/energy, inertia/movement) – as though everything had to be either one thing or another (Irigaray, 1985a, p. 313). All these principles are based upon the possibility of individuating, or distinguishing one thing from another, upon the belief in the necessity of stable forms.[4] An equation is made between the (symbolic) phallus, stable form, identity and individuation. Irigaray explains in *This Sex Which Is Not One* (1985c) that the logic of identity is male, because it is phallomorphic:

> The *one* of form, of the individual, of the (male) sexual organ, of the proper name, of the proper meaning . . . supplants, while separating and dividing, that contact of *at least two* (lips) which keeps woman in touch with herself (p. 26).

For the female imaginary, there is no 'possibility of distinguishing what is touching from what is being touched' (ibid., p. 26). The possibility of individuating is absent; woman '*is neither one nor two*' (ibid., p. 26):

Perhaps it is time to return to that repressed entity, the female imaginary. So woman does not have a sex organ? She has at least two of them, but they are not identifiable as ones. Indeed she has many more. Her sexuality, always at least double, goes even further: it is *plural*.

(Ibid., p. 28)

But if the female imaginary were to deploy itself, if it could bring itself into play otherwise than as scraps, uncollected debris, would it represent itself, even so, in the form of *one* universe?

(Ibid., p. 30)

It is not that the female is unidentifiable, but that there is 'an excess of all identification to/of self' (*Speculum*, p. 230). The principle of non-contradiction does not apply. The female imaginary is mobile and fluid: 'a proper(ty) that is never fixed in the possible identity-to-self of some form or other. It is always *fluid*' (*This Sex*, p. 79). In *Éthique de la différence sexuelle* (1984), the undifferentiated maternal/feminine is described as that which underlies 'all possibility of determining identity' (p. 98). Like the womb, it is the 'formless, "amorphous" origin of all morphology' (*Speculum*, p. 265, trans. adapted).

The reader will note the correspondence between the descriptions of the male and female imaginary, and the Pythagorean table of opposites, described by Aristotle in the *Metaphysics* (986a). On this table, Genevieve Lloyd (1984) comments:

In the Pythagorean table of opposites, formulated in the sixth century BC, femaleness was explicitly linked with the unbounded – the vague, the indeterminate – as against the bounded – the precise and clearly determined. The Pythagoreans saw the world as a mixture of principles associated with determinate form, seen as good, and others associated with formlessness – the unlimited, irregular or disorderly – which were seen as bad or inferior. There were ten such contrasts in the table: limit/unlimited, odd/even, one/many, right/left, male/female, rest/motion, straight/curved, light/dark, good/bad, square/oblong. Thus 'male' and 'female', like the other contrasted terms, did not here function as straightforwardly descriptive classifications. 'Male', like the other terms on its side of the table, was construed as superior to its opposite; and the basis for this superiority was its association with

the primary Pythagorean contrast between form and
formelessness.   (p. 3)

This correspondence between the imaginary (a concept deriving in
the first instance from psychoanalytic theory) and the ontological
categories of the pre-Socratics, is not, of course, accidental. I will
suggest later, in the third section, that the male and female imaginary
should be seen as political rather than psychoanalytic categories. I
interpret the female imaginary, for example, not as an essentialist
description of what women are really like, but as a description of the
female as she appears in, and is symbolised by, the Western cultural
imaginary. And I interpret Irigaray's work as a Derridean attempt to
deconstruct the pair in order to undermine its constraining power,
beginning by privileging the subordinate element.[5]

THE IMAGINARY

In this section, I shall trace briefly the development of the concept of
the imaginary in Irigaray's work. It seems to me that there is a shift
between *Speculum* and the work which follows it; the initial fairly
cautious appropriation of the term in a relatively uncontroversial
way is succeeded by a bolder and more extensive deployment with
much more far-reaching connotations. The points to which I want to
draw particular attention in this paper are:

(a) the importance of the imaginary body in philosophy;
(b) the introduction of the notion that the imaginary may be male or
    female;
(c) the description of rationality as imaginary.

As most readers of French theory know by now, the imaginary is a
psychoanalytic concept developed by Lacan in his reading of Freud.
The concept, if not the term, is introduced by Lacan in his article
entitled, 'The Mirror Stage as formative of the function of the I as
revealed in psychoanalytic experience' (Lacan, 1977, pp. 1–7). The
Imaginary is a developmental moment in the formation of the Ego or
'I': the baby, whose experience of its body until then had been
fragmented and incoherent, is enabled, by means of a mirror (or an
image of itself mirrored from a parental figure or figures) to see a
reflection of itself as a whole body or unity, with which it can then

identify 'in anticipation' (p. 4). However, it must be stressed that Lacan's Imaginary has its origins in Freud's theories of the Ego and of narcissism (see Rose, 1981; Benvenuto and Kennedy, 1986, ch. 2), and for my purposes here, it is the Freudian corpus which is more pertinent.

Freud does not use the term Ego entirely consistently (see the editorial comments in Freud, 1923, pp. 7–8), but it is possible to pick out three strands which shed light on Irigaray's concept of the imaginary. Firstly, the Ego is something which develops: 'a unity comparable to the ego cannot exist in the individual from the start; the ego has to be developed' (Freud, 1914, p. 77). Freud (1923, p. 17) describes it as 'a coherent organization of mental processes'. Thus the unity of personal identity is constructed out of a preceding state of lack of organisation of mental processes, which is described variously by psychoanalysts as undifferentiation, fragmentation and so on. (Lacan describes identity as illusory.) What is important is that it is not given from the beginning of life, but is developed in the context of the profound and literally life-giving relationship with the parental figure(s), and is thus completely suffused with affect. Since it is something which develops, it is therefore capable of modification under certain conditions in later life (such as psychoanalysis).

Secondly, the Ego is not equivalent to consciousness; part of the Ego is unconscious (Freud, 1915, pp. 192–93; 1920, p. 19; 1923, pp. 17–18). Thirdly, the Ego is a bodily Ego. This third point needs explaining in some detail. Freud's comment that 'the ego is first and foremost a bodily ego' (Freud, 1923, p. 26) is expanded by a later footnote as follows: 'I.e. the ego is ultimately derived from bodily sensations, chiefly from those springing from the surface of the body. It may thus be regarded as a mental projection of the surface of the body, besides . . . representing the superficies of the mental apparatus' (ibid.) Freud describes at several points how in phantasy, the ego represents its activities (mental or physical) to itself as equivalents of bodily activities. Probably the most well-known example of this is the identification whereby gifts or money (gold) or babies are equated with faeces (see Freud, 1905, pp. 186 and 196; 1908a, pp. 173–4; 1908b, pp. 219–20; 1917, pp. 128ff. and pp. 130–3). These equations or identifications may be shifting and provisional, or they may stabilise during the course of a person's development into a particular set of characteristics, as Freud describes in his paper 'Character and Anal Erotism' (Freud, 1908a).[6]

A more pertinent example of phantasy here is Freud's essay on 'Negation', in which the intellectual faculty of judgement (such as the capacity to assign truth or falsity to an assertion) is traced to this very primitive type of thinking in which everything is perceived/conceived on the model of the body:

> The function of judgement is concerned in the main with two sorts of decisions. It affirms or disaffirms the possession by a thing of a particular attribute; and it asserts or disputes that a presentation has an existence in reality. The attribute to be decided about may originally have been good or bad, useful or harmful. Expressed in the language of the oldest – the oral – instinctual impulses, the judgement is: 'I should like to eat this', or 'I should like to spit it out'; and, put more generally: 'I should like to take this into myself and to keep that out.' That is to say: 'It shall be inside me' or 'it shall be outside me'.
>
> (Freud, 1925, pp. 236–7)

To judge that something is true is, in phantasy, to swallow it or to incorporate it; to judge that something is false is to spit it out or to expel it.[7] Freud comments on the way in which a repressed thought may return in the form of a negative assertion: 'That is *not* what I was thinking', which is a kind of phantasy expulsion of the forbidden or repressed thought.

This is not a reductive account; to show the origins of conceptual thought in bodily phantasy does not entail any judgement about the truth or falsity of that thought. Phantasy is neither true nor false, and truth and falsity are judgements which belong to a different order and are governed by different rules. And further, as Freud (1908b) shows in his paper on the sexual theories of children, phantasmatic representations are not necessarily accurate perceptions of biological or social processes, but *interpretations* of them. These unconscious (mis)representations can coexist in the mind with the knowledge acquired at a later stage, providing, for example, an affective substratum which determines a person's attitude towards that later knowledge. (I will return to this point in the third section.)

The Freudian account of the (bodily) Ego and its relation to more intellectual activities in (unconscious) phantasy is explicitly subsumed by Lacan under the explanatory concept of the Imaginary: 'the symbolic equation [e.g. money=faeces] . . . arises from an alternating mechanism of expulsion and introjection, or projection and absorption, that is to say, from an imaginary game' (Lacan, 1975a, p. 96, trans. Rose, 1981, p. 139).[8] Thus what pre-Lacanian psychoanalysis describes as unconscious phantasy, Lacan describes as imaginary (though he then goes on to build a much more complicated edifice on the Imaginary and its relation with the Symbolic and the Real).

Let us return now to Irigaray. In *Speculum*, she takes the Lacanian term imaginary, and applies it to what psychoanalysis had previously called unconscious phantasy. At one point, for example, she attributes anachronistically the imaginary to Freud himself: 'elsewhere, Freud insists that in the childish imaginary the production of a child is equated with the production of feces' (p. 36), or refers to Freud's 'imaginary economy' (p. 101). At another point, she describes gold, penis and child as terms interchangeable with excrement 'in the current imaginary of any "subject"' (p. 125). When she refers to Lacan, it is not so much to argue with him, as to play with his concepts. She talks at some length in *Speculum* about the mirror (the concept of the imaginary was first introduced and developed in Lacan's theory of the mirror stage), but rather than giving an alternative account of women's psychosexual development, as might at first appear, she is offering a critique, or deconstruction, of a dominant conceptualisation or representation of sexual difference. Taking Lacan's mirror as an image of representation in the West, she asks him why he used a flat mirror, 'in that the flat mirror reflects the greater part of women's sexual organs only as a hole' (*Speculum*, p. 89, note): there is no penis, there appear to be no sexual organs, and 'she' appears to be defective. For the exploration of women's sexual specificity, a different sort of mirror (literal or figurative) might be needed – a speculum or a concave mirror.[9] Elsewhere she suggests that women are the components of which the mirror is made (*This Sex*, p. 151).

This is a point about conceptualisation, not about women. It is not so much that Irigaray is disputing Freud's or Lacan's theories, since she is in any case making use of their theories herself; it is rather that in *Speculum* she is psychoanalysing the psychoanalysts, analysing *their* imaginary, i.e. the unconscious phantasy underlying the Freudian or Lacanian explanatory systems. Her interpretation is that Freud's account of sexuality is anal, and that in the Freudian phantasy, the stage in which children are believed to be born through the anus (see e.g. Freud, 1908b), continues to underlie his theorisation. Freud's model of sexuality is male, according to Irigaray, quoting Freud: 'we are . . . obliged to recognise that the little girl is a little man' (Freud, 1933, p. 118). And since his phantasy is anal, a phantasy in which the specificity of women continues to remain unrecognised, women can *only* appear in this scenario as defective males.

But the point is also that an anatomical difference is perceived in the light of the conceptual frameworks available. In an important transition, Irigaray goes on to argue that this is not an example of the individual phantasy of any particular philosopher/psychoanalyst, but that speculation itself in the West is dominated by anality; sexuality and thinking, in an imaginary operation, have become equated both with each other and with one and the same bodily activity. The imaginary jumps, then, out of the domain of the technically psychoanalytic into the domain of social explanation,[10] and becomes a social imaginary signification which, as explained by another psychoanalyst and social critic, Castoriadis (1975), has almost unlimited extension:

> Compared with individual imaginary significations, [social imaginary significations] are infinitely vaster than a phantasy (the underlying schema of what is referred to as the Jewish, Greek, or Western 'world-picture' has no bounds) and they have no precisely located existence (if that is to say one can ascribe to the individual unconscious a precisely located existence).
>
> (pp. 200–1)[11]

By appropriating the term imaginary for his particular version of Freudian theory, Lacan was colonising a term which was already in current use in aesthetics and literary criticism, and changing its meaning radically. Irigaray, in a similar fashion, wrests Lacan's concept out of its Lacanian context in order to extend its significance; the imaginary emerges from its relatively subordinate position in *Speculum*, to become, in *This Sex* and *Éthique*, one of the key notions of an ambitious *social* critique.

To put it as succinctly as possible, the problem as defined by Irigaray is that the female has a particular function in symbolic processes: to subtend them, to be that which is outside discourse. Using the language of bodily phantasy and of the representations of the female body, one could say that 'She functions as a *hole* . . . in the elaboration of imaginary and symbolic processes' (*Speculum*,

p. 71). Any organisation of the real, whether it be linguistic, social or individual, is an organisation which carves out of an undifferentiated continuum a set of categories which enable the real to be grasped. But it is impossible to organise the world in this way without residue. The emergence of distinctions, determinate identities or social organisations always implies something else, that original state of non-differentiation from which they have emerged (Castoriadis's magma[12]), such as a pre-social nature[13] or the unconscious.[14] This outside, which is non-graspable in-itself, since it is by definition outside the categories which allow one to posit its existence, is traditionally conceptualised as female (the unlimited or the formless of the pre-Socratics). Within this sexual symbolism, the determinate, that which has form or identity, and so *ipso facto* rationality, belongs to the other half of the pair, and is therefore male.

Referring to this traditional conceptualisation, then, Irigaray describes women as a 'residue' (*This Sex*, p. 114), or as a 'sort of magma . . . from which men, humanity, draw nourishment, shelter, the resources to live or survive for free' (*Éthique*, p. 102). In *Speculum*, she had already described this 'outside' of discourse as the womb (*le matriciel*), and by extension the maternal body: 'formless, "amorphous" origin of all morphology' (p. 265, trans. adapted); in *Éthique* she adds that the undifferentiated maternal/feminine underlies 'all possibility of determining identity' (p. 98). Or women are described as resembling the unconscious: 'Thus we might wonder whether certain properties attributed to the unconscious may not, in part, be ascribed to the female sex, which is censured by the logic of consciousness' (*This Sex*, p. 73).

The unconscious is a realm in which the laws of identity and non-contradiction do not apply. So when Irigaray writes that for the female imaginary too, the laws of identity and non-contradiction (A is A, A is not B) do not apply either, it may sound like a dangerously irrationalist description of women that merely reinforces a traditional denigration. The practical value of these principles, without which rationality would be inconceivable, is so evident that it appears unquestionable. The logic of identity is the prerequisite of any language or any society at all. However, the point is that there will always be a residue which exceeds the categories, and this excess is conceptualised as female:

In other words, the issue is not one of elaborating a new theory of which woman would be the *subject* or the *object*, but of jamming the theoretical machinery itself, of suspending its pretension to the production of a truth and of a meaning that are excessively univocal. Which presupposes that women . . . do not claim to be rivalling men in constructing a logic of the feminine that would still take onto-theo-logic as its model, but that they are rather attempting to wrest this question away from the economy of the logos. They should not put it, then, in the form 'What is woman?' but rather, repeating/interpreting the way in which, within discourse, the feminine finds itself defined as lack, deficiency, or as imitation and negative image of the subject, they should signify that with respect to this logic a *disruptive excess* is possible on the feminine side.   (*This Sex*, p. 78)

The reader may remember the definition of the female in *Speculum* as 'an excess of all identifications to/of self' (p. 230).

From Irigaray's point of view, she is not *prescribing* what the female should be, but *describing* how it functions within Western imaginary and symbolic operations, *in order to* show how what is taken to be the unalterable order of reality (discursive or otherwise) is in fact *imaginary* and therefore susceptible to change. So she comments on Lacan that:

The topology of the subject as it is defined by certain theoreticians of psychoanalysis (cf. the *Écrits* of Jacques Lacan . . .) . . . would use the symbolisation of the feminine as a basis or basement for the (masculine) subject.   (*Éthique*, p. 103)

Any particular organisation is taken to be the real in an imaginary operation, since the real cannot be grasped without the framework of a set of categories. However, if one takes the imaginary to be equivalent to the real, and implies for example that the real is co-extensive with the categories of discourse, then of course the only possibilities for change will be permutations within the same set of categories; no totally different reorganisation could emerge.[15] Her objection to Lacan, then, is the way in which he takes a particular discursive organisation to be unchangeable:

What poses problems in reality turns out to be justified by a logic that has already ordered reality as such. Nothing escapes the circularity of this law.   (*This Sex*, p. 88)

This *ahistorical* (*This Sex*, pp. 100 and 125) conflation of the present categories of Western discourse with the real, thus eliding the question of social change, is Lacan's *imaginary* (*This Sex*, p. 99), which is also the imaginary of Western metaphysics. For,

> we note that this 'real' may well include, and in large measure, a *physical reality* that continues to resist adequate symbolization and/or that signifies the powerlessness of logic to incorporate in its writing all the characters of nature.
>
> (*This Sex*, pp. 106–7, trans. adapted)

Her particular argument against Lacan is that he excludes in advance the possibility of any real social change, because he does not ask the question about the relationship between real women and Woman – or awoman (*l'afemme*) as he prefers to say since, '*the* woman does not exist' (Mitchell and Rose, 1982, p. 167). For the problem for real women is that although they may be symbolised as the outside, they are not *in fact* outside the society they live in, and its symbolic structures.

In summary, then, Irigaray begins with an analysis of the imaginary of Western philosophical and psychoanalytic discourse (*Speculum*), aiming to show that the conceptualisation of sexual difference in this discourse is governed by an imaginary which is anal, that is to say which interprets sexual difference as though there were only one sex, and that sex were male (women are defective men). For our culture, identity, logic and rationality are symbolically male, and the female is either the outside, the hole, or the unsymbolisable residue (or at most, the womb, the maternal function). In *This Sex* and *Éthique*, Irigaray goes on to argue that the imaginary is not confined to philosophers and psychoanalysts, but is a social imaginary which is taken to be the real, with damaging consequences for women, who, unlike men, find themselves 'homeless' in the symbolic order. Unlike Lacan, she does not believe this imaginary to be fixed and unalterable; like Castoriadis, she is arguing that radical transformations in the social imaginary *can* take place, and that a new and previously unimaginable configuration could take shape.

   In 1966, in an early paper on the imaginary, she referred to 'the impossible return to the body' (Irigaray, 1985a, p. 15). In *Éthique*, she deplores the modern neglect of the body, and emphasises the fact that 'man's body is the threshold, the porch, of the construction of his universe(s)' (p. 99). Is there a contradiction here? Not if one remembers that the relation to the body is always an imaginary or symbolic one; it is the *real* body, like the real of the world, which is always out of reach. The importance of the imaginary body is that it underlies Western metaphysics, in which the subject is always identified as male. Thought is still, as it were, in the anal stage; sexual difference does not yet exist in the social imaginary of the West;[16] the female body is symbolised as outside. 'But this fault, this deficiency, this "hole", inevitably affords woman too few figurations, images or representations by which to represent herself' (*Speculum*, p. 71).

There might be another problem here. Since Lacan describes identity as imaginary, and if identity, according to Irigaray, is male (as described in the first section), the problem arises: either the idea of a female imaginary is self-contradictory, or the female imaginary, in so far as it attributes identity to the female populace, would still fall within the parameters of male thought, would be a male definition of the female. I think Irigaray's answer to that would be that precisely what we need to analyse is the unconscious of Western (male) thought, i.e. the female imaginary. Not until this repressed imaginary has been more adequately symbolised will we be able to articulate the relation between male and female elements in a different way. Which leads on to the question of strategy and the final section.

THE POLITICS OF MALE–FEMALE SYMBOLISM

I hope to have shown in the previous section that Irigaray's imaginary, although a concept which derives from psychoanalysis, cannot be understood in purely psychoanalytic terms, but also has an irreducible social dimension which makes its anatomical reference a symbolic or cultural one. She is not referring to a direct and unmediated relation to the body, but to an imaginary and symbolic representation of the body, an 'ideal morphology' which, as she puts it, leaves residues that are unsymbolised (or in which the female body may be symbolised as residue). I now want to conclude by discussing briefly the implications of using male–female symbolism to describe rationality as male and the female as unconscious/magma/residue in what might appear to be a symbolically retrograde move. Is it not politically dangerous to regard women as the irrational, or as the unconscious of culture? The problem is that one cannot alter symbolic meanings by *fiat*.[17] One cannot simply *reverse* the symbolism; and it is not enough to claim that women are in fact rational, since that is not the point. (The point is the relation of women to the symbolic structures which exclude them.) Irigaray's own strategy is mimicry, or mimesis:

> One must assume the feminine role deliberately. Which means already to convert a form of subordination into an affirmation, and thus begin to thwart it . . . To play with mimesis is thus, for a woman, to try to locate the place of her exploitation by discourse, without allowing herself to be simply reduced to it. It means to resubmit herself – inasmuch as she is on the side of the 'perceptible', of 'matter' – to 'ideas', in particular to ideas about herself that are elaborated in/by a masculine logic, but so as to make 'visible', by an effect of playful repetition, what was supposed to remain invisible: recovering a possible operation of the feminine in language.   (*This Sex*, p. 76, trans. adapted)

She insists though that mimesis is only a strategy (*This Sex*, p. 77), not a solution. And again, to understand her strategy, I think we need to refer back to the psychoanalytic model.[18]

In the individual psyche, unconscious phantasy is determining to the extent that it remains unconscious. When, in the psychoanalytic process, it achieves an access to consciousness via language (what Irigaray refers to as symbolisation or 'the operations of sublimation'), it becomes possible to effect a shift or change in the phantasy which enables the analysand to change and brings about real transformations in the personality, in the direction of greater flexibility and creativity, and less rigidity or repression.[19] I would suggest that one way to read Irigaray is to see her as conceiving of her work as initiating a process of change at the level of the social unconscious (or imaginary), by offering interpretations of the 'material' offered by society in its philosophical or metaphysical discourse:

> This process of interpretive rereading has always been a *psychoanalytic undertaking* as well. That is why we need to pay attention to the way the unconscious works in each philosophy, and perhaps in philosophy in general. We need to listen

(psycho)analytically to its procedures of repression, to the structuration of language that shores up its representations, separating the true from the false, the meaningful from the meaningless, and so forth.   (*This Sex*, p. 75)

These interpretations would verbalise the unconscious phantasy and begin the process of lifting the repression, a process which, on the model of psychoanalysis, might lead to change. On this reading of Irigaray, what is described as the female imaginary is not the essential feminine, common to all women, but a place in the symbolic structures.

In the first section, discussing the development of the Ego and its phantasies, I pointed out that the individual Ego, in psychoanalytic theory, is said to take shape in the context of a relationship with parental figures. Putting this another way, one might say that the acquisition of one's knowledge of the world is passionately motivated. Later, epistemology loses touch with its sources. This is precisely Irigaray's diagnosis of what has gone wrong with the rationality of the West. In *Éthique*, she suggests:

contrary to the usual methods of dialectic, love should not have to be abandoned in order to become wise or learned. It is love which leads to knowledge [*science*] . . . It is love which leads the way, and is the path, both.   (pp. 27–8)

As I indicated earlier, for Irigaray the conceptualisation of rationality is inseparable from the conceptualisation of sexual difference. The scission of epistemology from its sources is linked to a model of rationality (symbolised as male) in which the symbolic female is dominated or repressed, and 'transcended'. Irigaray suggests that this has led to the apotheosis of rationality – modern technology – and to apparently unstoppable processes of destruction.

To describe rationality as male is not to restrict rationality to men. Rather it is to argue against exclusion models of rationality, as Irigaray states more or less explicitly:

What has been needed, in effect, is a discourse in which sexuality itself is at stake so that what has been serving as a condition of possibility of philosophical discourse, or rationality in general, can make itself heard.   (*This Sex*, p. 168)

Exclusion is a process governed by the male imaginary (i.e. identity, or A is A, involves exclusion: A is not B); another way of putting it is to say that it is the way the male imaginary deals with sexual difference. What is important is that rationality is categorised by Irigaray as male, not in order to oppose it, which would be self-defeating, but in order to suggest a more adequate conceptualisation, in which, in psychoanalytic terms, the male does not repress or split off the female/unconscious, but acknowledges or integrates it. For the psychoanalytic model, the relation between the different parts of the person, however they are named: reason/passions, body/mind, superego/ego/id, consciousness/unconscious, need not be a clear-cut one; the boundaries may fluctuate, there may be a possibility of intercommunication which is not necessarily experienced as threatening or overwhelming. In Irigaray's terms, the sexual relationship (i.e. the relationship between the symbolic male and the symbolic female) should ideally be like a chiasma, in which each could offer a *home* (*lieu* or *sol*) to the other (*Éthique*, p. 16), in 'exchanges without identifiable terms, without accounts, without end' (*This Sex*, p. 197).

In her capacity as analyst of the social psyche, Irigaray can only offer interpretations, not programmes or solutions. But if one remains within her symbolism, one might say that the creative source for change lies in the unconscious, the magma, the outside – and therefore precisely in the female.

NOTES

Note on the translations. References to *Speculum* and *This Sex Which Is Not One* are taken from the available English translations (Irigaray, 1985b and 1985c respectively) except where otherwise indicated. Translations from *Éthique de la différence sexuelle* and *Parler n'est jamais neutre* (Irigaray, 1984 and 1985a respectively) are my own.

1. Alice Jardine (1985), in her impressive book on woman-as-effect in modern French theory, *Gynesis*, points out the problems of trying to read French theory out of context. A further problem is the term 'feminist'. Since many French women theorists see 'woman' as a metaphysical concept, they are reluctant to call themselves feminist because of the unacceptable theoretical implications of this term (see Jardine, pp. 19ff. and p. 82).

2. Irigaray indicates the 'political' aspect of her work as follows: 'Every operation on and in philosophical language, by virtue of the very nature of that discourse – which is essentially political – possesses implications that, no matter how mediate they may be, are nonetheless politically determined' (*This Sex*, p. 81).

3. Cf. Freud's account of hysterical symptoms, which do not correspond to neuro-physiological pathways but to symbolic or phantasmatic patterns: '*hysteria behaves as though anatomy did not exist or as though it had no knowledge of it*' (Freud, 1893, p. 169).

4. '*The object of desire itself*, and for psychoanalysts, *would be the transformation of fluid to solid*? Which seals – this is well worth repeating – *the triumph of rationality*. Solid mechanics and rationality have maintained a relationship of very long standing, one against which fluids have never stopped arguing' (*This Sex*, p. 113). (Irigaray's italics.) See also 'Le sujet de la science est-il sexué?' (Irigaray, 1985a, pp. 307–21), and 'Éthique de la différence sexuelle' (Irigaray, 1984, pp. 113–24, trans. in Moi, 1987), for an account of the 'maleness' of the human and physical sciences.

5. For an account of Derrida's deconstructive method, see his *Positions* (1981), title interview, and also Wood (1979). See also Moi (1985), pp. 138ff., for a brief account of Irigaray's use of Derrida.

6. For a moving and almost entirely non-technical account of the operations of unconscious phantasy and their possible effects on the personality and activities of adult life, see Milner (1969).

7. See Wollheim (1973), pp. 189–90.

8. Lacan's Imaginary is, of course, a much more far-reaching notion than this remark indicates. It should be pointed out that, as various Lacan commentators have indicated, Lacan's terms and concepts are not completely stable (Bowie, 1979, p. 122; Benvenuto and Kennedy, 1986, p. 102); they are mutually self-defining, and their implications alter in different contexts. I am not attempting here to do justice to the differences between Lacan's Imaginary and Irigaray's imaginary, but these differences are crucial, since as I pointed out in an earlier paper (Whitford, 1986, p. 4), Irigaray appears to be ignoring Lacan's essential distinction between the Imaginary and the Symbolic, and conflating the two. This strategy needs much more careful examination than it has so far received; in passing, I would just point out that Irigaray's position is that 'from a feminine locus nothing can be articulated without a questioning of the symbolic itself' (*This Sex*, p. 162). Any discussion of her differences with Lacan would need to take into account the fact that she is attempting to go *beyond* Lacan, and is not simply missing the point.

9. The deconstruction of the 'mirror' is central to *Speculum*, so I have not attempted to document it with page references.

10. In *Speculum*, Irigaray is dealing with the history of Western philosophical discourse. In *This Sex* and *Éthique*, however, particularly the latter, the social implications of her work become more apparent.

11. My translation. An English translation of part of the work from which this quotation is taken, in which Castoriadis puts forward his theory

about the imaginary institutions of society, can be found in Castoriadis (1984). The complete English translation (Polity Press, 1987) was not available at the time the present book went to press. Castoriadis gives as examples of social imaginary significations: religious belief (Castoriadis, 1975, pp. 196ff., trans. pp. 23ff.); reification (in slavery or under capitalism) (pp. 197ff., trans. pp. 23ff.); the modern bureaucratic universe and its pseudo-rationality (pp. 222ff.). To call social institutions like slavery or capitalism 'imaginary' might give the misleading impression that they are 'all in the mind'. Castoriadis stresses that 'the social imaginary, as we understand it, is more real than the "real"' (p. 197, trans. p. 24). The problem is rather that 'society lives its relation with institutions in the form of the imaginary; . . . it does not recognize the institutional imaginary as its own product' (p. 184, trans. p. 15). I should like to thank Dr Jay Bernstein of the University of Essex, for drawing my attention to Castoriadis's work on the imaginary.

12. 'A magma is that from which one can extract (or in which one can construct) an indefinite number of ensemblist organisations, but which can never be reconstituted (ideally) by an ensemblist composition (finite or infinite) of these organizations . . . We assert that everything that can be effectively given – representations, nature, signification – exists in the mode of a *magma*; that the social–historical institutions of the world, things, and individuals, in so far as it is the institution of the *Legein* and the *Teukhein*, is always also the institution of identitary logic and thus the imposition of an ensemblist organisation on a first stratum of givenness which lends itself interminably to this operation. But also, that it is never and can never be *only* that – that it is also always and necessarily the institution of a magma of imaginary social significations. And finally, that the relation between the *Legein* and the *Teukhein* and the magma of imaginary social significations is not thinkable within the identitary–ensemblist frame of reference – no more than are the relations between *Legein* and representation, *Legein* and nature, or between representation and signification, representation and world, or 'consciousness' and 'unconscious' (Castoriadis, 1975, pp. 461–3, trans. in Howard, 1977, p. 297). Howard provides a useful introduction to Castoriadis's ideas.

13. 'In any case, the attempt to find an existent state of nature cannot, in principle, succeed. This is not a problem of the limitations of our existing knowledge (the possibility of an as-yet undiscovered people living in a purely natural state). The reason why it cannot succeed is . . . that the term "nature" is in the end defined only by reference to the social, as that which is the non-social' (Brown and Adams, 1979, p. 37).

14. See Castoriadis (1975), pp. 372ff. for a discussion of the essential heterogeneity of the unconscious on the one hand and the logic of identity on the other.

15. Lacan, for example, writes: 'There is no pre-discursive reality' (Lacan, 1975b, p. 33). Cf. Castoriadis's criticism of Lacan (Castoriadis, 1975, pp. 7–8). Castoriadis's point is that from a Lacanian perspective, it becomes impossible to understand the emergence of a social

organisation that did not previously exist. This is not a question of an (impossible) return to a prediscursive reality, but of the possibility of creation *ex nihilo*. In this context, see MacIntyre's point about the unpredictability of future inventions (MacIntyre, 1981, ch. 8).

16. This is Irigaray's interpretation of Lacan's view that there is no relation between the sexes since 'woman does not exist' (see Mitchell and Rose, 1982, pp. 137–71). Irigaray's discussion is in 'Così fan tutti' (Irigaray, 1985c, pp. 86–105).

17. The traps of the symbolism that one inherits are usefully discussed in Lloyd (1984), ch. 7.

18. In a recent article I have developed this argument in more detail (Whitford, 1986).

19. In the technical language of Freud's metapsychology, this point is expressed as follows:

the conscious presentation comprises the presentation of the thing plus the presentation of the word belonging to it, while the unconscious presentation is the presentation of the thing alone. The system *Ucs.* contains the thing-cathexes of the objects, the first and true object-cathexes; the system *Pcs.* comes about by this thing-presentation being hypercathected through being linked with the word-presentations corresponding to it. It is these hypercathexes, we may suppose, that bring about a higher psychical organization and make it possible for the primary process to be succeeded by the secondary process which is dominant in the *Pcs.* . . . A presentation which is not put into words, or a psychical act which is not hypercathected, remains thereafter in the *Ucs.* in a state of repression.   (Freud, 1915, pp. 200–1)

REFERENCES

BENVENUTO, Bice and KENNEDY, Roger (1986), *The Works of Jacques Lacan: An Introduction* (London: Free Association Books).

BOWIE, Malcolm (1979), 'Jacques Lacan', in John Sturrock (ed.), *Structuralism and Since: From Lévi-Strauss to Derrida* (Oxford: Oxford University Press), pp. 116–53.

BRENNAN, Teresa (forthcoming), 'An Impasse in Psychoanalysis and Feminism'.

BROWN, Beverley and ADAMS, Parveen (1979), 'The Feminine Body and Feminist Politics', *m/f*, vol. 3, pp. 33–50.

CASTORIADIS, Cornelius (1975), *L'Institution imaginaire de la société* (Paris: Seuil). English translation: *The Imaginary Institution of Society* (Cambridge: Polity Press, 1987).

CASTORIADIS, Cornelius (1984), 'The Imaginary Institution of Society', trans. Brian Singer in John Fekete (ed.), *The Structural Allegory: Reconstructive Encounters with the New French Thought* (Manchester: Manchester University Press), pp. 6–45.

DERRIDA, Jacques (1981), *Positions*, trans. Alan Bass (London: Athlone Press).

FREUD, Sigmund. (All references are to the *Standard Edition of the Complete Psychological Works of Sigmund Freud* (SE), trans. and ed. James Strachey (London: The Hogarth Press, 1951–73). Dates given are those of original publication.

FREUD, Sigmund (1893), 'Some Points for a Comparative Study of Organic and Hysterical Motor Paralyses', SE I, pp. 155–72.

FREUD, Sigmund (1905), 'Three Essays on the Theory of Sexuality', SE VII, pp. 123–245.

FREUD, Sigmund (1908a), 'Character and Anal Erotism', SE IX, pp. 167–75.

FREUD, Sigmund (1908b), 'On the Sexual Theories of Children', SE IX, pp. 205–26.

FREUD, Sigmund (1914), 'On Narcissism: An Introduction', SE XIV, pp. 67–102.

FREUD, Sigmund (1915), 'The Unconscious', SE XIV, pp. 159–215.

FREUD, Sigmund (1917), 'On Transformations of Instinct as Exemplified in Anal Erotism', SE XVII, pp. 125–33.

FREUD, Sigmund (1920), 'Beyond the Pleasure Principle', SE XVIII, pp. 1–65.

FREUD, Sigmund (1923), 'The Ego and the Id', SE XIX, pp. 1–66.

FREUD, Sigmund (1925), 'Negation', SE XIX, pp. 233–9.

FREUD, Sigmund (1933), 'New Introductory Lectures on Psychoanalysis', SE XXII.

GALLOP, Jane (1982), *Feminism and Psychoanalysis: The Daughter's Seduction* (London: Macmillan).

GALLOP, Jane (1983), '*Quand nos lèvres s'écrivent*: Irigaray's Body Politic', *Romanic Review*, vol. 74, pp. 77–83.

GRIMSHAW, Jean (1986), *Feminist Philosophers: Women's Perspectives on Philosophical Traditions* (Brighton: Wheatsheaf).

HARDING, Sandra and HINTIKKA, Merrill B. (eds) (1983), *Discovering Reality: Feminist Perspectives on Epistemology, Metaphysics, Methodology, and Philosophy of Science* (Dordrecht: Reidel).

HOWARD, Dick (1977), 'Ontology and the Political Project: Cornelius Castoriadis', in Dick Howard, *The Marxian Legacy* (New York: Urizen), pp. 262–301, 328–33.

IRIGARAY, Luce (1974), *Speculum de l'autre femme* (Paris: Minuit).

IRIGARAY, Luce (1977), *Ce Sexe qui n'en est pas un* (Paris: Minuit).

IRIGARAY, Luce (1984), *Éthique de la différence sexuelle* (Paris: Minuit).

IRIGARAY, Luce (1985a), *Parler n'est jamais neutre* (Paris: Minuit).

IRIGARAY, Luce (1985b), *Speculum of the Other Woman*, trans. Gillian C. Gill (Ithaca and New York: Cornell University Press).

IRIGARAY, Luce (1985c), *This Sex Which Is Not One*, trans. Catherine Porter with Carolyn Burke (Ithaca and New York: Cornell University Press).

JARDINE, Alice A. (1985), *Gynesis: Configurations of Woman and Modernity* (Ithaca and London: Cornell University Press).

LACAN, Jacques (1975a), *Le Séminaire livre I. Les Écrits techniques de Freud* (Paris: Seuil).

LACAN, Jacques (1975b), *Le Séminaire livre XX. Encore* (Paris: Seuil).

LACAN, Jacques (1977), *Écrits. A Selection*, trans. Alan Sheridan (London: Tavistock).

LLOYD, Genevieve (1984), *The Man of Reason: 'Male' and 'Female' in Western Philosophy* (London: Methuen).

MacCORMACK, Carol and STRATHERN, Marilyn (eds) (1980), *Nature, Culture and Gender* (Cambridge: Cambridge University Press).

MacINTYRE, Alasdair (1981), *After Virtue: A Study in Moral Theory* (London: Duckworth).

MILNER, Marion (1969), *The Hands of the Living God: An Account of a Psycho-Analytic Treatment* (London: The Hogarth Press).

MITCHELL, Juliet and ROSE, Jacqueline (eds) (1982), *Feminine Sexuality: Jacques Lacan and the École Freudienne* (London: Macmillan).

MOI, Toril (1985), *Sexual/Textual Politics: Feminist Literary Theory* (London: Methuen).

MOI, Toril (ed.) (1987), *French Feminist Thought* (Oxford: Blackwell).

RAGLAND-SULLIVAN, Ellie (1986), *Jacques Lacan and the Philosophy of Psychoanalysis* (Urbana and Chicago: University of Illinois Press).

ROSE, Jacqueline (1981), 'The Imaginary', in Colin McCabe (ed.), *The Talking Cure: Essays in Psychoanalysis and Language* (London: Macmillan) pp. 132–61. Reprinted in Jacqueline Rose, *Sexuality in the Field of Vision* (London: Verso, 1986), pp. 166–97.

ROSE, Jacqueline (1985), 'Dora: Fragment of an Analysis', in Charles Bernheimer and Claire Kahane (eds), *In Dora's Case: Freud – Hysteria – Feminism* (London: Virago), pp. 128–48.

SAYERS, Janet (1982), *Biological Politics: Feminist and Anti-Feminist Perspectives* (London: Tavistock).

SAYERS, Janet (1986), *Sexual Contradictions: Psychology, Psychoanalysis, and Feminism* (London: Tavistock).

WHITFORD, Margaret (1986), 'Speaking as a Woman: Luce Irigaray and the Female Imaginary', *Radical Philosophy*, vol. 43, pp. 3–8.

WOLLHEIM, Richard (1973), *Freud* (London: Fontana).

WOOD, D. C. (1979), 'An Introduction to Derrida', *Radical Philosophy*, vol. 21, pp. 18–28.

8

Feminism, Feelings and Philosophy

Morwenna Griffiths

Women are more emotional than men, or such is the commonly held belief in present day Western society. But is the belief true? And does it matter? The answers are not easy ones to find because the meaning of the statement is so unclear. It might mean, for instance, that women are less in control of their emotions, or it might mean that they feel things more deeply, or that they are more irrational than men. None of these statements necessarily implies any of the rest – though they often come as a package. Indeed, the statement that women are more emotional than men has no clear meaning. However, it has a considerable political force because it is used to justify or explain the position of women. The usual justification/ explanation runs: since women are more emotional they are less suited to public life. But this is not the only possible political use of the statement. It has been taken up recently by some feminists and used in celebration of women's values and as a criticism of men and their personal, moral or social arrangements. In other words, feminists have stood the argument on its head. It now goes: since men are so unemotional, they are unfit to run public life.

In this article I shall examine what lies behind this difference of opinion. I shall begin by looking further at commonly held beliefs about emotions and feelings and how they relate to various groups in our society. I then go on to look at recent feminism and show that the relationships it assumes to hold between emotion and reason, mind and rationality, feelings and bodies, are not those which are usually assumed in recent mainstream Western philosophy, particularly in the Anglo-Saxon analytical tradition. If these feminist conceptions of emotion and feeling are right, they constitute a significant criticism of that philosophy and I shall argue that this criticism is justified. I shall then go on to make a suggestion about how these negative criticisms may have positive implications both for academic philosophy and for feminist theory. In other words, instead of considering beliefs about feelings, emotions and women in the terms of an accepted model in which questions about sex differences and emotions could be answered empirically, I am challenging the model itself in the light of feminist theory.

COMMONLY HELD BELIEFS

Related to the belief that women are more emotional than men go a number of other commonly held beliefs about men, women and emotion. According to the public voice, the dominant view of our society, these include women being more sensitive to feelings, their own and other people's, and women being closer to their bodies and more in tune with nature and natural rhythms. Men, by contrast, are often thought to be more in control of their bodies and feelings, freer, and able to manage the world's affairs coolly, rationally, logically and objectively. To show weakness, especially as a result of emotion and feeling, is to be 'unmanned' (OED). The public voice continues: the relationship with the body is very different for the two sexes. Women are in thrall to their bodies. Their lives are interwoven with their reproductive capacities: their face is their fortune and their biology is their destiny. By contrast, male pride in the body is pride in control and performance. Men may even view their bodies as highly efficient 'well-tuned' machines. An example of this male view of the self is shown by another source of male pride, sexual prowess, a concept which depends on sexuality being thought of in terms of the performance of feats of strength and endurance. In short, women are 'in tune with', 'in harmony with', 'close to' or 'part of' natural things; men are in control of them.

There is an assumption implicit in this set of beliefs that to be emotional, or sensitive to feelings, close to one's body, or in tune with nature is opposed to being rational and logical. Thus it would seem, if this assumption were right, that being emotional, or close to one's body and feelings, would mean being less rational, and therefore less free, and therefore less able to participate in all aspects of human life as a mature adult – less than fully human.

It is interesting and instructive to notice the race and class dimensions of the argument along with the sex/gender ones. In the dominant view I am describing, black people, 'primitives' and the working classes have been thought to be closer to feelings and nature and to be more emotional than white, 'civilised' and middle or upper class people. Sometimes the view is merely patronising. White women, black people, those from small-scale societies, and the working classes have been described as though they were childlike: innocent, thoughtless and natural (see Rowbotham, 1983, p. 302). In other words, the view is that all these groups of people are unfit for full participation in public life. Sometimes the view is more vicious. For example, myths surround black sexuality and lead directly to the suffering of black men, stereotyped as black rapists, drawing attention away from the white rapists of black women. Historically, this is well documented for the United States, and it was also true of British Imperialism (Amos and Parmar, 1984). History also shows that in the nineteenth century there was a strong belief that uncontrolled savages and the lower orders would be tamed by education. These views are not dead today.[1] The conception of a male out of control of his emotions and body is still a conception of a black, primitive or lower class male rather than a civilised middle class one. (Among current folk heroes the uncontrolled Incredible Hulk is not a gentleman while the cool and intelligent Superman is.)

It must be emphasised that not everyone shares these beliefs. The members of the groups in question may well dissent from them. They may do this by simply denying their truth. Or they may agree with the belief as stated, but not in spirit, by redefining the relevant concepts. Thus women may reclaim concepts like 'human nature' and 'natural' by conceptualising them in a number of different ways (Jaggar, 1983). Alternative structures of explanation also provide sources of dissent. Marxist explanation emphasises the alienation of members of the working classes, not their naturalness. For the time being I shall not go on considering the race and class aspects of this argument, but I shall return to them towards the end of the article.

To sum up: there is a commonly held, publicly voiced view that to be fully human you need a rational mind which is in control of a strong body. Feelings and emotions are dangerous because they threaten both the rationality and the control. Since women are more emotional they are less than fully human, neither wholly rational nor wholly in control of their bodies. There are those who do not hold to these views, but they are not widely heard.

FEELINGS AND FEMINISM

Feminist writing questions and challenges the assumption that emotion, feeling, nature and bodies are in opposition to rationality, mind and freedom, such that the relationship between them is one of hierarchical control. This challenge is implicit in a wide variety of feminist concerns. Feminism is not monolithic and feminists do not all speak with one voice. It is all the more striking then that the different concerns expressed in feminist writing and the variety of different voices which make themselves heard, all point, time and again, in a similar direction with regard to emotion and reason.

Quite rightly, women have not begun their criticism of masculinism with the abstract categories found useful to describe masculine viewpoints. They have begun with the concrete and particular, for instance, rape, depression, abortion, pay. Out of these concrete, particular concerns, abstractions are generated. One which keeps recurring is the close relationship between feelings and thought, emotion and reason, mind and body, and the need to break down current dualism in thinking about them. An extension of all this is the kind of relationship we perceive ourselves to have with the rest of the natural world, and the damage that is done to us and to it if that relationship is misconceived. How these concerns are theorised varies. But however deep the differences they are focused on a shared concern, that of the fundamental significance of feeling.

A recent book demonstrates the way that these abstract concerns have recurred. Hester Eisenstein (1984), in a particularly concise and thoughtful survey, identifies the main themes that underlie the concrete issues of 'second wave' (i.e. post 1960) feminist thought. The themes she identifies are not idiosyncratic, as a look at other recent collections and overviews shows. In her book the themes of feeling, emotion, bodies and nature run like threads through the variety of topics raised. The book can be read as a demonstration of the centrality of feelings to feminist thinking, and, further, as a demonstration of the way feminist thinking insists that feelings be part of the areas of discourse usually reserved for embodied minds, dispassionate arguments and impersonal, rational objectivity. This insistence has occurred because feelings have been understood to be related both to intelligence and to bodies – neither inexplicable promptings of the body nor some kind of pure disinterested 'higher' emotion.

Eisenstein begins her survey with the slogan 'the personal is political' and the arguments demonstrating the connections between the personal, private, intimate world of personal relationships and the public, social, political world of impersonal duties and rules. Sexual relationships are the next major theme: feminists have shown the connections between rape and power relations, and have made lesbianism a political issue. The connections are made in both directions. On the one hand, sexual relationships of all kinds are shown not to be mere urges of the body or rushes of unintelligent, irrational emotion. On the other, feelings are interwoven with what was previously taken to be impersonal and objective: politics and public life. These issues are fairly familiar outside feminist circles by now. I think the next ones Eisenstein deals with are less so: the production of knowledge itself and the way feelings are relevant to it; the critique of 'culture' and 'science' as being part of masculine gender identity; and the way that standard psychology's 'normal man' is not expected to have developed his emotions and feelings. Each of these issues raises the question of the relationship of rationality to feeling, and the effect of power structures on both.

The production of feminist knowledge is grounded in feeling. So far from feelings being seen as mere subjectivity, something to be overcome in the search for objectivity, they are seen to be a source of knowledge. The knowledge gained is distorted, however, unless power relations deriving from personality, race, class, etc., are acknowledged and allowed for. All of this can be seen directly in the theory and practice of the activity known as 'consciousness-raising' in which feelings are the subject matter, and their expression is a means of arriving at the truth, a truth about public, political life rather than about individual personalities. Feelings and their expression are likely to be a part of the process of obtaining rational objective knowledge, rather than being a hindrance to it (Eisenstein, 1984, pp. 35–6).

Further, truth and knowledge become distorted when feelings are not acknowledged. Most seriously, one way in which distortion has occurred is in the conceptualisation of truth and knowledge themselves. Evelyn Fox Keller has discussed this process for science. She argues (1985, pp. 75–6) that the kinds of rational objectivity and technical control taken to be constitutive of science are distortions introduced by unacknowledged and unexamined myths of masculinity which have their roots in typically masculine ways of feeling and which pervade scientific thought.

I have said that politics and the production of knowledge are two areas in which feminism asserts the significance of feelings, a significance which has not generally been acknowledged. The theme is taken up by feminist psychology which not only asserts the need to acknowledge feeling, but also warns about the distortions of understanding that result from accounts of normal adult rationality as including an ability to control and dominate one's emotions (Eisenstein, 1984, p. 64). In the last part of her book, Eisenstein looks at how these early themes are taken up and extended in the current writing of radical feminists such as Mary Daly and Susan Griffin. These feminists hold that the closeness of women to the natural world and male hatred of the flesh are causally related to men's systematic violent domination over women, and to their false forms of knowledge.

Daly and Griffin have developed the idea that women are more emotional, closer to their bodies and feelings, and part of the natural world in a way that men are not, and, further, they believe that this is a source of power and freedom unavailable to men and their masculine way of living. Both of them want women to become 'woman-identified'. For Daly this is a radical feminist separation, necessary for women to release the flow of 'Elemental energy' (Daly, 1984, pp. 370–3). Griffin, on the other hand, sees the 'culture within culture' that women on their own can create as a step on the road to a deeper understanding of the human (Griffin, 1982, pp. 11–12).

This development in radical feminist thinking celebrates feelings and nature in a way that overturns the standard views of rationality and control. It is a way of thinking that agrees with the statement that women are more emotional than men, but that reconceptualises and explains it such that it is now women rather than men who are better able to understand the world and live in it successfully. The development of this thought would have been difficult, perhaps impossible, using language straightforwardly, since the language we use reflects and shapes our conceptual frameworks as well as being shaped by them. The writing of Daly and Griffin relies, as much feminist writing does, on the reader's ability and willingness to read between the lines. It is allusive, poetical, polemical and utopian, and it is meant to jolt us out of the old ways of thinking. The accounts of women or of nature, for instance, are not meant to be empirically verifiable. They are, rather, accounts which suggest new ways of organising our thought, ways which should lead to a better understanding of humanity and the rest of the world.

The work of Daly and Griffin needs some critical examination, for while it has considerable value, as I shall argue, I believe it also makes serious mistakes. Its greatest value is in the impetus it gives us to reconceptualise and recategorise in a way that reinstates feelings and emotions and does not simply define them as part of the mind or part of the body. Eisenstein does not see this, and indeed she criticises radical feminists for retreating into psychological individualism and separatism, and for ignoring political needs. In doing so she has not taken into account the political significance of recategorising and renaming which enables people to see themselves in new ways.[2] Nor does she take into account the immediate political dimension of such ideas which can be seen in the identification of peace, ecology and technology as an important part of a feminist politics. Such a politics includes, for instance, the women's peace camp at Greenham Common, the international concern about the uses of science and technology and a concern for the complex pattern of life on earth (Caldecott and Leland, 1983; Seller, 1985).

Other parts of their work need a more severely critical examination because they pay insufficient attention to the social basis of the intelligence of feeling. Here I am in agreement with Eisenstein that radical feminism is not enough on its own, however important it is as a strand in the fabric of feminism. From the stance of radical feminism it is difficult to develop a basis from which to understand class and race factors, or the different views of women from other parts of the world. Indeed all these points of view tend to be missing in their writing. This is true even of Griffin who obviously has awareness of both race and class, but does not manage to include either of them in her main argument. I think this is because she does not explore the ways in which sexism is different and ways in which it is the same as discrimination directed at other groups (which often include women). So while she mentions them, their experience cannot appear in her argument.[3] Both Daly and Griffin talk as though women have an essential nature, distorted by patriarchy, but waiting discovery. Daly talks of dis-covery, a-mazing, exorcism and unveiling; Griffin (1982) of

a deeper self, a self untouched by convention, a self not moulded to society's idea of who a woman should be. This was an earlier, pre-social being who had come to life in me.   (p. 7)

This theory of an essential nature untouched by social influence ignores the importance of other people in the development of any human person, and in the end cannot account for the sheer variety in patterns of human life – including women's lives – that enrich the world.

FEELINGS AND PHILOSOPHY

In this section I shall argue that feminist views on feeling constitute a significant criticism of much mainstream Western philosophy of mind, and that these criticisms need to be taken into account if a better understanding of ourselves, both men and women, is to be reached. I have been summarising the way in which feminist writing implicitly questions and challenges assumptions about feeling and its relationship to reason, bodies and objectivity, assumptions which have been widely accepted in modern Western societies and by modern Western philosophers. I shall focus on three ways in which feminist writing challenges these assumptions. In doing so I shall be focusing on the tradition of modern Anglo-Saxon analytical philosophy and I shall make broad generalisations about it, which I believe to be justified, but which I have no space to justify here. I shall also make occasional mention of an alternative tradition which is more influential in Europe and outside the English-speaking world.[4]

The first two criticisms are to do with the concepts used to describe people and the third is to do with the focus of attention. The first criticism is that human beings have been discussed in terms of just the two categories of mind and body (or of embodied minds), so feelings and emotions have been thought to be some uneasy mixture of the two. Secondly, the relationship between mind and body (and feelings where they have been noticed at all) has been thought to be one of hierarchical control. Thirdly, the contradictions inherent in this view of people as embodied minds remain unnoticed because feelings have largely been ignored in philosophical discussions. If feelings were taken more seriously as feminism suggests they should be, the view would be harder to maintain.

The first implied criticism that arises from feminist views is that the conceptualisation of human beings has generally been into just two categories. This criticism seems justified. Philosophy of mind has been dominated by considerations of minds as rational, reasonable, reasoning or, sometimes, rationalising.[5] Philosophers also notice bodies, but they have little to say about feelings or emotions as a separate category. This lack of attention can be obscured by the way it is sometimes simply assumed that feelings and emotions are of the body or of the mind.[6]

This dualism is particularly obvious in the analytical tradition where one of the famous, and intractable, problems in philosophy of mind is the 'mind–body' problem, that is, the problematic nature of the relationship of minds to bodies. In this respect it is not much of an exaggeration to say that philosophy is less a series of footnotes to Plato than a series of footnotes to Descartes whom Mary Daly (1984) calls 'modern philosophy's severed head' (p. 253). Many contemporary philosophers now find themselves thinking of an even more disembodied phenomenon, the 'brain in a vat'.[7] It is true that the similarity is disguised. In analytical philosophy the language has changed from Descartes's pineal gland, corporeal and thinking substances to neurones, intentional objects and physical matter, or to the metaphors of computer programs, software and hardware. Glover (1976, p. 6) calls this series of footnotes a history of reactions against dualism, but as his summary makes clear, Descartes's mind stuff has been replaced by another abstraction, whether of patterns of behaviour or of mental states. Of course, I do not want to suggest that any particular details of Descartes's system are accepted by those philosophers who try to solve the 'mind–body' problem:[8] my point here is that Descartes set the terms in which the discussion is conducted.

Descartes paid some attention to feelings and emotions, trying to fit them into the structure of his philosophy. In his book, *The Passions of the Soul*, Descartes begins by noting that the passions affect and are affected by both soul and body. He defines the passions of the soul as:

> The perceptions, feelings, or emotions of the soul which we relate specially to it, and which are caused, maintained, and fortified by some movement of the spirits. (Art. 27)

The 'spirits' are 'animal spirits', i.e. of the body. He continues:

> Of all the kinds of thought which it [the soul] may have, there are no others which so powerfully agitate and disturb it as do these passions. (Art. 28)

He is making clear that the passions are not a perception of an outside object like sound, scent or colour, nor of a state of body like hunger, thirst or pain, but neither are they a pure activity of the soul, because the most proximate cause is the spirits. He seems unable to sustain this initial position within the framework of his dualism. By the end of his account he is describing a split between *intellectual* emotions and *bodily* ones. For instance, in Art. 91 he distinguishes the passion 'joy' from purely intellectual 'joy'. The latter has an obscure relationship with the body. He says:

> It is true that while the soul is united to the body this intellectual joy can hardly fail to be accompanied by that which is passion.
>
> (Art. 91)

But he does not explain what is meant by the phrase 'can hardly fail to'. In effect he abandoned his original definition but did not replace it with another. Feelings and emotions do not fit easily into a two-category system consisting of mind and body, and Descartes failed to solve the problem of making them do so.

Descartes's dualism has been much criticised. Many writers on emotions and feelings begin by criticising him. They declare themselves to be in reaction against him. It is striking though that these critics end up by adopting a very similar solution to Descartes to the problems of fitting feelings and emotions into the philosophy of mind. It is rare nowadays in philosophical circles for emotions to be thought of as pure physical prompting of the body. More often, emotions are defined as 'intentional', that is, of the mind.[9] Feelings are then contrasted with them and are said to be of the body. We end up with emotions (of the mind, rational) contrasted with feelings (of the body, natural).

Sometimes this position is extreme. Both Bedford (1957) and Solomon (1977), for instance, identify emotions with judgements and argue that the consciously experienced feelings are irrelevant to understanding an emotion. Others, like Kenny (1963), try to find some role or place for conscious experience, but it turns out to be a non-essential one. Kenny argues that sensations are interpreted as emotions only in the context of judgements which motivate patterns of action. However, such judgements and their resultant emotions do not *require* the sensations, so the sensations are non-essential to the account of emotion. In short, in all this recent Anglo-American philosophy the nature of the body is inessential to the emotions which have a life only in the mind. Thus Boden (1977):

> Philosophers who have used the methods of conceptual analysis generally agree that emotions are *not* mere feelings, or bodily sensations, but contain a strong cognitive component relating to the background circumstances in which the emotion is experienced . . . Feelings are *cues* to emotions, cues that are interpreted in relation to psychological schemata with varying cognitive content, such as pride, shame, vanity and humiliation.
>
> (p. 441)

Scruton (1980) summarises this even more strongly:

> It is now widely accepted that all emotion involves both understanding and activity and, indeed, that nothing important is left to an emotion when those two have been removed from it.
>
> (p. 524)

Hofstadter and Dennett (1981) say succinctly:

> Emotions are an automatic by-product of the ability to think. They are implied by the nature of thought. (p. 81)

In this dualist conception of mind, it is this insistence that emotions are of the mind that makes them rational. Since to be rational is to have choice and to be free, it then becomes clear that in so far as emotions are rational they are under the control of reason. They are contrasted with 'feelings', which being of the body are not reasonable, but like the rest of the physical world can be controlled indirectly by the exercise of intelligence.

Beginning with the assumptions that bodies and minds are the only fundamental categories and that they are separate and different, the Cartesian solution is not a surprising one. There are other solutions. For instance, if emotions and feelings are taken to be of the body, the controlling relationship may be reversed, and the rational mind controlled by the bodily promptings of feelings.[10] However, none of these dualist solutions are satisfactory. Feelings and emotions do not fit comfortably into a twofold division. This is true both of the 'bodily feelings' and of the 'mental emotions'. The feelings of sexuality and hunger, for instance, are dependent on understanding as well as on physical promptings. The emotions of fear, love, ambition and pride have associated feeling as well as judgement, and it is not at all clear that all of them are rational. And even if all this were resolved, a whole range of other psychological terms associated with feelings such as mood and character are left unaccounted for and unexplained. These problems have been noted by a number of commentators but they remain unresolved.

My first criticism of philosophy of mind, a criticism which is implicit in feminist writing, was that human beings have been wrongly described in terms of minds and bodies only. It is clear from the above summary that the second criticism, that the relationship between them is taken to be one of hierarchical control, appears to be justified too. I am not going to consider this one in detail. Briefly, whether emotions and feelings are thought to be rational or bodily, the relationship between mind and body – and therefore of emotion and the rest of the person – has been taken to be one of hierarchical control. This second criticism is independent of the first. For instance, Strasser (1977), who has a threefold categorisation which includes emotion as separate, describes a hierarchy of control.

I turn now to the third criticism, that feelings have largely been ignored as a focus of attention in philosophy. The question as to why feelings and emotions are not taken to be of much significance is an interesting one. Feeling and emotion present intractable problems to arguments that assume minds and bodies to be the only categories necessary to describe human beings, so it would seem that they should attract attention. They do not. Broadly speaking, feelings are ignored as a serious topic of discussion. There has been little sustained attention to them. Books on emotion are not widely read by philosophers. For instance, the books on the passions by Descartes, like those of Hume or Aristotle, are *not* the widely read ones by comparison with the rest of their work. Very little space is given to the subject on philosophy bookshelves or in journals. Such lack of sustained attention and argument means that the complexities are not noticed and oversimple accounts remain acceptable.

To sum up, philosophers continue to contribute to the commonly held belief in the value of hard heads in control of tough bodies. Feeling and emotions have to fit into this framework as best they can, and, since it is a Procrustean fit, a distortion of experience is the result. However, since feelings and emotions are not paid sufficient attention, this distortion is not noticed. To change the metaphor, complexities of feelings and emotions are like a loose thread in the material making up the philosophy of mind. If it were pulled it would not come away tidily, as most philosophers hope and assume, but would unravel the whole closely knit garment.

There have been some recent attempts to clarify the nature of feeling, which build on complexities instead of ignoring them. These accounts attempt to take into consideration both physical and intelligent aspects of feelings.[11] Unfortunately, such attempts are few and far between and so as yet inconclusive. A lot more of them are needed. In this spirit I shall now tentatively put forward the bare bones of an alternative.

AN ALTERNATIVE SUGGESTION

An adequate account of emotion has to take into consideration the process by which feelings come into being, the process by which our feelings become human feelings. To say that our feelings are human feelings is to draw attention to the fact, on the one hand, that they will be different from those of other species simply because of our different genetic inheritance. On the other hand, they will reflect the way human beings create themselves through their social interactions. That is, we have to take into account the history of an individual, and the time and place in which she lives her life. A snapshot of one instant in her life is insufficient to give any depth of understanding. To say this is firstly to emphasise both 'nature' and 'culture' rather than one at the expense of the other, and secondly to look at whole lives. The suggestion that I am making here about human feelings depends on both of these.

It is common enough to discuss either social relationships or genetically given feelings as constrained by each other, but this is usually done with respect to adults. By contrast, I begin by looking at the development of the individual from babyhood, and this makes my account significantly different. The feelings of newborn babies may be genetically given, but from the moment of birth they interact with the understandings and perceptions of the growing baby. Until they do so they are not fully human – but human feelings develop out of the feelings of babies. The process of coming to have human feelings comes about as a result of the interactions of those not yet quite human feelings inherent in human babies with the knowledge, understanding, perceptions and beliefs that people develop as a result of growing up and living in the world. As these feelings interact and reinteract with all the other understandings and perceptions of the individual, new feelings are formed which may be only partly conscious. That is, they are intelligent and the result of intelligence, but they are not necessarily susceptible to cool calculation. In sum, coming to have human feelings involves the understanding of the individual agent: the feelings are her own feelings. But they are not hers quite independently of the rest of the world. The feelings she has also depend on the kinds of understanding available to her: she lives her life in specific historical and geographical circumstances. Finally, they depend on the physical ground of her being: she has a human body.

The account I have outlined has implications for our understanding of how people conduct themselves. Rather than fill in the outline I shall describe some of the claims that follow from it. If the account is right, it suggests *both* that human understanding and actions are essential to human feelings and *also* that human feelings are essential to human understanding and actions. The first of these two claims is easy to see, I think, given what I have said about learning and feelings. A few examples may help to make it clear. Depression about the arms race, fear of going into debt, love of landscape, and the pain of losing a friend are all examples of human feelings that are dependent on being born a human being but that are incomprehensible without human understanding. In non-humans depression, fear, love or the pain of losing a friend may be as sharply felt but must be significantly different.

My claim that understanding is essential to feelings applies to all feelings, not only to those feelings that are sometimes called emotions. In particular, it is true of those feelings that are often called sensations. Pain, hunger and tiredness all vary with the meanings they have to the individual experiencing them. This conclusion gets support from medical descriptions and psychological research into pain in which there is evidence that pain varies with the meaning it has to the sufferer. The pain of battle wounds, the pain of amputated limbs, the pain of torture or the pain of an injection are not explicable only in terms of physiology – though they are not independent of physiology either (Melzack, 1973). (This claim directly undermines many of the classic discussions of pain in the 'private language' argument, for instance.)

It can also be seen that feelings are essential to human understanding. Perhaps this will be the more startling of my two claims, especially to those who think of feelings as getting in the way of understanding. I shall gesture at some of the arguments that would support this claim, if only I had space to develop them. They depend on a view of language and communication as well as on the continuing interaction and reinteraction of feelings and understandings which lead to new feelings and understandings (the model which I outlined briefly at the start of this section).

Some theories of language begin with adults. However, I want to emphasise here that language has to be learnt. I also want to emphasise that this is something which happens in early childhood, that is, at the same time as understandings and feelings are developing. That language has to be learnt is widely recognised.[12] The significance of the fact that this is done in early childhood is not always understood. Quine (1960), for instance, develops his account assuming that the primary concern for language learners is to match physical sensation to public names. He takes shared activity and interests as of secondary importance (pp. 20ff). For example, his account of the naming of a rabbit (or rabbit part) is:

A rabbit scurries by, the native says 'Gavagai', and the linguist notes down the sentence 'rabbit' (or 'Lo, a rabbit') as tentative translation, subject to testing in further cases.   (p. 29)

Not all accounts are quite as stark as this. For example, Jonathan Bennett (1976) assumes the need to communicate in shared activities, but he forgets shared interests of other kinds. It is evident that some language is learnt in both these ways, naming and doing. Children do indeed like to name objects. Parents and children share a common interest in, for instance, eating and getting dressed. But the richness of adult human language needs more than this. It also depends on a variety of shared feelings about a situation. Examples might be that walking to Daddy is fun, that some foods taste better than others, that a baby's cry is a significant noise, or that a cuddle is comforting. No doubt the very young the world over share these feelings which can be entered into by the adults teaching them language. When adults try to learn a strange language ambiguity of purpose is much more likely. What is significant and salient in adult situations and how people feel about their mutual activities or their environment, is much more variable among adults than among babies, and mistakes are more likely. To return to Quine, he apparently assumed that any people, however different, greet each other and hunt rabbits, or for that matter think rabbits worth pointing at. It is quite possible that his foreign informants would not think the rabbit worth pointing at. Or there could be a variety of concepts that the rabbit could be part of, religious, aesthetic, or something else radically unimaginable. In short, language and mutual understanding must both begin in shared feelings.

Thereafter, the process is a continuing one. Adult understanding depends on shared language which depends on shared feeling; the understanding then contributes to both language and feeling. Thus the understanding of a situation will depend on the feelings as well as on the reasoning abilities that are brought to it. Some examples will illustrate the point. Keller (1985) describes the process by which the aggregation of slime mould became understood. On the face of it, this is a problem in mathematical biology far removed from personal feelings. Keller suggests that the process was slowed down because of the shared feelings of most of the (male) participants that hierarchical control was the most likely model of operation. The point here is *not* that their feelings interfered with their understanding. It is rather that this is an example of how understanding the world depends on feelings about it. An alternative set of feelings contributed to a different possible hypothesis to be tested. Another example of this sort is discussed by Gross and Averill (1983). They suggest that shared feelings about scarcity and competition have restricted the number of hypotheses available to explain evolution. A different kind of example is provided by the practice of consciousness-raising. As I have already said (in the section on 'Feelings and Feminism'), feelings are necessarily included as subject matter in consciousness-raising groups, and the sharing of feelings is a means of arriving at knowledge. The communication of feelings (by intonation, use of names of emotions, inarticulate expression, descriptions of emotional states) allows a sharing of experience which generates new understandings of social or political relationships and connections, or of power structures, and of their influence on our own self-understanding. This is only possible because the feelings themselves developed out of a perception and understanding of social and political relationships. Although, of course, feelings are not infallible guides, because the perceptions and understandings may have been mistaken or misinterpreted, they are starting points to better understanding.

The process I am describing is dialectical. Our feelings prompt the articulation of our beliefs about the world, and the pattern of conceptualisation of it. They reflect both factual and evaluative judgements. The articulations are learnt in social interactions. But the articulation also moulds the feelings. The process is a continuing one which is why an ahistorical snapshot approach, looking at feelings at just one particular moment, must be distorting.[13]

If the foregoing is correct, it is evident that people's feelings are not simply private and individual. They could not be anything other than social. This follows from the fact that the understandings which help determine feelings are shared in a large part with other groups of people. Understanding about the world depends on access to information about it, and to experiences within it. It also depends, of course, on sharing public language with others.

One particularly influential effect is the social world. The understandings and therefore the feelings of people are systematically related to the person's position in society. An obvious example here is class. People who share a class position will share a particular set of viewpoints, that is, have easy access to certain information and language in which to discuss it. Of course, there are many factors influencing anyone's point of view and they may intersect in a variety of ways. Nothing I have said suggests that points of view are entailed by class position, only that they are influenced by it.[14]

Similarly, human understandings and feelings are systematically related to differences in biology, in so far as human beings have different biologies. A clear example here is that of age. The different ways of understanding and acting available to different age groups affect their feelings about the world. Children the world over share feelings unavailable to their grandparents, and, possibly, vice versa.

Both of the factors I have described, the effect of society and the effect of biology, combine to make feelings gender-related. The understandings and perceptions available to females are different from those available to males. Males and females are treated differently from each other and perceive themselves differently. Physiological differences, such as menstruation, pregnancy and the menopause in women, and erections and ejaculation in men, will also give the two sexes different understandings and feelings about the world.

The argument that physiological differences are likely to remain significant in the lives of future generations should not be taken as implying that 'biology is destiny'. For instance, at present, it is often argued that the facts of pregnancy and lactation imply that women ought to care for young infants. The opposite implications could be drawn just as straightforwardly, with the significance of the sex difference being kept. The argument could run: women have to take the responsibility of nine months of pregnancy, and, moreover, are in some danger during childbirth. It follows, in the name of justice, if for no other reason, that men should take primary responsibility for the infant.

IMPLICATIONS AND CONCLUSIONS

The argument in the paper and the suggested model have implications for more than one area of philosophy. They also have implications for feminist theorising.

The main implication for analytical philosophy is to do with the fundamental categories in the philosophy of mind. Trying to explain adult human beings as though they are embodiments of rational understanding is a futile activity. The feelings of adults cannot be understood in terms of brute sensations acted upon by rational thoughts. Nor can emotions be understood as by-products of thought, independent of human sensations or bodies. An altogether more complex model is needed. The one I have suggested is an interactive one in which feelings and emotions have to be understood in terms of the history of an individual's life, and in terms of the social context in which that life is lived. Clearly, if this suggestion is right, the concepts of rationality and of mind would change accordingly.

Following from this is another implication for philosophy, that feelings are a source of knowledge and should be treated seriously as such since both need to be taken into account in coming to understand the world. In effect, feelings are a route to truth: they both provide us with our beliefs about the world and also provide a basis for assessing these beliefs. Control of feelings and emotions by the rational mind is a wrong understanding of how human beings ought to conduct themselves. In other words, a rational agent is required to attend to and reflect on feelings, not to attempt to control them, except in so far as a rearticulation of feelings might be appropriate in the light of reflection.[15] The complex interactions of feelings in ourselves are open to reflection and change. One part does not dominate the other. We must be 'in harmony with' our feelings, rather than 'in control of' them.

There are implications for feminist theory as well as for philosophy. The idea that we can shrug off our patriarchal straitjackets and find our pre-social selves is misleading. It is particularly misleading over the way sexism relates to the issues of class and race. The model I have gestured at in this article helps to explain why feminists must take account of class and race. It shows how the issue of sex/gender is similar to them and also why it is different because it is rooted in physiology.

The purpose of this article was to examine some questions about women and emotion. The answers have not been forthcoming because the concepts in which the questions are couched are themselves in doubt. Satisfactory answers depend on overhauling these concepts using the insights of feminists but using them carefully and critically. From a preliminary examination it appears that the place of feelings in human conduct has not been properly understood. Attention to its significance is important because any proper running of private and public life depends on it.

NOTES

1. Midwinter (1980, pp. 31ff.) describes the history of the belief. Bantock (1967) presents a particularly explicit statement of it.
2. Alice Walker is illuminating on this point in her writing about the Civil Rights movement in the USA (Walker, 1983, p. 119ff.).
3. Compare Lorde's letter to Daly (Lorde, 1984).
4. This other tradition includes Hegelianism, post-Hegelianism, Marxism and phenomenology. Generally ignored by the Anglo-American philosophical establishment, it has influenced other English-speaking academics, as the current interest in hermeneutics, structuralism and Lacanian psychoanalytic thinking demonstrates. It is strongly influenced by the Romantic opposition to the objectifying Enlightenment view of humanity. Criticisms about the subsuming of feelings and emotions into minds or bodies also apply to substantial areas of the European traditions but so differently that I could not usefully consider the latter together with the Anglo-Saxon analytical tradition.
5. See Lloyd (1984) for some of the meanings attached to these terms.
6. Schopenhauer discusses feelings, but he identifies them with the body.

Sartre discusses emotions but begins by defining them as of the mind (1962), and not of the body, which he discusses separately (1957).
7. See, for instance, Hofstadter and Dennett (1981).
8. Putnam (1975) for instance, takes pains to distinguish his position from that of Descartes.
9. Davidson (1980) contains a number of articles on intentionality and its philosophical meanings. Kenny (1963) and Wilson (1972) discuss it with reference to emotion.
10. This is Schopenhauer's view. See, for instance, *The World as Will and Idea* (1961).
11. A particularly useful collection is edited by Amélie Rorty (1980).
12. The considerable philosophical literature on translation is an indication of this.
13. I am grateful to Kathleen Lennon for clarifying my thinking here.
14. See, for instance, Caroline Steedman's discussion (1986).
15. See note 13.

REFERENCES

AMOS, Valerie and PARMAR, Pratibha (1984), 'Challenging Imperial Feminism', *Feminist Review*, vol. 17, pp. 3–19.

BANTOCK, Geoffrey (1967), *Education, Culture and the Emotions* (London: Faber).

BEDFORD, Errol (1957), 'Emotions', *Proceedings of the Aristotelian Society*, vol. 60, pp. 281–304.

BENNETT, Jonathan (1976), *Linguistic Behaviour* (Cambridge: Cambridge University Press).

BODEN, Margaret (1977), *Artificial Intelligence and Natural Man* (Hassocks: Harvester).

CALDECOTT, Leonie and LELAND, Stephanie (eds) (1983), *Reclaim the Earth* (London: The Women's Press).

DALY, Mary (1984), *Pure Lust: Elemental Feminist Philosophy* (London: The Women's Press).

DAVIDSON, Donald (1980), *Essays on Actions and Events* (Oxford: Oxford University Press).

DESCARTES, René (1972), *The Passions of the Soul* in *The Philosophical Works of Descartes*, vol. 1, trans. Elizabeth S. Haldane and G. R. T. Ross (Cambridge: Cambridge University Press).

EISENSTEIN, Hester (1984), *Contemporary Feminist Thought* (London: Allen & Unwin).

GLOVER, Jonathan (ed.), (1976), *The Philosophy of Mind* (Oxford: Oxford University Press).

GRIFFIN, Susan (1982), *Made from this Earth* (London: The Women's Press).

GROSS, Michael and AVERILL, Mary Beth (1983), 'Evolution and Patriarchal Myths of Scarcity and Competition', in S. HARDING and M. HINTIKKA (eds).

HARDING, Sandra and HINTIKKA Merrill B. (eds) (1983), *Discovering*

Reality: Feminist Perspectives in Epistemology, Metaphysics, Methodology, and Philosophy of Science (Dordrecht: Reidel).

HOFSTADTER, Douglas R. and DENNETT, Daniel C. (eds) (1981), *The Mind's I: Fantasies and Reflections on Self and Soul* (Brighton: Harvester).

JAGGAR, Alison M. (1983), *Feminist Politics and Human Nature* (Brighton: Harvester).

KELLER, Evelyn Fox (1985), *Reflections on Gender and Science* (New Haven: Yale University Press).

KENNY, Anthony (1963), *Action, Emotion and Will* (London: Routledge & Kegan Paul).

LLOYD, Genevieve (1984), *The Man of Reason: 'Male' and 'Female' in Western Philosophy* (London: Methuen).

LORDE, Audre (1984), 'An Open Letter to Mary Daly', in Audre Lorde, *Sister Outsider* (Trumansburg, NY: Crossing Press), pp. 66–71.

MELZACK, Robert (1973), *The Puzzle of Pain* (Harmondsworth: Penguin).

MIDWINTER, Eric C. (1980), *Schools in Society* (London: Batsford).

PUTNAM, Hilary (1975), *Mind, Language and Reality* (Cambridge: Cambridge University Press).

QUINE, Willard Van Orman (1960), *Word and Object* (Cambridge, Mass: MIT Press).

RORTY, Amélie O. (ed.) (1980), *Explaining Emotions* (Berkeley: University of California Press).

ROWBOTHAM, Sheila (1983), *Dreams and Dilemmas* (London: Virago).

SARTRE, Jean-Paul (1957), *Being and Nothingness: An Essay on Phenomenological Ontology*, trans. Hazel E. Barnes (London: Methuen).

SARTRE, Jean-Paul (1962), *Sketch for a Theory of the Emotions*, trans. Philip Mairet (London: Methuen).

SCHOPENHAUER, Arthur (1961), *The World as Will and Idea*, trans. R. B. Haldane and J. Kemp (New York: Doubleday).

SCRUTON, Roger (1980), 'Emotion, Practical Knowledge and Common Culture', in A. RORTY (ed.), pp. 519–36.

SELLER, Anne (1985), 'Greenham: A Concrete Reality', *Journal of Applied Philosophy*, vol. 2, pp. 133–41.

SOLOMON, Robert C. (1977), *The Passions* (Garden City, NY: Doubleday).

STEEDMAN, Caroline (1986), *Landscape for a Good Woman: A Story of Two Lives* (London: Virago).

STRASSER, Stephan (1977), *Phenomenology of Feeling: An Essay on the Phenomena of the Heart*, trans. Robert E. Wood (Pittsburgh: Duquesne University Press).

WALKER, Alice (1983), *In Search of Our Mothers' Gardens* (London: The Women's Press).

WILSON, J. R. S. (1972), *Emotion and Object* (Cambridge: Cambridge University Press).

9

Subject, Body and the Exclusion of Women from Philosophy

Joanna Hodge

Descartes's declaration in part 4 of his *Discourse on Method*: 'cogito ergo sum', 'I think, therefore I am', installs the theme of subjectivity at the centre of philosophical enquiry for the next three hundred years. Now, however, the usefulness, indeed the availability of a conception of subjectivity is increasingly open to question, from angles as diverse as Derek Parfit's post-utilitarianism[1] and the phenomenological hermeneutics of Martin Heidegger.[2] This questioning makes indispensable a critique and reconstruction of the terms of reference of philosophical enquiry, in order to complete the displacement of subjectivity as a central term. That critique and reconstruction will be all the more effective if it can at the same time identify and take into account the way in which certain conceptual structures, for example that of subjectivity, have played a part in the exclusion of women from philosophical enquiry and from the processes of determining the parameters of such enquiry. The critical task of this essay is to show how the concept of the subject, produced in Descartes's enquiries, has served both to exclude women from philosophy and to obscure how that exclusion has been effected. The positive result will be to show how the displacement of this concept makes it more possible to begin to criticise and dismantle an illegitimate gender specificity, which has been a characteristic feature of the Western philosophical tradition.

This essay falls into three parts. First, it must outline the centrality of subjectivity to Cartesian and post-Cartesian philosophy, and indicate how the empiricist critique of the Cartesian concept of the subject substitutes an analysis of subjectivity, of the epistemological function of subjective processes, which retains some of the misogyny of the Cartesian concept. Secondly, it will show how the

Cartesian concept of the subject introduces a separation between rational consciousness and sensual embodiment. This separation mobilises themes concerning sexual difference, which date back to the Pythagorean table of opposites, reported on by Aristotle in his *Metaphysics*[3] and recently retheorised by Jacques Derrida[4] and Luce Irigaray[5] in their discussions of sexual difference. The theme of sexual difference is implicitly, if not explicitly, deployed in Cartesian philosophy. The Cartesian taking-for-granted of a conception of a sexually undifferentiated body is a way of both affirming and ignoring the questions of sexual difference and of gender specificity, whereby men constitute the terms of reference of philosophical enquiry and women are excluded. Thirdly, there is an important political dimension to the supposed gender blindness of concepts of the subject and of subjectivity, for that false appearance of gender blindness is reproduced in democratic theories about the 'rights of man'. The question to the adequacy of formulations of political goals in terms of the 'rights of man' is then also a question to the adequacy of the Cartesian concept of the subject, and to the adequacy of accounts offered of the relation between subjectivity and the body.

A liberal feminist theorising would claim that the conception of political agency made available in democratic theory can be extended to include women as well as men, with minor modifications. The problem then becomes how to disconnect theories of the rights of man and of political subjectivity from the Cartesian notion of the subject which, as argued in the second part of this paper, is implicitly connected to a male experience of the world and to a masculine body. While no doubt in the eighteenth century this political retheorising of subjectivity in terms of the 'rights of man' posed the problem of the political and rational status of women with a new urgency, the argument of this paper is that this political conception of subjectivity cannot provide a solution to the problem, since the terms in which the problem is posed must also be challenged. The status of women as political and rational agents cannot cease to pose problems while the domains of politics and rationality are constructed as masculine, and as pertaining to men, rendering the domains of domesticity and sensuality feminine, and pertaining to women. In the third part of the paper, it will be argued that maleness and masculinity are inherent in the conception of subjectivity, thus making a critique of both the subject and of subjectivity indispensable, if women are to claim effective access to politics and to philosophy.

Feminist critiques of philosophy, identifying the ways in which women have been excluded from and silenced within philosophical enquiry, become possible precisely as a result of the formation and subsequent disintegration of conceptions of subjectivity, made available in Cartesian thinking. The formation of subjectivity is a theme stressed by liberal feminist theory,[6] while its subsequent disintegration is the theme emphasised in radical and deconstructionist feminist thinking.[7] In order to analyse the implications of conceptions of subjectivity for women, both its formation and its disintegration must be taken into account, making both liberal and radical deconstructionist feminist theory indispensable. The central theme of the paper is, then, that presupposing the availability of a concept of the subject or of a conception of subjectivity elides the feminist question about the absence of women from the practice of philosophy in the post-Cartesian epoch. Putting in question the availability of these two conceptions makes possible a feminist critique of the illicit assumption that the body of the subject is in fact male. The supposed sexually undetermined status of the body of the subject, like the supposedly gender-neutral term 'the rights of man', operates as a mechanism for the exclusion of women and the silencing of the feminist critique of that exclusion. Thus a gender specificity in the modern period of Western philosophical enquiry is masked by the appearance of gender neutrality, in one of its central themes, the theorising of the subject and of subjectivity.

SUBJECTIVITY AND MODERNITY

In his *Lectures on the History of Philosophy* (1971), Hegel explicitly claims that with Cartesian philosophy, the modern period of Western philosophy begins:

> Now we have arrived really for the first time at the philosophy of the new world and begin this philosophy with Descartes. With this, we enter into autonomous philosophy, a philosophy, which knows that it comes autonomously from reason and that self-consciousness is an essential moment of truth. Here we can say that we feel at home and can cry 'land', like sailors after a long reconnaissance on the violent sea. Descartes is one of those people, who have started all over again from the very beginning;

and with him begins the development, the thinking of the modern age.   (p. 120)

But Hegel is merely making explicit the presumption implicit in the combination of deference and disputation with which philosophers, contemporaneous with and subsequent to Descartes, treated his work. Locke and Kant, Spinoza and Berkeley all address themselves to Descartes's thought and the objections to Descartes produced in his lifetime, by Caterius, Mersenne, Hobbes, Arnauld, Gassendi and Bourdi, indicate the importance attributed to his work, already in his lifetime.

Hegel identifies two key elements in Descartes's thinking, which are linked together, but which, when variously emphasised, produce different readings of Descartes. The first element is the epistemological connection for Descartes between self-consciousness and the articulation of truth; the second is the ontological connection posited by Descartes between thinking and existence. The epistemological link between the subjective processes of self-conciousness and truth provides the basis for Descartes's refutation of scepticism; the ontological link between thinking and existence, to be established in a concept of the subject, provides the metaphysical basis for this epistemological move. The epistemological element provides a conception of subjectivity, of the processes of a subject of knowledge, while the ontological element seeks to show in what material form these processes are incorporated, thus gesturing towards a concept of the subject. For Descartes and for Hegel, the epistemological arguments and the metaphysical commitments about the nature of the entities involved, in particular about the knowing subject, are closely linked together. Thus for both Hegel and Descartes the two key elements in Descartes's thinking are inseparable.

Once all such metaphysical commitment has become liable to be suspected of dogmatism, however, the metaphysical commitments contained in the concept of the subject must also become suspect. This disrupts the Cartesian linkage between a quest for truth, the analysis of subjective epistemological process and of self-consciousness, and the concept of the subject. An empiricist, anti-metaphysical reading of Descartes seeks to retain a conception of subjectivity, while remaining sceptical about the metaphysical commitments of a concept of the subject, thus attempting to keep the refutation of scepticism contained in the link between the evidence of self-consciousness and truth, without making the metaphysical and possibly dogmatic claim about the availability of a completely specified concept of the subject. For empiricist readings of Descartes, the availability of a concept of the subject, which Descartes takes himself to have established, has always been in question, but the suggested unavailability is not taken to undermine the analysis of subjectivity and of self-consciousness, required for the refutation of scepticism. Thus the empiricists have a conception of subjectivity which does not posit the availability of a concept of the subject. The rationalist readings of Descartes offered by Leibniz and Spinoza, on the other hand, regard a concept of the subject as indispensable, but as not yet available, and they therefore address themselves to attempting to make good what they see as the shortcomings of Descartes's account.

For empiricist readings of Descartes, then, the availability of a conception of the subject has always been in doubt. Hume, for example, does not accept the inevitability of a linkage between an epistemological theory concerned with subjectivity and an ontological theory of the subject. Instead of positing with Descartes the givenness of a subject position, Hume gestures towards the actual functioning of subjectivity, and appeals to the common sense supposition that there is no good reason to doubt the continued functioning of something, which has functioned in the main reliably up until now. For Hume, there is no concept of the subject, but only a conception of subjectivity, acquired through access to a structure with a certain set of functions in relation to knowledge and experience. For Hume, subjectivity converts into objectivity as a result of the contribution of subjective functions to the constitution of what counts as reality, to the constitution of the objective, interpersonal domain. Thus, for Hume a conception of subjectivity is useful and indispensable, and there is no need for a concept of the subject; for Spinoza, conversely, and for Hegel, it is the unavailability of a concept of the subject which leads them respectively to construct their conceptions of *deus sive natura* and *Geist*. In order to make possible a properly post-Cartesian conception of philosophy, from which women are no longer excluded, the mechanisms whereby both the concept of the subject and subjectivity serve to exclude women from philosophical practice must be revealed.

RATIONAL CONSCIOUSNESS, SENSUAL EMBODIMENT

In the Second Meditation,[8] Descartes sets up a distinction between
the degrees of certainty assignable respectively to perceptions of the
mind and of the body. The Second Meditation concludes:

> I see that without any effort I have finally got back to where I
> wanted. I now know that even bodies are not strictly perceived by
> the senses or the faculty of imagination but by the intellect alone,
> and that this perception derives not from their being touched or
> seen but from their being understood; and in view of this I know
> plainly that I can achieve an easier and more evident perception of
> my own mind than of anything else.   (p. 34, trans., pp. 22–3)

This epistemological distinction between degrees of certainty in the
perception of different entities is restated in the Sixth Meditation as
the 'real distinction', an ontological distinction, between mind and
body, signalled in the subtitle of that meditation, a distinction
between different kinds of entity. The intervening Third and Fifth
Meditations introduce considerations about the nature and
existence of God, thus providing a theological and ontological
context for the preceding epistemological discussion. This
theological context brings with it the constraint of the dogmatic
necessity of making room for the separability of the immortal soul
from the perishable flesh, as Descartes indicates in the following
remark from the Synopsis of the *Meditations*:

> Since some people may expect arguments for the immortality of
> the soul in this section, I think they should be warned here and
> now that I have tried not to put down anything which I could not
> precisely demonstrate. Hence the only order which I could follow
> was that normally employed by the geometers, namely to set out
> all the premises on which the desired proposition depends,
> before drawing any conclusions about it. Now the first and most
> important prerequisite for knowledge of the immortality of the
> soul is for us to form a concept of the soul which is as clear as
> possible and is also quite distinct from every concept of body; and
> that is just what has been done in that section.
>   (p. 3, trans., p. 9)

The theological and ontological context makes available a series of substitutions with different inflections between spirituality, soul and mind, and between materiality, flesh and body. The necessity in translating of choosing one of these pairs of terms, for instance mind and body, obscures the metaphysical dimensions of Descartes's discussion, and confirms the secularising tendency to separate issues in philosophy and science from theological and eschatological questions. The separation is misleading in the context of a thinker for whom such a separation is not yet firmly established. The importance of analysing the ontological commitments of any epistemological theory is, of course, much greater when there are theological and eschatological questions at stake, and thus the elision of the theological context makes it less pressing to address the metaphysical dimension of Descartes's thinking.

In the Second Meditation, thoughtfulness is presented by Descartes as the distinguishing feature of mind:

> Here is a deceiver of supreme power and cunning who is deliberately and constantly deceiving me. In that case too I undoubtedly exist, if he is deceiving me. And let him deceive me as much as he can, he will never bring it about that I am nothing so long as I think that I am something. So after considering everything very thoroughly, I must conclude that this proposition, I am, I exist, is necessarily true whenever it is put forward by me or conceived in my mind.   (p. 25, trans., p. 17)

The restatement of the distinction between mind and body in the Sixth Meditation picks up on these elements of thoughtfulness, reflexivity and self-consciousness, through which Descartes seeks the distinctness of mind:

> On the one hand I have a clear and distinct idea of myself, so far as I am simply a thinking, non-extended thing and on the other hand I have a distinct idea of body, insofar as this is simply extended non-thinking thing. And accordingly it is certain that I am really distinct from my body and can exist without it.
>
> (p. 78, trans., p. 54)

Thus the distinguishing characteristic of body as opposed to mind is that it is non-thinking and extended.

Descartes continues his presentation of the difference between body and mind by introducing the notion of divisibility:

The first observation I make at this point is that there is a great difference between the mind and the body inasmuch as the body is by its very nature always divisible, while the mind is utterly indivisible. For when I consider the mind of myself, insofar as I am merely a thinking thing, I am unable to distinguish parts within myself; I understand myself to be something quite single and complete. (p. 86, trans., p. 59)

This distinction between the divisibility of the body and the supposed indivisibility of the mind makes way for Descartes's likening of the body to a mechanical construct, like a watch:

When I consider the purpose of a clock I may say that it is departing from its nature when it does not tell the right time; and similarly when I consider the mechanism of the human body, I may think that, in relation to the movements which normally occur in it, it too is deviating from its nature, if the throat is dry at a time when drinking is not beneficial to its continued health. (p. 85, trans., p. 58)

The intriguing point about such functionalist views of the body is the way in which, as Susan Möller Okin argues in her book *Women in Western Political Thought* (1980),[9] this functionalism has been used primarily with respect to the specific female function in reproduction, rendering that single element central to the definition and process of being a woman, whereas the unique male capacities have not similarly been argued to be the only proper occupation of men. In Descartes's discussion, however, there is no reference to the gross biological fact that among human bodies there are two standard variant kinds of machine, one male with its specific capacities and role in reproduction, and one female, with its own role. He is thereby prevented from addressing himself to the question of a difference in the natural functions of human bodies.

In his paradoxical conclusion to the *Meditations*, Descartes asserts that his previous doubts about the evidences of the senses are in fact laughable, since the senses are by and large reliable, and can be submitted to the scrutiny of rational process, in cases of doubt:

I know that in matters regarding the well-being of the body, all my senses report the truth much more frequently than not. Also, I can make use of more than one sense to investigate the same thing, and in addition I can use both my memory, which connects present experiences with preceding ones, and my intellect, which has by now examined all the causes of error. Accordingly I should not have any further fears about the falsity of what my senses tell me every day: on the contrary, the exaggerated doubts of the last few days should be dismissed as laughable.

(p. 89, trans., p. 61)

In the Synopsis to the *Meditations*, Descartes reverts to this clarification of the method of doubt. The doubt was not intended to, and indeed could not, achieve a disruption of all belief and expectation. It is intended to establish what is most incontrovertible:

> The great benefit of these arguments is not, in my view, that they prove what they establish – namely that there really is a world and that human beings have bodies and so on – since no sane person has ever seriously doubted these things. The point is that in considering these arguments we come to realise that they are not as solid or as transparent as the arguments which lead us to knowledge of our own minds and of God, so that the latter are the most certain and evident of all possible objects of knowledge for the human intellect. (p. 17, trans., p. 9)

So it is the seriousness of sanity which permits Descartes to render the subversions of doubt laughable.

In the Sixth Meditation, Descartes makes reference to the problem of non-veridical perception. This problem is set up by the plurality of possible causes of a single brain state, which corresponds with one and only one mental state:

> My next observation is that the mind is not immediately affected by all parts of the body, but only by the brain, or perhaps just one small part of the brain, namely the part which is said to contain the 'common' sense. Every time this part of the brain is in a given state, it presents the same signals to the mind, even though the other parts of the body may be in a different condition at the time.

(p. 86, trans., pp. 59–60)

Although Descartes talks about the human body as a machine, the vital connection between the body and the mind, as articulated through the brain, is not one of single determinate causal connection. Thus he is forced to conclude:

It is clear from all this that, notwithstanding the immense goodness of God, the nature of man as a combination of mind and body is such that it is bound to mislead him from time to time. For there may be some occurrence, not in the foot but in one of the other areas through which the nerves travel in their route from the foot to the brain, or even in the brain itself; and if this cause produces the same motion which is generally produced by injury to the foot, then pain will be felt as if it were in the foot. This deception of the senses is natural, because a given motion of the brain must always produce the same sensation in the mind; and the origin of the motion in question is much more often going to be something which is hurting the foot, rather than something existing elsewhere. (p. 58, trans., p. 61)

But as far as Descartes is concerned this multiplicity of causes in no way disturbs the obviousness of the embodiment of the thoughtfulness in which the mind consists. Plainly Descartes in no way anticipated that the obviousness of this incorporation and the possibility of communion between the two elements, mind and body, would become the central issue for dispute, already in his correspondence with Arnauld and Gassendi, and increasingly importantly in the reception of his work by Spinoza and Leibniz.

Curiously, one of the correspondents in his lifetime who particularly shook his confidence in the self-evidence of the link between mind and body, and in the capacity of the one to affect the other, despite the differences in their composition, is Princess Elizabeth of Bohemia. In his *Principles of Philosophy* Descartes gives a curiously revealing dedication to her, where despite the adulation of her intellectual capacities, she is clearly confined to being the representation of knowledge, objectified as wisdom incarnate, to be studied and made the object of the philosophical project of analysis, and made the object of the philosopher's desire:

Finally, I see that all the necessary conditions for perfect and sublime wisdom, both on the side of knowledge and on the side of will, shine forth in your character. For together with your royal dignity, you show an extraordinary kindness and gentleness which though continually buffeted by the blows of fortune, has never become embittered or broken. I am so overwhelmed by this that I consider that this statement of my philosophy should be offered and dedicated to the wisdom which I so admire in you – for philosophy is nothing else but the study of wisdom. And indeed my desire to be known as a philosopher is no greater than my desire to be known as, Your Serene Highness's most devoted servant. (p. 8A, trans., p. 192)

The sex of this correspondent poses the challenging problem of a differential relation between men and the body, and women and the body. The issue of there being two different kinds of body, with different meanings and cultural inscriptions, becomes unavoidable.

*   *   *

The constitution of women's bodies in cultural practice in general, and pornography in particular, as the reified object of the male gaze and of masculine desire, renders women's bodies both more and less than the mechanical structure, appended to thoughtfulness, which Descartes constructs. They are less than such an appendage, since they are not complete in themselves, subordinate only to the appended thinking process. Their meaning is constituted by structures over and above the thoughtfulness of the particular mind to which each is attached. They are more than such an appendage, since they disrupt the false notion of autonomous self-constitution, which Descartes seems to be positing. This disruption raises the important suggestion that cultural attitudes and expectations play a part in the formation of subjectivity and the development of individuality. In so far as women's bodies are conceived as mechanical structures, appended to some rational process, that rational process is not taking place in the mind of the woman to whom that mechanical structure is appended, but in the minds of men. The bodies of women are thus constituted as appendages of men's desire, not as the appendages of rational processes attributable to women. Descartes's model of taking the body for granted as an appendage of rational processes excludes women as possible bearers of the structure, since for cultural reasons, it is not possible for the bodies of women to function in the required way. Women therefore have reason for doubting the existence of an objective world, as women have reason for doubting that there is available to them a body, in which their rational processes are incorporated, since both world and body are culturally constructed by men as belonging not to women but to men.[10] Women are put by the Cartesian system in the position of the insane person, who cannot see the laughability of Cartesian doubt. Thus in the Cartesian system there is already inscribed the position of the humourless feminist, who cannot see the joke.

There is then a double manoeuvre at work here, of simultaneously attributing lesser importance to the body and to the evidences of the senses, as opposed to the mind and the evidences of rational process, while at the same time taking the body absolutely for granted. This is a taking-for-granted which has different implications for men and for women, for men over against women, and for women over against men. It is a rationalisation and remobilisation of the early modern suspicion of the flesh articulated in the Calvinist and Loyolan reworkings of Protestant and Catholic disciplines of the body. Instead of the body and the flesh being construed as requiring discipline, on the grounds that they are prime sites for the defiance of divine injunctions, they are construed as the site for the production of sensory illusion, subverting the epistemological project of establishing truth and certainty, and perhaps undermining faith in reason altogether. Thus Descartes sets about producing an account of the body and the mind, such that the body can be safely ignored, having been shown to be subject to the discipline of reason, and not subversive of it.

LIBERAL HUMANISM AND THE RIGHTS OF WOMAN

Descartes himself is not particularly concerned with the metaphysical problem of showing just exactly what kind of connection between body and mind there might be, nor is he particularly concerned with the epistemological problem of how there might be knowledge of that connection. He seems to suppose that knowledge of that connection is just immediately given, and is thus both primary and self-evident as a clear and distinct idea. In his Synopsis to the *Meditations*, he states his commitment to such a union as follows:

Lastly, in the Sixth Meditation, the intellect is distinguished from the imagination; the criteria for the distinction are explained; the mind is proved to be really distinct from the body, but is shown notwithstanding to be so closely joined to it that the mind and the body make up a kind of unit . . .   (p. 15, trans., p. 11)

But as he gives no thorough definition of this 'kind of unit', in which the unity of body and mind is supposed to consist, the empiricist readings of Descartes which emphasise the epistemological dimension and ignore or indeed denounce the metaphysical dimension of Descartes's thinking do receive some licence from Descartes himself. Rejecting the metaphysical element in Descartes's thought, however, makes it even more difficult to identify and criticise the implicit assumption that the body to which the processes of subjectivity are attached is a male body, since processes of subjectivity are inevitably more tenuously attached to a material bodily dimension, although still in some sense attached, than is a set of embodied mental processes. The empiricist rejection of the metaphysical dimension in Descartes's thought makes it all the more difficult to pose the question of the differences between the two kinds of body in which minds may be embodied. Feminism and political issues, however, like theology and eschatological issues, make it impossible not to address metaphysical questions about the difference between different kinds of entity and between different kinds of existence.

The issue is posed with unavoidable urgency by the political debates surrounding the French Revolution, in particular, of course, by Mary Wollstonecraft, in her *Vindication of the Rights of Woman* (1792),[11] in which she questions the contemporary assumption that claims for natural rights and political participation for all men did not automatically extend to women. She argues the connection between the possession of rationality and the claim to rights, in her dedicatory letter to M. Talleyrand–Perigord:

> But if women are to be excluded, without having a voice, from a participation of the natural rights of mankind, prove first, to ward off the charge of injustice and inconsistency, that they want reason, else this flaw in your NEW CONSTITUTION will ever show that man must, in some shape, act like a tyrant, and tyranny, in whatever part of society it rears its brazen front, will ever undermine morality.   (pp. 11–12)

Quite properly, Wollstonecraft then proceeds to devote most of her text not to an analysis of citizenship and rights, but to an analysis of 'the prevailing opinion of sexual character', correctly identifying differential expectations concerning women and men, with respect to education, physique and morality, to be the key social practices through which the exclusion of women from political participation and enjoyment of rights is achieved.

Wollstonecraft interestingly links her denunciation of the double morality, one for women and one for men, to a denunciation of enslaving:

> A truly benevolent legislator always endeavours to make it the interest of each individual to be virtuous; and thus private virtue becoming the cement of public happiness, an orderly whole is consolidated by the tendency of all the parts towards a common centre. But the private or public virtue of woman is very problematical, for Rousseau, and a numerous list of male writers, insist that she should all her life be subjected to a severe restraint, that of propriety. Why subject her to propriety – blind propriety – if she be capable of acting from a nobler spring, if she be an heir of immortality? Is a sugar always to be produced by vital blood? Is one half of the human species, like the poor African slaves, to be subject to prejudices that brutalise them, when principles would be a surer guard, only to sweeten the cup of man? Is not this indirectly to deny women reason? for a gift is a mockery, if it be unfit for use.   (p. 158)

However, gender privilege does continue to exist, despite the fact that the vote has been extended to women, and some notion of natural rights attributed to them. This demonstrates Wollstonecraft's point that a more radical critique of cultural expectation and of conceptual structures is required, in order fully to include women into political process. Wollstonecraft's appeal for respect for women as rational implies a claim that women too are bearers of subjectivity, bearers of the epistemological functions, through which standards of objectivity are set up. The kinds of subjectivity attributable to women and to men were, however, radically different in Wollstonecraft's day, as indeed they still are now.

Subjectivity in epistemological terms implies the capacity to adopt the stance of the independent observer, identifying and fixing the objects of the observer's gaze. This kind of subjectivity plays a part in constituting the domain of objective fact, and thus has the status of neutrality and indeed of objectivity, in the sense of there being no specificity and no particularity about the site of observation. This neutrality, however, is available only to those who are not marked as deviant with respect to a socially, culturally constituted standard of normality. That standard of normality in both Wollstonecraft's time, and in the twentieth century, involves among other things being male, and having a male body. Women are thus subjective in a different sense from that in which the bearer of epistemological processes is subjective. The latter form of subjectivity is convertible into objectivity. The subjectivity attributed to women is not convertible into objectivity, and therefore does not bring with it the attribute of rationality. To women is attributed the kind of subjectivity which must be contained and controlled by moral prescriptions and by physical and intellectual constraints, in order to prevent women from transgressing the roles and rules laid down in cultural expectation and practice by the bearers of full rational subjectivity.

Liberal feminism makes claims in terms of rights and in terms of a conception of humanity, which are predicated on the hope of extending the full, rational notion of subjectivity to women. Liberal feminism has undoubtedly made space for a wider audience for the more radical critique which Wollstonecraft begins to develop. The problem is that the claims in terms of rights and in terms of humanity presuppose a conception of self-determining subjectivity, attached in some unspecified way to a body. This last lack of specificity again abstracts away from the actually existing differences between being embodied in a male body and being embodied in a female body, which, as analysed above, make it difficult to attribute to women fully rational status and the kind of subjectivity which has a role in the constitution of objectivity. As a result of this lack of specificity, campaigns to extend the control of women over their lives, in the name of equal rights, can be subverted, as the Equal Rights Amendment campaign was subverted. It is argued, for example, that the abolition of those practices of discrimination, which feminists suppose to disempower women, must entail the abolition of other discriminatory practices, which protect the interests which are specific to women as a result of physical and physiological difference. Thus to prevent the latter undesirable consequence, it is mistakenly thought undesirable to proscribe any discriminatory practices at all.

The more radically critical project, then, cannot just claim that women too can take up subject positions, that a conception of subjectivity can be extended to women, just as to men, nor claim that a gender-neutral concept of the subject can be made available. The very notions of the subject and of subjectivity are embedded in a system of distinctions, which must be challenged in order to reveal the way in which women and men do not enter into the domains of the political and of the rational on the same terms. The alignments of the political and the rational with maleness and masculinity, and of the domestic and the sensual with femaleness and femininity run deep not just in the meanings functioning in European philosophy, but indeed in the social institutions and cultural practices of European societies. Thus a feminist critique cannot simply question a few definitions of terms, and challenge the terms in which problems are posed. It is a question of a thoroughgoing critique of the values implicit in all existing social and cultural practice.

NOTES

I should like to thank Morwenna Griffiths and Margaret Whitford for their encouragement in drafting this paper.

1. See the discussion of identity and impersonality in Parfit (1986).
2. See the disruptions of conceptions of temporality consequent on the attempt to provide a phenomenological description of the self in Heidegger (1962).
3. For Aristotle on the Pythagorean table of opposites, see *Metaphysics* 986a ff. On the interpretation of the effects of this table on Greek philosophy in particular, and more generally, I am indebted to Sabina Lovibond.
4. For Derrida on sexual difference, see Derrida (1986).
5. For Irigaray on sexual difference, see Irigaray (1984).
6. Alison Jaggar's enormously interesting book, *Feminist Politics and Human Nature* (1983), accepts the struggle of an individual to achieve full subjective autonomy as a given of democratic political thinking.
7. Radical feminists such as Mary Daly identify the constraints imposed by language and by the available concepts as the primary target for feminist critique. Daly does not suppose that extending the scope of conceptions of subjectivity to include women would help in any way to reduce the constraints on women, since that reduction is the work not of an individual developing autonomy, but of a collective, collectively redefining meaning. See Daly (1979). Deconstructionist feminists, such as Irigaray, similarly see the collective production of meanings as a more significant site for intervention than the individualist project of self-determination, affirmed under the conception of subjectivity. See in particular Irigaray (1974).
8. For all references to Descartes's works, see *The Philosophical Writings of Descartes* (1985), which gives running reference to the standard twelve-volume edition of Descartes's works, *Oeuvres de Descartes* (1964–1976).
9. See Okin (1980), especially Part 5, 'Functionalism, Feminism and the Family'.

10. For different angles on the constitution of women's bodies in cultural practice, see Dworkin (1981), Coward (1984) and Kappeler (1986). For broad perspectives on issues around the constitution of sexuality, see the two collections Snitow *et al.* (1984) and Vance (1984).
11. For references to Wollstonecraft, *A Vindication of the Rights of Woman*, see Wollstonecraft, *The Rights of Woman* (1970).

REFERENCES

COWARD, Rosalind (1984), *Female Desire: Women's Sexuality Today* (London: Paladin).

DALY, Mary (1979), *Gyn/Ecology: The Metaethics of Radical Feminism* (London: The Women's Press).

DERRIDA, Jacques (1986), 'Geschlecht 1', *Cahier de l'Herne*, vol. 45, pp. 416–39.

DESCARTES, René (1964–76), *Oeuvres de Descartes*, 12 vols., ed. Adam and Tannery (Paris: Vrin/CNRS).

DESCARTES, René (1985), *The Philosophical Writings of Descartes*, 2 vols., ed. John Cottingham, Robert Stoothoff and Dugald Murdoch (Cambridge: Cambridge University Press).

DWORKIN, Andrea (1981), *Pornography: Men Possessing Women* (London: The Women's Press).

HEGEL, G. W. F. (1971), *Vorlesungen über die Geschichte der Philosophie*, vol. 20 of *Werke*, 20 vols. (Frankfurt: Suhrkamp Verlag). English trans.: *Hegel's Lectures on the History of Philosophy*, trans. E. S. Haldane and Frances H. Simon (London: Routledge & Kegan Paul, 1974).

HEIDEGGER, Martin (1962), *Being and Time*, trans. John Macquarrie and Edward Robinson (Oxford: Blackwell). (First published 1927).

IRIGARAY, Luce (1974), *Speculum de l'autre femme* (Paris: Minuit). English trans.: *Speculum of the Other Woman*, trans. Gillian C. Gill (Ithaca and New York: Cornell University Press, 1985).

IRIGARAY, Luce (1984), *Éthique de la différence sexuelle* (Paris: Minuit).

JAGGAR, Alison M. (1983), *Feminist Politics and Human Nature* (Brighton: Harvester).

KAPPELER, Susanne (1986), *The Pornography of Representation* (Cambridge: Polity Press).

OKIN, Susan Möller (1980), *Women in Western Political Thought* (London: Virago).

PARFIT, Derek (1986), *Reasons and Persons* (Oxford: Oxford University Press).

SNITOW, Ann, STANSELL, Christine and THOMPSON, Sharon (1984), *Desire: The Politics of Sexuality* (London: Virago).

VANCE, Carole S. (1984), *Pleasure and Danger: Exploring Female Sexuality* (London: Routledge & Kegan Paul).

WOLLSTONECRAFT, Mary (1970), *The Rights of Woman*, Everyman series (London: Dent).

10

Realism versus Relativism: Towards a Politically Adequate Epistemology

Anne Seller

INTRODUCTION

Within feminism, the argument between realism and relativism appears to be both acute and political. I shall examine this argument, primarily from a political point of view. My philosophical education taught me to follow reason wherever it went and to distrust political considerations. My experience as a feminist has taught me to stick by my political commitments even when I appear to have lost the argument. In this paper I am trying to reconcile this conflict and I hope to demonstrate that, at least in social and political spheres, the political is, and should be, given equal consideration to the epistemological. I shall do this by first looking at the strengths and weaknesses of the two positions, and suggest that the differences are not as great as first appears, because both need to appeal to the same community, in the same way, in order to decide what is the case and what we should do about it. I call this community a 'community of resistance', borrowing the term from liberation theology,[1] and I see it not merely as a way of being with other people, but as a way of being in, and knowing, the world; a way which sees both politics and knowledge as process, rather than as achievement. While the paper appears to be about relativism, my main concern is to make explicit the way in which this community offers the democratic epistemology which I seek.

This, then, is not so much an exercise in what feminism and philosophy might contribute to each other, as an attempt to reconcile the two in my own life; to do them together.

THE APPEAL AND PROBLEMS OF REALISM[2]

Some preliminary definitions: I characterise realism as the view that there is an objective order of reality, which can be known by the human observer. The claim that it is a fact that women's wombs do not wither if they use their brains, or that it is in multinational corporations' interests to maintain women's obsessions with food are both examples of realism. For the moment, I define relativism as the view that every woman's experience is valid, not false, illusory or mistaken, and that all ways of making sense of the world are equally valid. I shall subsequently revise this to the view that the truth of a claim is relative to the group within which that claim is made. Thus, eventually, I wish to distinguish relativism, which may be a coherent position, from subjectivism, which is certainly not.

The primary appeal of realism is political. If all views are equally valid, so are sexist ones, and relativism appears to disarm me. We also all now agree on certain truths. It is false to say that a woman's womb withers if she uses her brain, irrational to use sexual characteristics rather than economic position as the deciding factor in granting a mortgage, and patently unjust to pay less to a woman than a man for completing identical tasks. A combination of careful observation, willingness to take account of the evidence, and a commitment to consistency will reveal these truths. They are not a matter of perspective, social position or gender.

But we have to ask how these truths are known, we need an epistemology. It is here that the realist runs into difficulties. For given that it is a combination of those intellectual virtues already mentioned (consistency, careful observation etc.) which enabled us to expose the bias and falsehood of sexist views; and given that these virtues are popularly recognised as the characteristics of a scientific attitude towards the world, we might look for an epistemology based on that scientific approach. For the truth to out, feminists need only to do rigorously what men have purported to do, and indeed, we owe a great deal to feminists who have, through rigorous intellectual effort, revealed that much purportedly impartial and objective scholarship and science is grounded in male bias.[3] We have a better knowledge of ourselves and our past because of them.

But although this epistemology, which I call rational–scientific, is politically appealing (it enables us to say to the sexist 'you are wrong') it also raises political problems. First, it is an élitist epistemology. Only some women have the resources (time, library, etc.) to conduct such research, other women will simply have to accept it on authority. This may not be a ground for rejecting it, but it means it needs to be supplemented with an epistemology for everyday life which answers the question, 'How do I know who or what to believe?' One epistemology for the élite, another for the masses is embarrassing. Secondly, women have often experienced the scientific–rational approach as oppressive both in its process and in its findings. It has been used to make women feel foolish because they have been unable to express themselves in its terms, and it has been used to 'prove' the inferiority of women. The claim about wombs and brains came out of a scientific community that was not deliberately dishonest and was committed to certain canons of observation and rationality. Why did it take so long to discover that it was false?

At this point, the realist may answer that ideology and false consciousness obscure the operation of intelligence and observation, or she may argue, as Grimshaw (1986) does, that we do not have to be positivists, committed to the view that it is possible to give an objective, value-free description of the world simply by observing the appropriate scientific method, in order to believe that there is an objective reality, often masked by ideology, but ultimately knowable. I define ideology as a system of beliefs, including values, which serves a particular group's interest. Thus there is a powerful motive, not always fully conscious, for a group to believe certain things. False consciousness is a system of beliefs and values which betrays the interests of the person or group with the false consciousness. It is puzzling to the 'enlightened', who, to explain it, must usually appeal to the mechanisms whereby a dominant group persuades an oppressed group to accept the former's view of the world. Clearly, the language of science, if not the spirit, would be a useful tool in this endeavour of keeping the oppressed ignorant. The realist, thus, maintains her view that there is an objective reality, there really are certain objective interests served in certain objective ways, regardless of what the people involved might think, and argues that one of the ways of finding out about that reality is to ask whose interests are being served by any particular belief, especially one suspected of being false. Knowing those interests would explain why false beliefs are held, and suggest ways in which we might redirect our attention so as to discover truth. But it does not tell us how to decide what is true, especially where there is conflict of opinion or interest as there often is within the feminist movement. This becomes critically important when it is a matter of knowing what our interests are and how these are best served: while it may only be authoritative to tell a woman that science proves mental activity will not affect her fertility, it is authoritarian to tell her what her interests are, and that she is falsely conscious if she thinks that they are best served through, for example, marriage.

So the political problems of the rational–scientific epistemology are made more acute when questions of ideology and false consciousness are introduced. At best, the use of this epistemology appears to be profoundly undemocratic. At worst, it is an exercise in domination. At best, some women are telling other women what they are like, what their interests are, and how they might best be served. At worst, some women are imposing their own interests on the movement as a whole. For example, while it is in white middle-class women's interests to show how women are like white middle-class men, in order to get their share of the jobs, money and status, it is not in black or working-class women's interests. How do we know when we are not simply being sold someone else's ideology if we cannot rely on our own judgement?

ON WHEN TO BELIEVE AN AUTHORITY

I think it is rational to accept authorities on two bases: that they can solve our problems, and/or that they can share their view of things with us. We accept the mechanic who successfully repairs the car. Many of us treat doctors in the same way, although some are progressively learning to doubt that view of the profession.[4] I think we are most willing to accept authority when the issue is most acutely one of control of a situation. If I am bleeding to death, or if my car stalls at every traffic light, I have a clear test of a solution to the problem, and I am probably not very interested in the mechanics of that response. For all the debate, Popper (1957) successfully isolates one test of knowledge with his notion of technological impossibility and its implication of control. But this only applies to certain areas of knowledge, and only under certain conditions. I am, for example, unwilling to accept control where the costs are too high. If I am told that the only way we can continue to feed the population is by increasingly large-scale agribusinesses and factory farms, my distress at the destructiveness of that method of food production makes me less likely to accept the solution on authority. If I live with acute famine, I might not balk at the solution. The costs are suddenly not so high. Where I have a clear problem, clear criteria for the successful solution to the problem, and reasonable costs for the solution, I have a test of knowledge, and a test for accepting other people's claims to knowledge. This is a conception of knowledge as control or power, and is central to our understanding and worship of scientific knowledge. Its roots go back at least to Bacon, and it is no accident that it developed contemporaneously with modern science. But as has been often said, it does not give us The Truth about the World. There can be more than one solution to a problem, more than one way of controlling a situation. We can eliminate non-solutions, but not establish *the* single correct solution. This is obvious (although not to Bacon) as soon as knowledge is conceived of in terms of control, much less obvious if knowledge is seen simply as a correct description of the world.

It is clear that such a view of knowledge only has limited application. As Carolyn Merchant (1982) has pointed out, implicit in it is the idea of domination. Most of us are unwilling to accept domination, even by 'scientific' knowledge, in social life, and many of us are unwilling to accept it even within so-called scientific areas. Thus many feminists have struggled to regain control over birthing from the scientific experts, and few would accept that the issue of how to achieve orgasm can be settled by anyone but themselves. Indeed, one of the reasons for the feminist distrust of science is that issues presented as scientific turned out to be political, for example, the control (knowledge) of women's sexuality and fertility. Issues of control and domination, and of what counts as a solution, then become relevant in deciding whether or not to accept a particular epistemological approach. Popper's notions of piecemeal social engineering (Popper, 1957) are unacceptable precisely because he treats social problems as technological problems to be controlled by technique rather than democratically resolved.

We also accept knowledge on authority where experts can share that knowledge with us, for example, where they have done surveys, or been in a position to make observations, which we cannot. Here it is necessary that we understand what is going on, unlike the problem-solving cases, and that we trust the expert, and this often gets very close to allowing our political commitments to decide our view of the truth. For example, my suspicion of the health risks run by people living near to nuclear power stations is confirmed by statistics about child leukaemia in such areas. But counter-surveys may be done, which show the rate not to be as much above normal as suspected, which refer to acceptable levels of radiation, and so forth, until I run out of time and expertise to judge the case on its 'merits' and instead decide on the basis of my prior commitment against nuclear energy. This decision is not irrational: BNFL and I are going to disagree about acceptable levels and risks, what constitutes a 'normal' rate of child leukaemia, and so on, through a complex of value judgements and decisions about the facts that do not necessarily involve either of us in distortion, dishonesty or even error. This becomes even clearer in the light of H. L. A. Hart's analysis of cause (Hart and Honoré, 1959), which shows how we use value judgements in picking out certain conditions as precipitating events. For example, background radioactivity and certain nutritional patterns may both be necessary conditions for the disease. BNFL and I will disagree over which to call the cause. Further, my grounds for deciding which set of statistics to accept are neither more nor less rational than the expert's. We have both decided as honestly as we can on the basis of our best efforts to assess the evidence, we have both thought within a complex of judgements, values and beliefs (which are also going to include our view of acceptable solutions to problems). At this point, the differences between the realist and the relativist do not look very great. The realist could end up saying that the claim that nuclear power stations cause child leukaemia is not false, the relativist saying that it depends on your general views about nuclear energy whether or not you believe it.

This leads me to consider another way in which knowledge is shared: where what is shared is an idea, vision or theory. Here we seem to be out of the realm of being told what is true, more into an exchange between someone who holds a view and others who try out that view for themselves. Much of the best teaching is like this, a matter of introducing people to ideas which they can then play with and use (or ignore) to create and correct their own views. Introducing someone to the idea that she lives in a sexist society, where she is frequently not counted as a fully human person, is an example of this (Frye, 1983, pp. 41–51). It is also an example of the sort of issue over which the differences between the relativist and the realist become critical. For the realist is often cast by the relativist as *telling* us, 'You really are oppressed regardless of what you feel.' The relativist insists that only our experience of oppression can show we are oppressed, and if we do not have that experience, we are not (Stanley and Wise, 1983). Some of us live in a sexist society, and others do not. The realist responds:

> Theories, ideas and ideologies are not *just* ways of making sense of the world. They may also be the means by which one group of people may dominate or exercise control over another. And the fact that one group has power over, or exploits another cannot be reduced to anyone's belief that this is so.
>
> (Grimshaw, 1986, pp. 160–1)

But that difference becomes less acute and critical as soon as we consider the question of how we can know, or decide, whether or not we are oppressed. I ask myself whether such claims and theories make sense of my experience, whether they articulate discomforts and frustrations that I had previously dimly apprehended but been unable to articulate, and so on. I do not look for 'an experience of oppression' which validates the theory, for it is only in the most extreme and repressive situations (the South African black, the Guatemalan peasant) that such experiences are so obviously identifiable. I look rather at a pattern (the double-bind, for example (Frye, 1983, pp. 2–4), or hidden discrimination in the classroom (Mahony, 1985)). I did not notice such a pattern until someone else pointed it out to me, but once it has been, I not only see a pattern of discrimination, I find myself reinterpreting behaviours and events. Small courtesies, for example, become subtle insults. This whole process looks to me like an attempt to get at what is really going on, but an attempt that is consistent with the relativist's insistence that we should not allow ourselves to be bullied into accepting views about ourselves which do not, in some way, match our experience. Furthermore, it seems to me that it is only through such checking that the theorist herself can test her hypotheses. Whether feeding disorders are expressions of self-hatred or political revolt depends ultimately on the experience and testimony of the women suffering or revolting.

This section anticipates the argument to come. For I am arguing that the ultimate test of the realist's views is their acceptance by a community, and that it is also in a community that the non-expert decides what to believe and what not. This is not to say that such acceptance makes those views true, or rejection makes them false, but rather to say these are the best methods available to us for making decisions which accord with reality.

THE APPEAL OF RELATIVISM

The appeal of relativism is political and epistemological, and it is often difficult to distinguish the two. Women's oppression has partly been understood in terms of the silencing of women, the denial of their experience as valid, or the treatment of it, when discovered, as neurotic. The woman who failed to find satisfaction in the fulfilment of domestic duties or who did not want to have babies was treated as a suitable case for treatment. The apprehension that such women were not sick but oppressed by a false view of what they should be came about only through women sharing these feelings and experiences with each other. The view of what they should be was seen as false, first, because it failed to tally with how they felt – women, apparently, did not become happy and fulfilled in the ways that they were supposed to, and furthermore experienced feelings of relief in being able to say this in public – and second, in the perception that the demand that they find fulfilment and happiness in these ways fitted the interests of men rather well, maintaining women's dependence upon men. It is wrong to undermine a person with the claim that she does not know what she wants or feels, or that what she wants or feels is inappropriate; and you cannot know *what* is wanted or felt and cannot discover oppression unless you listen to people. A clear example of this can be found in the abortion debate. Unless we listen carefully to women opposed to abortion, the feminist movement will simply ignore (be *ignor*ant of) them and cut them off. Further, the woman charged with false consciousness is charged with not really understanding where her interests lie. But she is likely to have a clearer view of her particular situation, than a more distant observer has.[5] For example, if she has few marketable skills, it may be in her immediate interests to emphasise her mothering and childbearing capacities (Luker, 1984). To reply that she fails to see her interest *as a woman* may be true, but to insist that she be a member of a group that she fails to identify with seems to me as oppressive as the insistence that we all keep to our place in the patriarchal family. If our communities are to be epistemologically effective, then they cannot be politically coercive.

Relativism also fits with the feminist experience of finding that the world is not what it appeared to be, that instead of relying on the descriptions she grew up with, she has to create her own descriptions. Bartky (1977) gives a clear account of this process of confusion. She speaks of a realisation that what is really happening is quite different from what appears to be happening, and a frequent inability to tell what is really happening at all. It is not so much that we are aware of different things, but that we are aware of the same things differently, and this is an experience of anguish and confusion. Is what I say in a meeting foolish and irrelevant, or am I being ignored because I am a woman? If I refuse to compete aggressively for promotion, am I acting out of timidity and self-denial that I have been educated into seeing as proper to women, or am I demonstrating my independence of a contemptible system of values? Everyone can make her own list, but several things are clear about the kind of question or doubt that is being expressed. These are doubts about who we are, what kind of people we think that we ought to be, and hence about what we ought to do, how we ought to behave. I no longer know how to describe myself, and my relations with others, and part of the reason is my uncertainty about meanings and values. It is not that I have discovered an identity that was denied expression within a particular system of values. Rather, a feminist more commonly has the experience of changing her identity as she takes a series of decisions. An existentialist account best fits the experience: there seems little basis for these decisions, no compelling evidence or desire. On the other hand, there may be a sense of compelling need to do something, without quite knowing what.

Under these conditions, facts, values and decisions become inextricably combined, I have to decide on them *together*. Contrast this with MacIntyre's (1962) account of the practical syllogism: greenfly harm roses (more of a fact than a value because of our clear agreement of what constitutes healthy and beautiful roses), spraying kills greenfly, and hence the obvious decision to spray. Now consider how this clear and compelling decision could be muddied: a realisation that all I ever see in my roses is potential defect from disease and pest might lead me to revise my aesthetic standards; I never see a perfect rose so much as a potential victim; a weariness with gardening might lead me to aspire to a different kind of garden (consider the dog roses of the hedgerow), and I may come to see the cultivated rose as artificial, gaudy, or, because of an awareness of the consequences of pesticide spraying, to see it as an expression of destructive values, an attempt to make nature conform to art, an example of destructive control. Or I may continue to appreciate the roses, while considering spraying to be too high a cost to pay for them or I might decide to let the greenfly weed out the weaker specimens. Raising questions about the way in which the rose is produced can cause questions about the value of the rose, but does not have to. My decisions about what I am willing to do will affect my decisions about how to view the rose, and vice versa. But it may be objected, it is not a matter of decision that spraying kills greenfly. Perhaps not, but I can take decisions which make that 'fact' irrelevant.

To return to the feminist example: I am arguing that you cannot prioritise the problems, in the sense of saying: decide what the facts are, what you want, and then what to do. Each of these decisions affects the others, they may be mutually supported, but it is impossible to claim that one follows from the others. My decision not to compete aggressively for promotion is a decision to see youthful fierce competitiveness as experiments in a dominant ethic which I have discovered does not suit; not as self-assertion. Or it may constitute another decision, to see myself as no longer having the energy for such self-assertion, and in this case I may find (decide?) that I am acting out of low-esteem.

Now the realist may wish to insist, but which? One of these descriptions will be correct, some decisions will be dishonest, some self-deluded, and some simply mistaken, and that suggests a standard of at least truthfulness, if not truth, and correctness, if not reality. This is a valid query. If the violence of a man against a woman is seen as an expression of love, of her desirability and the strength of his desire for her (as it has been seen in so much literature), it cannot be said to be aggressive assault. Rape in the marriage bed is not simply a discovery of a previously unnoticed fact, it is a decision to understand behaviours in a different light, a decision involving men and women in a process of scepticism about what we were really doing and really meant. Our subjective consciousness is critically important in this, but we cannot wilfully decide what it is or was. We painfully try out concepts and descriptions, which partly create it but are also constrained by the need to fit. So how do I find out when I am being honest, when self-deluded?

THE COMMUNITY OF RESISTANCE

The answer for me is through painstaking questioning and checking of precisely the kind that went on in women's consciousness-raising groups. For this, a commitment to listen, to care for and to support each other, and to express ourselves honestly is necessary. Only when all feel safe to speak of hidden or barely recognised experiences can knowledge of our desires and our situation emerge. I can only discover whether my experience of 'passionate' intercourse as assault means that I am frigid by making comparisons with other women's experiences, and discovering the possibilities in love-making. We will need to discuss the meaning of passion, violence and frigidity, which must include comparing cases. Our agreement in judging sameness will determine these meanings, and recreate our pasts and our futures.[6] In this process, we also decide what is really there. Our feelings, for example of inadequacy or alarm, are indicative of reality, but it is only through intersubjectively checking that several of us have those feelings that we can feel confident that they are a response to something real, and know what those feelings are.[7] There is a close analogue with perception here. We do not have necessary and sufficient tests of the truth, which we can individually apply, such as Descartes and so many since him have sought, but a process of conversation which may allow the truth to emerge, and which each of us may individually be able to judge at the end, albeit with identities and frameworks of understandings which may have only emerged through that conversation. For example, as the abortion debate developed in the seventies, women developed an understanding that they, rather than their biology, could determine their roles in society. This gave the issue a new symbolic importance in terms of who controls our lives, changed the terms of the debate from one about crime to one about rights, and led reformers to identify themselves as women rather than reformers. None of this could have happened if the unspeakable had not become speakable:

As one early activist put it: 'I was alone at first, but every time I gave a speech I was no longer alone because people came from everywhere saying, "You've said what I felt, but I didn't know how to say it".'   (Luker, 1984, p. 120)

She might have added that she was no longer mad or bad, although she was not necessarily right.

Each individual's experience, as an unconsidered given, cannot show what is going on. As an isolated individual, I often do not know what my experiences are. There can be no argument for subjectivism here, but rather for an intersubjectivism which begins in individual experiences, but instead of multiplying them (we *all* saw flashes in the sky) seeks to understand them through conversation. (Lightning or Reagan's secret weapon or group fear?)

This commitment to engage in conversation to find out what the world is like is a moral or political commitment to a community, to be with a group through growth and change. It involves me in an act of faith, not only that we will each struggle honestly for our understanding, but to a view of knowledge and politics as process, rather than achievement. In multiplying heads, we do not simply multiply intelligences and confirmations, but we produce knowledge in the exchange of views, multiple, slightly different, sometimes opposed, and in the questioning, perhaps precisely because of our differences. This is unlike the working out of an argument. Putting two heads together produces a bigger and better computer, but once you have a computer adequate to the task, multiplying it gets us no further. This suggests that the *kind* of knowledge we seek is the sort that *requires* all our contributions, requires us to act together, in conversation (Buber, 1965). The shifts in meanings and values exemplified in the abortion debate above show this. Neither knowledge *nor* political solutions are final, they consist rather in continual doing. This is not a coincidental similarity; the two are inextricably bound up with each other. Knowledge tells us how to make sense of the world, how to adapt to it, what demands realistically to make of it. It tells us what is there. Politics too is trying to make sense, to live with, adapt to. Put another way: we won't so much finally achieve peace as continuously make it, and that will mean continuous efforts at understanding. We will not achieve a final equality of persons, so much as continuously make it. In doing these things we will doubtless discover previously unimagined meanings to peace and equality. I say 'discover' because they will be implicit in, or prompted by, previous understandings and decisions. In that sense they lie beyond the individual, are not simply an arbitrary choice. But neither is the knowledge of what peace and equality are something that can be bumped into by an individual with a map and compass, as Columbus bumped into the West Indies. What peace and equality are discovered to be will depend on the decisions that various communities have taken. Through our decisions with a community, we decide how we want to belong to the world, how we want to set about understanding it, living in it and changing it. We have nothing else to rely upon except each other in taking those decisions.

THE COMMUNITY AND THE PROBLEMS OF RELATIVISM

Using the community to take our decisions seems to retain the appeal of relativism without its problems (which amount to the paradox of claiming that all views are valid while aspiring to the truth). This is seen clearly in two examples: what can I say about those who *fundamentally* disagree with me, (e.g. sexists, Nazis), and about my own past?

First, my past: as I became engaged with feminism, I found myself changing in ways that are most simply and honestly described as: I used to think . . . feel . . . but I was wrong. The relativist seems either committed to saying that I was right then, and that although I now disagree with what I thought then, I am also right now, or to abandoning the use of such terms as 'right' and 'wrong'. Either of these paradoxical positions seems to commit me to denying that I have developed in a progressive way. This denies the experience I have of progress and commits the relativist to the claim that while I might *feel* as if I have developed in fact I have only changed. The relativist is then validating *all* my experiences except that which I might count as the most important in my life.

Let me briefly consider some of the ways in which I vindicate my later position, for I think that these will show the way in which appeal to community resolves the problem. I can now acknowledge and recognise feelings and experiences which I previously barely took account of or tried to rationalise as irrelevant or insane. (For example, feeling deeply insecure in the nuclear state.) I recognise that in some ways I have always thought this way but not always been able to articulate it properly. (For example, that doctors have no right to control my life.) I do not as frequently have to pretend about what I feel or like. I now find patterns of behaviour that make better sense of my life, and I also find I can honestly acknowledge inconsistencies and be prepared to live with them, while I try to work them out with others. I am no longer bullied into accepting consequences that I really do not believe. The list could be longer, and no one item on it is conclusive. Each item could be demonstrated with autobiographical details, which show how conversation, being listened to and listening, enabled me to see these things. I would summarise these vindications as a progressive release from feeling isolated, finding the world an alien and unfathomable place, into finding a community that enables me to live in the world rather than trying to escape it and, no matter how confusing these attempts are at times, to make some sense of it. This again brings out the importance of the distinction between subjectivism and relativism. I pay attention to my subjective experiences in order to find what Arendt (1963) called 'the world'. It is not that every individual's unexamined and undiscussed experience is true, much less her opinions, but it is only *through* examining and discussing individuals' experiences that we can do what the realist calls finding truth, what the relativist calls contributing to the construction of reality as opposed to simply being the victims of other people's constructions. Again, there seems little importance in the difference between the realist and the relativist.

I find it more difficult to deal with those who fundamentally disagree with my politics and I can only sketch a solution. If I am honest, I believe that if only they examined their lives, they would find all the things that I have found, that is, that life could be better. This is a Socratic position, and maybe too close to wishful thinking to be persuasive. I do not have much evidence for it, although I have progressively come to approach them in that spirit. There are, I think, two problems involved: how to persuade them to change their ways, and how to persuade bystanders not to join them. The realist would do this by pointing to false beliefs. This might work for bystanders, but not for the committed Nazi or sexist, and raises again the problem of why 'the truth' is not compelling. The relativist engages in a struggle to see that her community prevails, a struggle that may include charges of inconsistency or dishonesty. My response is not merely that I don't want to live with such people as Nazis and sexists, but that their approach is based on the assumption that some people are not persons and therefore cannot be fully participating members in creating their communities and hence the world. Thus they make it impossible to the majority of us to live with them, at least in the way that persons might live together. We are communities in a state of war, and although it does not necessarily follow that our relations are violent, I think that they may necessarily be subversive. This vindicates neither the relativist nor the realist position. Once again, it indicates that the differences between them become less important in the light of questions about what to do.

CONCLUSION

Reasonable people who are located in different parts of the social world find themselves differentially exposed to diverse realities, and this differential exposure leads each of them to come up with different – but often equally reasonable – constructions of the world. (Luker, 1984, p. 191)

Quite so, and we require that our constructions fit, in a *real* way, our needs and desires, which are decided upon together with the constructions. This is neither realism nor relativism, but finding the best way to recreate our world, which can only be done through a genuinely democratic movement based on a genuinely democratic epistemology of the kind I have sketched above.

NOTES

1. See Welch (1985) for an excellent example.
2. 'Realism' is the term that comes closest to capturing the range of beliefs that I want to discuss. I hope that the context of the paper makes it clear that I am not concerned with various theories in the philosophy of science, but rather with a view that, especially in the context of feminism, and more generally in the social and political sphere, is best understood in opposition to relativism. It is the view that there is an objective order in human affairs, independent of people's beliefs about it, which can be discovered by some methodology generally characterised as rational and scientific. Thus, on this view, both Marxists and positivists might be characterised as realists because they believe in a social reality discoverable by the use of a method they specify as scientific.

3. Several examples in Harding and Hintikka (1983).
4. For the reasons, see Ehrenreich and English (1979).
5. This is reminiscent of J. S. Mill's defence of individualism, but leads to a different conclusion.
6. The influence of Wittgenstein (1958) and Winch (1958) is apparent here.
7. See the paper on 'Feminism, Feelings and Philosophy' by Morwenna Griffiths in this volume.

REFERENCES

ARENDT, Hannah (1963), *On Revolution* (Harmondsworth: Penguin).
BARTKY, Sandra Lee (1977), 'Toward a Phenomenology of Feminist Consciousness', in M. VETTERLING-BRAGGIN, F. ELLISTON and J. ENGLISH (eds), pp. 22–34.
BLOOR, David (1983), *Wittgenstein: A Social Theory of Knowledge* (London: Macmillan).
BOURQUE, Susan C. and DIVINE, Donna R. (eds) (1985), *Women Living Change* (Philadelphia: Temple University Press).
BUBER, Martin (1965), *The Knowledge of Man* (New York: Harper & Row).
CABEZAS, Omar (1985), *Fire from the Mountain: The Making of a Sandinista* (New York: Crown Publishers).
CAGAN, Leslie (1983), 'Feminism and Militarism', in Michael Albert and David Dellinger (eds), *Beyond Survival: New Directions for the Disarmament Movement* (Boston: South End Press), pp. 81–118.
DALY, Mary (1979), *Gyn/Ecology: The Metaethics of Radical Feminism* (London: The Women's Press).
EHRENREICH, Barbara and ENGLISH, Deirdre (1979), *For Her Own Good: 150 Years of Experts' Advice to Women* (London: Pluto Press).
EISENSTEIN, Hester (1984), *Contemporary Feminist Thought* (London: Allen & Unwin).
FEYERABEND, Paul (1977), *Against Method* (London: New Left Books).
FEYERABEND, Paul (1979), *Science in a Free Society* (London: New Left Books).
FREEMAN, Jo (1975), *The Politics of Women's Liberation: A Case Study of an Emerging Social Movement and its Relation to the Policy Process* (New York: Longman).
FRYE, Marilyn (1983), *The Politics of Reality: Essays in Feminist Theory* (Trumansburg, NY: Crossing Press).
GORNICK, Vivian (1977), *The Romance of American Communism* (New York: Basic Books).
GRIMSHAW, Jean (1986), *Feminist Philosophers: Women's Perspectives on Philosophical Traditions* (Brighton: Wheatsheaf).
HARDING, Sandra and HINTIKKA, Merrill B. (eds) (1983), *Discovering Reality: Feminist Perspectives on Epistemology, Metaphysics, Methodology, and Philosophy of Science* (Dordrecht: Reidel).
HART, H. L. A. and HONORÉ, A. M. (1959), *Causation in the Law* (Oxford: Clarendon Press).

HESSE, Mary (1978), 'Value and Theory in the Social Sciences', in Christopher Hookway and Philip Pettit (eds), *Action and Interpretation: Studies in the Philosophy of the Social Sciences* (Cambridge: Cambridge University Press), pp. 1–16.

JAGGAR, Alison M. (1983), *Feminist Politics and Human Nature* (Brighton: Harvester).

JAMES, William (1896), 'The Will to Believe', *New World* (June), reprinted in Melvin Radar (ed.), *The Enduring Questions* (New York: Holt, Rinehart & Winston, 1980), pp. 67–80.

KUHN, Thomas (1970), *The Structure of Scientific Revolutions* (Chicago and London: University of Chicago Press).

LAKATOS, Imre and MUSGRAVE, Alan (eds) (1970), *Criticism and the Growth of Knowledge* (Cambridge: Cambridge University Press).

LUGONES, María C. and SPELMAN, Elizabeth V. (1983), 'Have We Got a Theory for You! Feminist Theory, Cultural Imperialism and the Element for "The Woman's Voice"', *Women's Studies International Forum*, vol. 6, no. 6, pp. 573–81.

LUKER, Kristin (1984), *Abortion and the Politics of Motherhood* (Berkeley: University of California Press).

MacINTYRE, Alasdair (1962), 'A Mistake about Causality in the Social Sciences', in Peter Laslett and W. G. Runciman (eds), *Philosophy, Politics and Society* (Oxford: Blackwell), pp. 48–71.

MACY, Joanna (1983), *Despair and Personal Power in the Nuclear Age* (USA: New Society Publishers).

MAHONY, Pat (1985), *Schools for the Boys? Co-education Reassessed* (London: Hutchinson).

MERCHANT, Carolyn (1982), *The Death of Nature: Women, Ecology and the Scientific Revolution* (London: Wildwood House).

MICHNIK, Adam (1986), *Letters from Prison and Other Essays* (Berkeley: University of California Press).

MILL, John Stuart (1910), *On Liberty*, Everyman series (London: Dent).

MITCHELL, Juliet and OAKLEY, Ann (eds) (1976), *The Rights and Wrongs of Women* (Harmondsworth: Penguin).

PEAVEY, Fran *et al.* (1986), *Heart Politics* (USA: New Society Publishers).

POPPER, Karl R. (1957), *The Poverty of Historicism* (London: Routledge & Kegan Paul).

PUTNAM, Hilary (1981), *Reason, Truth and History* (Cambridge: Cambridge University Press).

RICHARDS, Janet Radcliffe (1980), *The Sceptical Feminist: A Philosophical Enquiry* (London: Routledge & Kegan Paul).

RORTY, Richard (1979), *Philosophy and the Mirror of Nature* (Princeton, NJ: Princeton University Press).

ROWBOTHAM, Sheila, SEGAL, Lynne and WAINWRIGHT, Hilary (1979), *Beyond the Fragments* (London: Merlin Press).

ROWLAND, Robyn (ed.) (1984), *Women Who Do and Women Who Don't Join the Women's Movement* (London: Routledge & Kegan Paul).

SCHELL, Jonathan (1986), 'A Better Today', *The New Yorker*, 3 February.

STANLEY, Liz and WISE, Sue (1983), *Breaking Out: Feminist Consciousness and Feminist Research* (London: Routledge & Kegan Paul).

STIEHM, Judith H. (1984), *Women's Views of the Political World of Men* (New York: Transnational Publishers).
VETTERLING-BRAGGIN, Mary, ELLISTON, Frederick A. and ENGLISH, Jane (eds) (1977), *Feminism and Philosophy* (Totowa, NJ: Littlefield Adams).
WELCH, Sharon D. (1985), *Communities of Resistance and Solidarity: A Feminist Theology of Liberation* (New York: Orbis Books).
WINCH, Peter (1958), *The Idea of a Social Science and Its Relation to Philosophy* (London: Routledge & Kegan Paul).
WITTGENSTEIN, Ludwig (1958), *Philosophical Investigations*, trans. G. E. M. Anscombe (Oxford: Blackwell).

11

Experience, Knowledge, and Responsibility

Lorraine Code

INTRODUCTION

Two central, interconnected tasks that face feminist philosophers working in theory of knowledge are that of finding appropriate ways of knowing women's experiences and the structures that shape them; and that of developing theoretical accounts of knowledge which retain continuity with those experiences. To perform the first task adequately, it is necessary, among other things, to break out of stereotyped perceptions of woman's 'nature' which work, persistently, to constrain possibilities of knowing well. In this connection, I shall argue that ways of knowing can be judged 'appropriate' partly on the basis of responsibility manifested by cognitive agents in making knowledge claims, and in acting upon assumptions that they know. Adequate performance of the second task requires a shift in perspective about the purpose of 'the epistemological project'. It involves moving away from theoretical positions which advocate a purity in knowledge that would leave experience behind in a search for an epistemic ideal of unrealisable clarity.

To perform these tasks successfully it will be useful, too, to eschew any idea that ethics and epistemology are separate and distinct areas of enquiry. This could provide scope both for the view that knowing well is good for its own sake – a moral *and* an epistemological point – and for a recognition of the extent to which the explanatory capacities of moral theories and of policies based upon them depend upon their having a basis in responsible knowledge of human experience. Hence, in the elaboration of feminist epistemological concerns that I shall present here, epistemic responsibility will figure as a central intellectual virtue, with the potential to play a regulatory role in cognitive activity analogous to the role moral virtues can play in moral activity.

Certain preliminary points need to be made before proceeding to a more detailed discussion of these tasks. First, in naming the task of coming to know women's experiences as one of the two central tasks I shall discuss, I mean to indicate from the outset that the notion of women's experience (in the singular) is an artificial construct. While it may often be expedient, in the course of the discussion, to use the term in the singular, it should always be read with a sensitivity to the fact that there is no such singular entity. To assume that there could be would be to mask crucial differences between and among women, and hence to break that continuity with experiences that it is important to maintain.

Secondly, it needs to be made clear that the point of this exploration is neither to provide a female-experience-based nor a responsibility-based epistemology, designed to *supplant* traditional epistemological modes, though running parallel to them in structure and content. Nor is it simply to *add* an account of female experiences and of the workings of epistemic responsibility to 'traditional' epistemological theories, leaving their presuppositions and structures otherwise intact. While it is by no means clear what theory of knowledge might look like when attention is directed towards maintaining continuity with experience(s) and clarifying the implications of epistemic responsibility, it seems to be highly probable that it must differ markedly, both in its aims and in its conclusions, from traditional epistemological enterprises. Some of these differences will become apparent in the discussion that follows; but my purpose is much more to offer an exploration, from a feminist perspective, of certain epistemological problems, and to give some indication of the directions one might take in trying to solve them, than it is to present a fully articulated feminist theory of knowledge.

These points reflect my conviction that, while feminist epistemological practice may indeed reject and/or seek to render problematic much of traditional 'malestream' epistemology, it can most fruitfully do so by remaining in dialogue with that tradition. In genuine dialogue, as contrasted both with polite conversation and with adversarial confrontation, both of the participants are changed.[1] So the process I envisage does not involve simply turning away from the malestream tradition in order to celebrate 'the feminine', however that might be understood. Rather, it involves engaging with that tradition, trying to see what can be learned from reading it 'against the grain' so that different of its facets are highlighted, and its gaps and exclusions understood and elaborated.[2]

But engagement with the *philosophical* tradition alone will not enable feminists to perform these tasks successfully. Disciplinary boundaries constitute some of the most intractable exclusionary structures impeding possibilities of insight and illumination. It is becoming a well-established aspect of feminist practice to move back and forth across such boundaries with the aims both of demonstrating their artificiality, and of tapping sources of understanding that fall outside the scope of traditional disciplinary orthodoxy. Hence feminist epistemological practice engaged in from a philosophical perspective is continuous with the epistemological concerns of feminists working in such traditionally disparate areas as sociology, anthropology, history and political theory. Feminists have much to learn from each other.

With respect to the practical effects that such learning might have, it should be mentioned that in commenting upon the *artificiality* of a conception of women's experience (in the singular), and upon the artificiality of disciplinary boundaries, my point is not to equate goodness with 'naturalness'. Rather, it is to draw attention to a connection between artificiality and contingency. What has been labelled or created by human beings out of contingent circumstances can likewise be labelled and understood differently by them, or altered when its flaws are revealed. Suspending such artificial constructs may reveal other possibilities, perhaps more creative ones, just as reading traditional texts, theories and presuppositions against the grain may reveal other perspectives on seemingly entrenched ideas.

STEREOTYPES AND RESPONSIBILITY

Stereotyped perceptions of women's nature, and actions based upon them, count amongst the most intransigent of constructs that shape women's experiences and make it difficult for women to move 'beyond domination'.[3] Manifestations of such perceptions are perhaps best known as they come across in anthropological, psychological and sociological studies and the (often unquestioned) assumptions about gender differences in terms of which such studies are conducted. But it is clear from a closer perusal of some of these studies that their implications are as much ontological, in their structuring effects upon women's possibilities of being, and epistemological, in their constraints upon responsible knowing, as they are practical. Indeed, such studies often work as self-fulfilling prophecies, leading people to *be* much as stereotype-governed research takes them to be.[4] It is because of these consequences that a principal requirement of epistemically responsible knowing centres about the need to become aware of the extent to which stereotypes govern perception and shape alleged knowledge (both one's own, and those of other members of one's epistemic community). It is part of responsible epistemic practice to work towards freeing cognitive activity from such constraining influences: this is an indispensable first step in the project of developing an epistemological approach that can maintain continuity with experience.

The point is not, however, that if stereotypes are stripped away, then experience will present itself 'pure' and untainted. Experience is always mediated by the location of experiencing subjects within a certain time, place, culture and environment, and it is always shaped as much by unconscious considerations and motivations. It is, arguably, also shaped by the gender of the experiencer. But stereotypes constitute a particular sort of knower-adopted overlay upon these structures, of whose effects one can become aware, and which one can work to rethink and restructure. It is especially for this reason that it makes sense to illustrate something of what is involved in epistemic responsibility by looking at some of the epistemological and political effects of stereotypes.

I have spelled out the features and implications of epistemic responsibility more extensively elsewhere.[5] My belief in its importance stems from my view that the Kantian conception of the creative synthesis of the imagination is one of the most important innovations in the history of philosophy, and that to think of knowledge as arising out of that synthesis is to take human cognition to be an active process of *taking* and *structuring* experience. Such activity is constrained by the (often fluid) nature of human cognitive equipment, and by the (also fluid) nature of reality. But within these constraints there is considerable freedom in making sense of the world. To take an example particularly relevant to this context, one is free to know, conduct one's life, and interact with other people on the basis of the alleged knowledge, that women are deficient in reason by comparison with an alleged masculine norm. Certainly it is possible to 'make sense' of many aspects of the world on these terms, and to construct a view of human relations and possibilities which depends upon this alleged 'knowledge'. Yet feminists are showing how serious a bias is at the basis of such knowledge claims, and how they provide the cognitive basis for devastatingly oppressive practices. And many other analogous examples can be cited from a wide variety of contexts. They show why imperatives are required to limit the kinds of sense that can responsibily be made of experience; and I take the notion of *epistemic responsibility* to stand for a cluster of considerations that work to constitute such imperatives.

Evidence for such responsibility is to be found in intellectual virtue, and in the recognition of a normative force that attaches to 'realism'. By the former, I mean a certain kind of orientation to the world and to one's knowledge-seeking self as part of the world. An intellectually virtuous person would value knowing and understanding how things 'really' are, to the extent that this is possible, renouncing both the temptation to live with partial explanations when fuller ones are attainable, and the temptation to live in fantasy or illusion. Such a person would consider it better to *know*, despite the comfortable complacency that a life indiscriminately governed by fantasy and illusion might offer. And this connects directly to the idea that 'realism' has normative force. In terms of this idea, the value of understanding how things are, to the best possible extent, is greater than, and supersedes, any value that might be taken to attach to consistent adherence to established theory or received opinion about how things might be. To achieve the 'right' perceptions implied by such an approach requires honesty and humility, the courage not to pretend to know what one does not know, the wisdom not to ignore its relevance, and the humility not to yield to temptations to suppress facts damaging to a cherished theoretical stance.

Now it seems to be beyond dispute that claims to know based in stereotypical perceptions and conceptions fail in just this respect. In their extreme crudity as epistemological tools, stereotypes violate the requirements of epistemic responsibility, opting, in its place, for what one might term both epistemic indolence and epistemic imperialism. The former is manifested in a stereotype-user's conviction that s/he knows what s/he is talking about and is absolved from any need to attempt to know better. This encourages a kind of intellectual *akrasia*, an entrenched reluctance to enquire further lest one face the necessity of having to 'reconsider a range of treasured beliefs'.[6] The latter is manifested in a belief that a stereotyped person or situation is summed up, that the putative knower has labelled it for what it is, and has thus claimed it as part of his/her stock of cognitive possessions.

From the minimal concern with knowing well that is apparent in such epistemic postures, it is clear that these are epistemically irresponsible ways of claiming to know. Here there is none of the humility, openness and concern with the normative force of realism that marks responsible cognitive endeavour. In fact, stereotypes close off possibilities of understanding; and this feature of their functioning is attributable, in part at least, to their resemblance, at once, to products of hasty generalisations, and to illegitimate appeals to authority. Both in its manner of selecting accidental characteristics of people and stretching them to sum up all people of that sort (be they women, blacks or men), and in its posing as a finished product, not open to amendment, the use of a stereotype has all the reprehensible features of pronouncements based upon hasty generalisations. Yet it is unlikely to have been derived by the overly simple (empiricist) process of simple enumeration by which hasty generalisations, in the main, are formed. Stereotypes are just as much the products of accumulated cultural lore, acquired as part of an acculturation process, and, as such, both deep-seated and tenacious. To allow them to pass for knowledge is to grant that cultural tradition undue authority and to abandon the critical perspective characteristic of responsible knowing.

Yet having said this, it is perhaps paradoxical to observe that something very like stereotypes is in fact needed if knowledge, or language, are to be possible at all. Categories and classifications, derived both from cultural traditions and from generalisations based on particular experiences, are part of the essential stuff of which both language and knowledge are made. So it is part of this epistemological task to devise responsible ways to distinguish open, potentially 'fallibilist' categories and classificatory devices from rigid, dogmatism-evincing stereotypes. It is as much part of responsible knowing to become mindful of the possibilities of acting according to stereotypes oneself, and of succumbing to stereotyped self-perceptions, as it is to avoid stereotyping others.

With special reference to stereotypes of women, feminists in several disciplines have documented the way in which actions and attitudes shaped by such stereotypes structure the ways in which women are perceived and know, and come thereby to know themselves. Much of this documentation is philosophically pertinent just because it shows, precisely with reference to people's experience of themselves as participants in the world, that how one comes to know oneself through 'received' doctrine has profound effects upon one's possibilities of being. In a complex process of reciprocal structuring and restructuring, what a person comes to believe that she (or he) *is* affects what that person can know, and to a large extent, structures what s/he is. In short, a stereotype is an unjust tyrant whose effects are both ontological and ethical. Two examples of such documentation are worth citing here to show something of what I mean.[7]

Margaret Rossiter's historical study of *Women Scientists in America: Struggles and Strategies to 1940* (1982) takes as one of its central themes a demonstration of the tyranny of stereotypes as they work to construct women's lives and to confine them both within certain possibilities for using their qualifications, and within certain modes of self-awareness which reinforce the stereotypes. Rossiter shows, for example, that if women can bring themselves to 'know', even within their professional lives, that it is more appropriate to seek employment compatible with what it is (stereotypically) to be a woman (the 'helpmate' role of a research assistant is an obvious example), then they make themselves less threatening to social structures, and hence more employable. In this mode, one simply buys into the 'complementarity' thesis and engages gratefully in mediocre work allegedly more suited to one's own different (=inferior) female capacities. One's possibilities of knowing both one's own experiences and 'the world' responsibly are thereby diminished.

A somewhat different manifestation of the feminine stereotype is evident in the case of Christine English who was found guilty not of murder but of manslaughter, in the 1981 killing of her lover. She successfully pleaded diminished responsibility as a result of severe premenstrual tension. Initial feminist enthusiasm for the decision in this case arose out of belief that doctors and lawyers had in fact granted reality to women's experiences of menstrual and pre-menstrual sufferings, long dismissed (on a common reading of the stereotype) as 'all in her mind'. But in a subtler way the decision contributes to a re-entrenchment of the very stereotype it appears to challenge. For the stereotype of female hysteria, emotional immaturity and irrationality might readily, now, be reinstated, on the basis of the expertise of highly accredited authorities.[8] Despite their rigidity, on the basis of which one is rightly critical of their usage, stereotypes also have a curious elasticity which enables them to stretch and shift so as to accommodate (and condemn) quite contradictory ways of behaving.

To return, then, to the complex interrelation between the avoidance of stereotypes, and epistemic responsibility, ordinarily I would take some version of the ancient Greek injunction 'Know thyself' to be one of the imperatives that responsible knowers would try to follow. I think one can work towards observing this injunction even while acknowledging that 'selves' are not fixed and are never fully conscious entities, and that claims to self-knowledge are not absolutely privileged by contrast with other people's claims to know one. Selves are constructed and reconstructed out of narratives, perspectives, experiences and events; and out of first-, second- and third-person accounts. But even within these acknowledgements there is a place for some version of self-knowledge, however provisionally it may need to be construed.

But when it comes to knowing oneself responsibly in defiance of stereotypes, the examples just cited indicate that this is an even more convoluted requirement than it seems to be, even with the ephemerality of 'selves' taken into account. Particularly in cases such as that of the scientific helpmate, *not* knowing oneself may be conducive to survival. On the other hand, to undermine a stereotype strengthened by evidence from the English case, the most responsible approach would seem indeed to be to know oneself as well as possible, to work to acquire a just perception of one's own capacities and incapacities, starting from the well-justified assumption that the authority of the experts is as fallible as any other human posture. Plainly there are no straightforward or universal solutions to the puzzles posed by efforts to know women's experiences, or to challenge structures that systematically distort them.

EXPERIENCE AND KNOWLEDGE

In Carol Gilligan's work on the responses of female moral agents to Lawrence Kohlberg's tests for measuring levels of moral maturity, it is the clash between the moral experiences of those female subjects and the requirements of the Kohlberg theory that leads her to conclude that women speak in a *different* (moral) voice (Gilligan, 1982). In fact, within the terms of the present discussion, one might take it to be Gilligan's (implicit) working hypothesis that the epistemological assumptions of Kohlberg's work preclude the possibility of accounting for women's experiences within the theoretical conclusions he draws.

Very much in keeping with traditional Kantian morality, Kohlberg assumes that moral maturity is characterised by a capacity for the autonomous endorsement of universalisable moral principles. The worthiness of such principles will be apparent from their applicability, with impartiality and following the dictates of duty alone, across all situations where moral judgement is required. Epistemologically speaking, it is tacitly assumed, although the question itself is not raised, that situations requiring moral judgement will be *known* in just the same way by all moral agents.[9] But it is a serious oversimplification to take for granted that perceptions are always unproblematically 'right'. Indeed, the moral quality of an action is dependent upon the cognition in which it is based, and this cognition is itself a proper object of evaluation.

Now Kohlberg's female and male subjects differ from one another as much in their *apprehensions* of the situations upon which they are called to pronounce as they do in their moral judgements. This cognitive asymmetry evidenced in their disparate responses seems to inspire much of Gilligan's dissatisfaction with the way those responses have been read so as to reinforce traditional stereotypes of the rational and morally mature male, and the irrational and morally immature female. Rather than considering an equally plausible interpretation to the effect that the complexity of female responses to Kohlberg's tests (statistically speaking) might be read as evidence of a finely tuned moral sense and a high level of moral sophistication, readers of these responses have tended automatically to favour the conclusion that female respondents are too much immersed in particularity to achieve the principled impartiality characteristic of mature moral being. It can at least be suggested that there has been a failure to maintain a responsible degree of openness on the part of these readers, too easy a willingness to structure their readings so as to confirm entrenched stereotypes and theoretical presuppositions.

In claiming that Gilligan's work lends itself to this kind of epistemological interpretation, I do not mean either to suggest that there *are* intrinsically incommensurable 'masculine' and 'feminine' ways of knowing, or that such statistical differences as emerge from female and male responses are essentially and/or 'naturally' female and male. Gilligan herself argues that although the moral voices she discerns have traditionally been differentiated along gender lines, this is a matter of historical contingency rather than biological necessity.[10] It is partially consequent, she suggests, upon the ways in which gender has been constituted in mother-dominated Western child-rearing practices.[11] Both voices, she maintains, are at least in principle accessible to women and to men.

None the less, a distinctive mode of moral discourse is discernible in Gilligan's work, especially in women's responses to her abortion study. This mode is markedly different from the kinds of deliberation commonly conducted within the rubric either of a Kantian or of a utilitarian approach to moral questions. While it is difficult to specify exactly how it differs, and quite inappropriate to see it either as arising out of, or as constituting a rival moral *theory*, certain of its features can be sketched out.

Both in the perceptions of relevance they reflect, and in their manner of apprehending and structuring situations, the responses Gilligan records are characterisable by what might be described as an analogue of practical reasoning (*phronimos*).[12] This is manifested in a kind of reflective posture, a thoughtfulness, which contrasts markedly with the Kantian-derived concentration upon achieving a principled moral stance that carries over into Kohlberg's work. But this is not the standard utilitarian contrast. The concern at its core is not so much with the consequences as with the *implications* both of motives and of actions, as much for other people, with whom one recognises a complex network of affinities and connections, as for oneself.

The possibility of discerning these implications seems to involve attempting to position oneself reflectively within a situation, in relation to various of its aspects, so as to achieve a stance which will allow one to take account of as many of these implications as possible, while not destroying one's capacity to act. To do this well one needs to cultivate an attitude perhaps best described, borrowing Annette Kuhn's useful and evocative phrase, as one of 'passionate detachment' (Kuhn, 1982, ch. 1). It is rather like the attitude a good therapist brings to a client: a kind of 'objective' sympathy, a mode of participation without intervention, of compassion without passion, which, at its best, succeeds at once in being involved and maintaining an appropriate distance. It is a matter of positioning and repositioning oneself within a situation until the best course of action comes to suggest itself; but always at points within the situation, for there is no removed, God's-eye vantage point. Whether such a mode of moral response is 'naturally' or contingently female remains an open question.

It is an advantage of Gilligan's methodological approach that she makes it possible for this moral voice to be heard, not as affording evidence of stereotypically muddled female thinking, but as worthy of a hearing equivalently thoughtful to that accorded to products of male deliberation. There is an evident *concern*, in her work, to maintain contact with, and derive insights from, accounts which not only arise out of experience and are firmly grounded in it, but which stay in touch with that experience in drawing their conclusions. This contrasts with methods of epistemological and moral theory construction which aim to transcend experience, to move beyond it, allegedly towards greater clarity and accuracy but at the expense, I believe, of the insight and understanding that a maintained continuity with experience can afford.

Gilligan listens to people's stories (to *women's* stories) as they recount their experiences; and her aim seems to be the laudable one of listening responsively, and so, I would maintain, responsibly, to these stories.[13] For responsiveness seems to be a necessary component of any approach that purports to retain continuity with experience: it signals an appropriate receptiveness and humility towards that recounted experience, from which one moves only cautiously in the direction of interpretation. Such caution is enjoined in recognition of the fact that subjective factors are bound to structure any interpretation, and it is important to to be cognisant of them, to the extent that one can. By no means the least significant of such factors is in the fact that a subject's account of her/his own experiences is as much structured by unconscious and semi-conscious forces as it is by conscious ones; and this is true, too, of any interpretation. Listening to, responding to and interpreting stories are acquired capacities. One has to put some effort into learning how to exercise them well. The need for *responsibility* in their exercise is particularly clear when one considers that there can be no uniquely True story, nor is there any uniquely right interpretation. But some are clearly better, or worse, than others, at least for now, and one can learn to recognise which ones.

In elaborating the potential value of Gilligan's methodological approach through these considerations, I do not mean to suggest that she herself shows a sensitivity to all of them. But the story-listening techniques she uses could be adapted and amplified so as to be more tentative, more qualified and nuanced in their interpretative moves. And even within the limitations of her own use of the approach, one sees some indication of how both epistemological and moral thinking might begin to move away from a preoccupation with transcending experience, not bothering about *who* the knowing subject, or the acting subject, really is.[14] Extrapolating from what Gilligan has done, it is possible to make sense of how it is that actual, historically situated, gendered epistemological and moral subjects know and respond to actual, complex experiences.

Clearly if any conclusions, however tentative and provisional, are to be derived from the process of telling and listening to stories, then the subject matter, the theme, of these stories must be specified, at least roughly. It is unlikely that randomly collected stories could be of much use in providing solutions – even tentative ones – to specific theoretical problems. So the investigator who would use such an approach must take a good deal of care to select stories both open enough *and* theoretically specified enough to elicit a range of responses which will neither predetermine possible conclusions, nor offer no possibility of discerning a common thread. If Gilligan is indeed committed to the view that this 'different' moral voice is accessible equally to women and to men, then I think one must have serious reservations about her use of a study of women's responses to abortion as a means of making it audible. She makes too little of an epistemological constraint that is built into the structure of the investigation.[15]

Leaving open the question as to whether there are essentially 'feminine' and 'masculine' ways of knowing, it is none the less reasonable to maintain that there is a range of experiences which could not be known in ways similar enough, from knower to knower, to produce 'common' knowledge in differently gendered subjects. Experiences which depend upon natural biological differences, in areas of sexuality, parenthood, and some aspects of physical and emotional being, must be different for women and for men to the extent that it would be impossible for them to know them in anything like 'the same' way.[16] Hence it cannot make sense to imply that conclusions about moral maturity *per se* could be drawn from biologically specific experiences available only to women, particularly if one grants the point that the quality of moral action is dependent upon, and a direct reflection of, the cognitive activity in which it is based. The abortion study could only work to generate a universally relevant new perspective on moral maturity if one could assume, with respect to the questions that arise within it, that women and men count as a group who have to make this kind of decision *as equals*. But to make such an assumption is to ignore the crucial practical respects in which women and men are not equally implicated in and affected by decisions about abortion. It is to gloss over the unequal impact upon women's and men's lives, at least within current social structures, of child-bearing and rearing. Hence it creates an intolerable discontinuity between experience and theory.[17]

On the other hand, stories must be specified sufficiently to provide experiential accounts of a *certain kind* of situation, if any substantive conclusions at all are to be drawn from them. And there is good reason to think that it is imperative to hear stories drawn from undervalued aspects of women's experiences, in view of the age-old imbalance in the standard selection of examples from stereotypically masculine experience. So the question arises as to what Gilligan's primary purpose is. If it is to make the 'different' voice audible as one in which both women and men can speak, then the abortion study does not serve her well. In advocating that a necessarily female kind of experience, and hence of knowledge and moral judgement, be allowed to generate an alternative standard of moral maturity she creates a structure for judging moral practice in which male knowledge, and hence male moral judgement, must equally necessarily be Other.

If, however, it is Gilligan's purpose to develop a specifically female morality, then perhaps the abortion stories are well chosen after all. But such a project would, I think, be of doubtful worth in the long run. Any celebration of specifically 'feminine' modes which would aim to revalue them, yet leave them intact, would be in danger of obscuring the constraints commonly attendant upon their manifestation. If 'connectedness', for example, were selected as a primary value, it would be important to keep in mind that, at least in the past, women's concentration upon 'connection' within the domestic sphere has limited their capacity to contest exploitation, and has contributed to their powerlessness and oppression. So if the project is to open the way for the development of an ethics of care and responsibility which could be juxtaposed *against* an ethics of rights and justice, the most likely consequences would be to reinstate and reinforce precisely those stereotypes Gilligan sets out to undermine. It would be but a short step towards the contention that the former – the caring morality – is female morality, attuned to women's softer, more emotional, and lesser concerns; the latter – the rights and justice morality – is male morality, appropriate to men's more serious moral endeavours.

Gilligan would, I think, be better advised to choose themes for her stories which might enable male and female responses to be more nearly commensurable. Then her readers could more readily entertain the possibility that her work contributes to a long-needed challenge to the tyranny of feminine *and* masculine stereotypes.

CONCLUSION

My discussion has centred on the question of how people and situations are known; and I have made a particular plea in favour of taking seriously a certain kind of story – first-person accounts of experiences. Such stories provide access to a kind of knowledge not ordinarily regarded as appropriate for epistemological consideration. Indeed, this is one of the gaps that shows up when one reads standard, 'malestream' epistemology against the grain, and wonders what has become of the *people* whose knowledge it allegedly analyses and explains. I have suggested that reflection upon epistemological and moral matters which is responsibly attuned to such narratives might be able to retain a kind of contact with human lives that is often lost in formalistic and abstract theoretical structures. Moreover, the subtlety and variety of narrative of this kind is such as to highlight the crudity of stereotypes, and their ineffectuality as putative cognitive devices. Responsible knowing simply has no place for them.[18]

The rejection of stereotypes as cognitive tools does not force one to fall back upon a belief in pure, unmediated experiences. Indeed, it would be a complete mistake to believe that stories, narratives, somehow provide unmediated access to experiences. Stories, even first-person stories, are not necessarily *truer* either than stereotypes or than standard philosophical analyses. Nor is there any kind of reliable criterion for determining their truth. Rather, the main point is that stories convey something about cognitive and moral experiences, in their manifold manifestations, which slip through the formalist nets of moral principles and duties, or standards of evidence and justification. The modest proposal urged here is that perhaps, by taking stories into account, theorists will be better able to repair some of the rifts in continuity that are so glaringly evident between moral theory and moral experiences, and theory of knowledge and cognitive experiences.

It is unlikely that this project could ever result in a seamless, invisible mending of these rifts. Theoretical structures and patterns that emerge from responsible reflection upon experience will more likely be piecemeal, comprised of interpretations of stories, and interpretations of interpretations. The point is not to generate a neat, comprehensive theoretical structure, but to learn how to let experience shape and reshape theory. In a word, the aim is to *understand* rather than to find methods of justification, verification and control. So the price to be paid in terms of loss of certainty, clarity and precision is, admittedly, high. The position is a vertiginous one, and understanding is fleeting. But the certainty, clarity and precision claimed for dominant theoretical structures is as illusory as the truth claimed for stereotypes. And the vertigo will not be the source of dismay that it may at first sight seem to be, if cognitive activity does, in fact, begin to move towards thoughtful, responsible practice. Such practice can generate theoretical accounts of knowledge which stand a good chance of retaining contact with women's experiences without, carelessly and dismissively, simply slotting them into stereotyped categories.[19]

NOTES

1. In her article, 'A Paradigm of Philosophy: The Adversary Method', Janice Moulton (1983) shows how adversarial argumentation, which is characteristic of most present-day philosophical discourse, is minimally productive of understanding, insight or change.
2. Some of the most significant of these gaps and exclusions are made clear in Lloyd (1984), where it is argued that reason itself is defined by exclusion of character-traits traditionally associated with femaleness.
3. Here I cite the title of Carol Gould's book, *Beyond Domination* (1983). Stereotyped perception of women's nature is, of course, continuous with stereotyping of any sort and shares its reprehensibly dogmatic, unthinking character. Nor could one argue that only women are stereotyped and hence, by implication, that it is only men who stereotype. Women are prone to stereotyping each other, anti-feminists to stereotyping feminists, and vice versa. It is the stereotyping of

women that concerns me here, whether by men or by other women. But epistemologically speaking, the use of stereotypes is always a crude and irresponsible way of not bothering to know, yet posing as though one does.

4. Classic feminist discussions of such practices are found in Hubbard (1983), Weisstein (1972) and Rubin (1975).

5. See Code (1983a, 1983b and 1984). The theory is still more fully elaborated in my *Epistemic Responsibility* (forthcoming). In the account given here, I borrow from the discussion of this idea that appears in Code (1983b).

6. This is Amélie Rorty's phrase in Rorty (1983).

7. For the sake of clarity, these examples are taken from patriarchal structures, where stereotypes are imposed upon women from the vantage point of male experience and alleged expertise. In coming to a philosophical understanding of the problem of stereotypes as such, one would have to take account of the facts, already mentioned, that women, too, stereotype other women; and that people are prone, also, to stereotype themselves. So the problem is more complex than these examples might suggest. But I think its solution would follow the same lines for its various manifestations, all of which, I think, are evidence of irresponsible cognitive practice.

8. I discuss these examples more fully in my 'The Tyranny of Stereotypes', in Storrie (ed.), (forthcoming).

9. Hence Lawrence Blum (1979) argues that there are two aspects to any occasion of moral judgement: the apprehension of a situation, and the action(s) based upon that apprehension.

10. Cf. Gilligan (1982) p. 2. But it should be noted, as Debra Nails (1983) points out, that the book is 'characterized by generalizations about the sexes, offered as descriptions of differences', hence that it has 'the power to exaggerate existing differences' (p. 662).

11. In this connection, Gilligan draws upon the work of Nancy Chodorow (1978).

12. Gilligan is not a philosopher, and would be unlikely to characterise them in this way. But it seems to be a potentially fruitful way of understanding something of what is at issue.

13. That she is not always successful in achieving this aim does not detract from its commendability as a guiding methodological principle. Gilligan seems often to interpret too swiftly, and it has been suggested that she quotes too selectively, and unjustifiably out of context (cf. Nails, 1983, esp. pp. 640–52). But the aim itself could be pursued somewhat differently, and its worthiness become more clearly apparent.

14. The use of narrative partially to effect this move is analogous to Alasdair MacIntyre's advocacy of the importance of narrative in understanding moral judgements and actions within the context of a life (see MacIntyre, 1981).

15. These reservations are also expressed in Code (1983b).

16. This is not to suggest that all women and all men would know these situations and aspects of their being in the same (stereotypical) way –

only that the lines of difference would be differently drawn in terms of their common starting points within one sex, and between the sexes.

17. I am indebted in my formulation of this point to Jean Grimshaw's discussion of philosophical writings on the ethics of abortion in her *Feminist Philosophers* (1986), pp. 31–3.
18. I discuss the epistemological value of story-telling in greater detail in my 'Stories People Tell' in the *New Mexico Law Review* (forthcoming).
19. Work on this paper was made possible by a Strategic Grant from the Social Sciences and Humanities Research Council of Canada, and by a Visiting Fellowship at the Humanities Research Centre at the Australian National University in Canberra.

REFERENCES

BLUM, Lawrence (1979), *Friendship, Altruism and Morality* (London: Routledge & Kegan Paul).

CHODOROW, Nancy (1978), *The Reproduction of Mothering: Psychoanalysis and the Sociology of Gender* (Berkeley: University of California Press).

CODE, Lorraine (1983a), 'Father and Son: A Case Study in Epistemic Responsibility', *The Monist*, vol. 66, pp. 268–82.

CODE, Lorraine (1983b), 'Responsibility and the Epistemic Community: Woman's Place', *Social Research*, vol. 50, no. 3, pp. 537–55.

CODE, Lorraine (1984), 'Toward a "Responsibilist" Epistemology', *Philosophy and Phenomenological Research*, vol. 45, no. 1, pp. 29–50.

CODE, Lorraine (forthcoming), *Epistemic Responsibility* (Hanover, New Hampshire: University Press of New England).

CODE, Lorraine (forthcoming), 'Stories People Tell', *New Mexico Law Review*.

CODE, Lorraine (forthcoming), 'The Tyranny of Stereotypes', in Kathleen Storrie (ed.), *Women, Isolation and Bonding: The Ecology of Gender* (Toronto: Methuen).

GILLIGAN, Carol (1982), *In a Different Voice: Psychological Theory and Women's Development* (Cambridge, Mass: Harvard University Press).

GOULD, Carol C. (ed.) (1983), *Beyond Domination: New Perspectives on Women and Philosophy* (Totowa, NJ: Littlefield Adams).

GRIMSHAW, Jean (1986), *Feminist Philosophers: Women's Perspectives on Philosophical Traditions* (Brighton: Wheatsheaf).

HARDING, Sandra and HINTIKKA, Merrill B. (eds) (1983), *Discovering Reality: Feminist Perspectives on Epistemology, Metaphysics, Methodology, and Philosophy of Science* (Dordrecht: Reidel).

HUBBARD, Ruth (1983), 'Have Only Men Evolved?' in S. HARDING and M. HINTIKKA (eds), pp. 45–69.

KUHN, Annette (1982), *Women's Pictures: Feminism and Cinema* (London: Routledge & Kegan Paul).

LLOYD, Genevieve (1984), *The Man of Reason: 'Male' and 'Female' in Western Philosophy* (London: Methuen).

MacINTYRE, Alasdair (1981), *After Virtue: A Study in Moral Theory* (London: Duckworth).

MOULTON, Janice (1983), 'A Paradigm of Philosophy: The Adversary Method', in S. HARDING and M. HINTIKKA (eds), pp. 149–64.

NAILS, Debra (1983), 'Social Scientific Sexisms: Gilligan's Mismeasure of Man', *Social Research*, vol. 50, no. 3, pp. 643–64.

RORTY, Amélie (1983), 'Akratic Believers', *The American Philosophical Quarterly*, vol. 20, no. 2, pp. 174–83.

ROSSITER, Margaret (1982), *Women Scientists in America: Struggles and Strategies to 1940* (Baltimore: Johns Hopkins University Press).

RUBIN, Gayle (1975), 'The Traffic in Women: Notes on the Political Economy of Sex', in Rayna Rapp Reiter (ed.), *Toward an Anthropology of Women* (New York: Monthly Review Press), pp. 157–210.

WEISSTEIN, Naomi (1972), 'Psychology Constructs the Female', in Vivian Gornick and Barbara K. Moran (eds), *Women in Sexist Society* (New York: Signet Books), pp. 207–24.

12

The Issue of Women's Philosophy

Paula Ruth Boddington

It may be easy for someone to wonder what all the fuss is about: if women can and do go to university to study philosophy, and there are women philosophers, women can't be very seriously excluded from philosophy. How odd to think that women would do philosophy any differently from men. For philosophy is claimed to be – in a way I shall only gesture at here – somehow a fundamental, suprapersonal methodology or account of things. But yet to many the point may seem obvious that women will tend to understand philosophy differently and bring different things to it. Many are already working, in various ways, under such an assumption.

This paper is going to look at the issues around which these views turn. I don't wish simply to address the 'adversaries' of the idea that there is a women's point of view in philosophy, or vice versa (see Moulton, 1983). This paper grew out of questions that arose out of trying to get to grips with the debate. Complexities arise and it may not be obvious exactly what view to take as to how far, if at all, and in what ways women have a special contribution to give to philosophy, or how far philosophy is and has been biased against women.

In a patriarchy it is to be expected that patriarchal influences may reach all sorts of seemingly 'innocent' areas of life; philosophy then is bound to be impregnated with maleness. Or one may focus one's feminist thought around more discrete injustices and such phenomena as sex-roles and wonder if both these extend as far as the sacred heart of philosophy. One will wonder this especially, if at all tempted to that end of the spectrum of opinion that sees philosophy as, in some ways, a neutral, an absolute, body of theory or activity; a giver of neutral theory relevant for all people (or even, bravely, for all sentient or rational beings). Conversely, such a picture could give extra cause for alarm. If philosophy is seen or sees itself in this way, it could be falsely influential, putting about as universal and absolute what is only male and relative. And the male–female, masculine–feminine issue of bias in philosophy can be seen to be especially pressing if philosophy is held to, at least partly, create and reinforce our theories of man/woman, masculine/feminine.

This points then to a reason for particular concern about women and philosophy, and may help to show why many are worried about the alleged absence of women in the subject – it's not simply taken as any old putative example of the onslaught of patriarchy and male dominance, not simply just another thing these wretched women have found to complain about. Another reason may be, given that masculinity or maleness is especially associated with reason, theory and the intellect, that plausibly philosophy is not polluted with unduly large doses of testosterone and associated muck merely from being another élite sort of academic activity in male-dominated society, but will in its self-conscious theoretical stance possibly turn out to be a veritable Rambo of the university world. I will look for specific issues about women that may keep them out of philosophy or lead them to philosophise differently from men; and how philosophy may be construed or constructed to keep out what women as women have to offer it. So this will involve looking at conceptions of philosophy as well as ideas about women and women's thinking. I hasten to add that, the details being so many, I can only give an outline and indicate a few general themes.

What indeed is the issue I am addressing? It can be pictured in three categories: a women's view of philosophy, based on a biological category; a feminine view of philosophy, i.e. a gendered view; a feminist view of philosophy, a theoretical stance.[1] The last is not being discussed in this paper. It seems apparent that there are *feminist* approaches to some areas in philosophy – in political philosophy, of course, and there has already been much work in feminist ethics. But bear it in mind, for it will often involve taking on a women's point of view. I address myself then to one of the first two – but which? I consider there is a large difference between the man/woman and masculine/feminine. These are different types of concepts; although, as a matter of fact, gender overlaps considerably with biological sex. Indeed, if one takes any of the various conceptions of masculinity and femininity that come to mind, the idea of a human being totally masculine or totally feminine hardly bears thinking about. Another complication one must remember is that these dichotomies may be only approximate dichotomies, and more like continua. But both pictures may be useful, one can still look to either end of the continuum and the dichotomy view colours current thinking to a large degree. It seems quite clear that femininity corresponds much more to the female: ideas of femininity are closely associated with what's considered suitable for (most) women. Ideas of what's considered suitable for someone of a certain gender act as blocks and encouragements to virtually the whole of the 'appropriate' sex. So I am addressing the question of a women's view of philosophy – in the main – and this will involve considering 'feminine' styles of thought or behaviour which will fit only approximately with biological sex. So in considering women I'll consider those affected by the social, psychological, etc. influences on that sex, roughly; it could be said, again, roughly, considerations affecting people in whom femininity is in the ascendant.

One of the phenomena to be looked at and considered – because it helps make the reasons for disagreement clear – is that of fuzziness about what women's philosophy would be when one considers the overlap between the sexes and mixtures within an individual, and different conceptions of what a woman is like or of what femininity is. The first of these is automatically accounted for by gender overlapping with biological sex. Many examples can be found. To take just one to illustrate: the ordinary-language philosophy of J. L. Austin, in its enormous precision, in its analytical approach and perhaps in its not using any old ordinary language but that of a certain area and class, -may be said to be masculine philosophy. However, traits that some have supposed to be feminine in philosophy include humour and lightness – the masculine is serious and takes itself seriously.[2] But here Austin's great wit can't go unnoticed.[3] It is such overlapping that could lead one to dismiss the whole sex–gender debate in philosophy. But no, I say, this is to be expected, and there could still be reason to claim that gendered thought-styles associated with sex could be identified. I shall say a little more on this later; it requires some delicate vision and brings in too the complication of different conceptions of men and women, masculine and feminine, which have varied historically, geographically and with factors such as class. But what does seem quite ubiquitous is some such division of thought; and it is known roughly what it is, with all its contradictions, in the current set-up. With these apologies this approximation is enough for me here, simply because the having of some such division is so pervasive.

So far I've talked in theoretical terms. There are also practical implications as to how philosophy is written, discussed, taught, learned; how it itself is conceptualised; how good and ill might be identified in philosophy. I can't answer all these fully here but wish to expose them to view. Is it regrettable (apart from the real issue of possible injustice to women) that women are relatively invisible in philosophy? What different effects might there be of male/female teachers, students or learning groups (especially general predominance of one sex)? Is it desirable indeed that use is made of the man–woman, masculine–feminine divisions in understanding, assessing and criticising philosophy? It may be possible to do philosophy consciously as a woman – awareness of these issues may lead a person to consider that their approach to philosophy has been through (false or faulty) male or masculine ideals, or to view the inadequacies of philosophy at least partly in these terms.

Potentially we have in our hands a revolutionary tool; if it is correct that these dichotomies are pervasive and point to fundamental grounds for change, then while the shattering work is going on we'd better stand back and hang on to something firm. That something should be our lack of fear at there being nothing firm; our willingness to abandon old ways of thinking whilst being prepared not prejudicially to anticipate the new, nor indeed to assume how much or how little might be left of the old.

*   *   *

In this section I discuss conceptions of philosophy, to air the thoughts behind seeing the whole issue of women's philosophy as, variously, daft, pointless, non-existent or fruitful. I draw for illustration on comments from philosophers chosen for their explicitness and boldness about the nature of philosophy. But first, consider the effects of varying one's conception of philosophy. It might be to describe differently an activity which is essentially the same elsewhere but under a different description. It might be simply to count some things as philosophy and some as not. More than just description, there might be substantial effects – it might make one stop or start doing some things that one might have done previously or not otherwise done. An effect might be to get respect (or abuse) for what one is doing, and along with this, it might be to criticise the activities of other philosophers. The substantial effects are obviously the most worrying.

Looking at conceptions of philosophy will help to shed light on the issue of philosophy's relation to women, and I wish just to air the possibilities. If philosophy does not admit women openly even when it's considered that there's an ideal situation with ideal philosophy going on, there are two main possibilities. One is that philosophy does in fact in some way exclude women – that women, as a whole, aren't allowed in or can't get in, or may be doing something else, instead of philosophy, or doing nothing comparable. Another possibility is that there are persuasive definitions of philosophy around, and women do do philosophy, but differently, in a way that's excluded. Consider two contrasting views, one that philosophy is a difficult subject only for an élite, and one that it's open to everybody. C. E. M. Joad (1975) gives us a breathtaking example of the first view – extreme, perhaps, but one affecting many people's thought to some extent:

> Philosophy is an extremely difficult subject and most books on philosophy are unintelligible to most intelligent people. This is partly, but not wholly, due to the difficulty of the subject-matter, which, being the universe, is not surprisingly difficult and obscure.
>
> (p. 7)

But Karl Jaspers (1954) gives us a welcoming, friendly response – philosophy is and must be open to all:

> The question is only whether a philosophy is conscious or not, whether it is good or bad, muddled or clear. Anyone who rejects philosophy is himself unconsciously practising philosophy.
>
> (p. 12)

The former view is endorsed by any account of philosophy as a very fixed and difficult activity or body of thought, which will be inclined to exclude people in so far as it introduces the possibility that there will be those who will choose to, or who will inevitably, take part in a somewhat different activity, when they might think they are doing philosophy (or perhaps just do it atrociously). In contrast, the Jaspers-type view is endorsed by those who want to allow any theorising or depth of thought as philosophy, and by those who consider that if we are to think at all we can't get away from such theory (see, for example, Fildes, 1983).

There are many different aspects to the various conceptions of philosophy. I propose to concentrate on what I see as of central relevance: the question of whether, and if so how, philosophy could admit of points of view. This question first arises most forcefully from the view of philosophy as absolute, ultimate, 'metahuman' if one likes, and transcending particular points of view, petty perspectives and biases. I break the investigation into a number of smaller questions. To whom is philosophy available? Does philosophy raise fixed questions? Does philosophy proceed in a fixed manner? Does philosophy strive towards fixed answers? Consideration of these will give more depth and content to the idea of a 'point of view'.

Is philosophy available only to fixed people? If so, it perhaps represents their point of view only. One answer given is that philosophy is only for the well educated. See Joad (1975, pp. 38–40) again for an answer, listing the amazing academic achievements of the ideal philosopher who must be 'in the commonly accepted sense of the term well-educated'. Lloyd charts how notions of philosophical skill evolved through history to require training in reasoning, training largely denied to women and many others (Lloyd, 1979, 1984). And Michèle Le Doeuff (1977) warns of the dangers of mere amateurism and doing philosophy outside an academic institution.

What position do I take? If one wants to assess what one is doing then some people will generally emerge as better or as worse or as total failures – and philosophy should be intrinsically self-aware and self-assessing. But the extreme Joad-type account, I think, should be discarded. Leanings towards it are perhaps more seductive if philosophy is considered as a body of results forming an entire, vastly difficult system. If philosophy is seen more as an activity, or at any rate comes a little more in bite-sized pieces, one may be quite happy to count dribs and drabs of it as philosophy, and the doing of it as philosophy even if nothing of value to anyone else is produced. In doing this some standards could be kept in philosophy without hiving it off to a tiny and privileged élite.

A rather different account is that only some are fired by philosophical questions. As well as the common view that philosophical questions are removed from everyday concerns, in Wittgenstein one can see an example of a view that philosophic questions strike us only from certain perspectives:

Look at the blue of the sky and say to yourself: 'How blue the sky is!' – When you do it spontaneously – without philosophical intentions – the idea never occurs to you that this impression of colour belongs only to *you*.   (Wittgenstein, 1958, pt. 1 no. 275)

Moreover, there is a complex relation between this philosophical stance and common sense – for whilst Wittgenstein implores us: 'SLOGAN "Don't treat your common sense like an umbrella. When you come into a room to philosophise don't leave it outside but bring it in with you"' (Diamond, 1976, p. 68), it's yet at a certain remove from common sense that philosophy begins: 'A philosopher is a man [sic] who has to cure many intellectual diseases in himself before he can arrive at the notion of common sense' (Wittgenstein, 1980, p. 16).

So, maybe, only some people will be driven by philosophical thirst. This is of especial interest to us since women have been considered more glued to common sense and everyday concerns – so less likely to entangle themselves in philosophy? Interestingly, this may be abusive or complimentary. And it has been claimed that women have a flimsier grasp on everyday reality (see, for example, Mora, 1980) – is this a remove from common sense? The relation – if we attempt to follow Wittgenstein – is at any rate complex. Women may be simultaneously not moved by philosophy and in possession of one of the ingredients for a good eye for a philosophical solution. Many find philosophy leaves them cold. But I think it likely that the experience of many women, that of having a worldview shattered, will draw them to philosophy; and I am in any case inclined to Jaspers's view that philosophical questioning can arise in anyone – it's a basic human reflectiveness. And, if people aren't interested, there's no need to shut them out and exclude them. Or, of course, they might not be interested because the discipline has made itself irrelevant and alienating to them. So I would consider it erroneous to suppose philosophy confined by ability or inclination to any one segment of the population (and I would be suspicious of the straightforwardness of claims that it is).

If the questions of philosophy are set, this could both exclude those who want to raise different questions and also not allow room for concentrating on certain questions in philosophy without accusations of neglect of 'the' philosophical questions. Look at Hospers (1956):

Virtually everybody who has studied the subject will agree that certain issues and problems are philosophical ones: the nature and extent of human knowledge; the relation of the knowing mind to the outside world; the problem of determinism and human freedom; the validation of statements about cause, about God, about the good, the beautiful and many other things

(p. 47)

and at Ayer (1971):

For if there are any questions which science leaves it to philosophy to answer, a straightforward process of elimination must lead to their discovery.   (p. 45)

These both leave the impression that it's settled as to what the philosophical questions are. Philosophy may be thought to be piecemeal (little bits of conceptual analysis here and there), or it may be seen as a vast monolith to be tackled all at once: all questions must be considered simultaneously – one can't just concentrate on some areas. The middle way must be correct, it seems to me. Philosophical questions are interlinked and the possibility of later revision must be kept open. But it can't seriously be done more than a bit at a time. Progress can be made on these bits but concentration must legitimately be allowed because of the hugeness of the task. Again, viewing philosophy as an activity rather than as a set of results will help in this.

As for the fixedness of philosophical questions, this must be faulty. At least one philosophical activity is looking at underpinnings and assumptions, and in doing this, different people may find different assumptions present, different assumptions questionable, or questionable for different reasons. For instance, look back at Hospers – the theory of knowledge will be affected if it is assumed that an amazing fact needs to be explained: how can anyone possibly know anything? The sceptic will wonder thus, but others may find no great cause for philosophical concern in so extreme a view and instead address themselves to, say, why different groups arrive at different pictures of knowledge. One may not be worried at all about human freedom and the extent to which one is determined by 'outside' forces of nature, brain chemicals, etc. if one doesn't think of oneself as divorced from that outside in that peculiarly alienating way. Both these examples might fit into feminist or women's thinking, but one doesn't have to come from those positions to see that this is so – that different perspectives will be fired by different philosophical puzzlements. Those from different cultures, training, of different personalities and political beliefs, and those of flexible mind, will also realise this. And no one can claim that any one set of assumptions is *the* set to expose and question, that any one set is the set it's OK to have – and no one can claim to make no assumptions. It's actually in this issue – different philosophical responses to the questioning of assumptions – that I consider greatest room for 'points of view' perhaps arises.

Does philosophy proceed in a fixed manner? Has it a fixed methodology? It's true that many have laid down a fixed method – Ayer again, or the Wittgenstein of the *Tractatus* for two of many examples in the philosophical traditions most familiar to these shores. And that 'ghastly mess' of Continental philosophy proceeds in a different manner entirely, so it's dimly gathered. But has Hospers in his introductory book brought these all together in a general way perhaps? He says that in answering philosophical questions,

> the method is always the same: once the tangled meaning-questions have been analysed, the philosophical enterprise with regard to each of these subject-matters will consist in a systematic and reasoned attempt to examine the ground for belief in each of these areas. (Hospers, 1956, p. 55)

This may offer hope that in some such way we can embrace all of philosophical methodology. But it must be instantly recognised that different things could count as 'reason' as in 'reasoned attempt', and there is or should be no monopoly on who's right about this. The feminists Lloyd and Moulton, amongst others, demonstrate this but again it's something that should be apparent anyway – different systems of thought in the world show this; there are different systems of logic, and within Western philosophy can be found such differing approaches. Differing opinions exist, for instance, on the status of transcendental arguments. There are a myriad methods, a myriad points of view as to which is right, associated with different ways of approaching the world.

Does philosophy reason towards fixed answers? From the foregoing discussion this is clearly a pretty remote aim. But certain pictures of philosophy seem to suggest this, such as seeing philosophy as conceptual analysis only, where there's a fixed method for how the analysis should go, or seeing philosophy as building up a system to answer fixed and universal generalised truths. I find it staggering that anyone could, in a self-conscious and rigid way, conceive of themselves as after truth in philosophy, in the light of the preceding discussion. Even if some truths might be arrived at, even if one feels the need to keep up ahead the inspiring target, keeping an eye too closely on the hoped-for result probably spoils chances of success. If two philosophers – unless obviously influenced by the same traditions – agree on more than a few random things, it's a cause of surprise and speculation. So if the search is for truth, what happens to the idea that there should be some convergence on truth after all this time? This may or may not be a depressing state of affairs. But as things are it seems apparent that one has to tread carefully with the idea that philosophy seeks the truth and is producing the goods. Which answers are right? A search for understanding is probably a more helpful picture, and one that allows for more variation – what helps me to understand may be only what you knew anyway, or may leave you still entirely baffled. And this picture brings with it more room for the notion of a 'point of view'.

The answer to all these questions is that there is and ought to be room for variation and for viewpoint in philosophy. On certain narrow conceptions of philosophy there is none and should be none. There seems no point in confining oneself to such an outlook and indeed it looks positively foolhardy to shut out other possible approaches to problems, to shut out other possible problems, to refuse to recognise that everyone comes loaded with different assumptions. Anyone who stresses the importance of the philosopher's role, the philosopher as human being, the human personal input, is not likely to fall for such an exclusive account of philosophy. To do so would be a narrowing of vision and a mistake.

*   *   *

In this section I consider how it could be claimed women's position relates to philosophy. Women may be thought to be excluded in terms of numbers and relative silence; amongst undergraduates, postgraduates, lecturers, writers and researchers, 'great thinkers', or from certain so-called 'hard-core' areas of philosophy. Firstly, and more briefly, I shall take a look at suggestions that women are shut out of philosophy, then go on to consider claims that women's contribution to philosophy will be different in some way to men's.

As I mentioned at the start, it could simply be the case that as an academic subject in a male-dominated society, philosophy will tend to exclude women. Some elements of such exclusions could well be found, through such well-known techniques as ridicule, described, for example, by Ruth (1979). And such a picture of general mechanisms of oppression, the claim that women's subordinate position in society is responsible for their views on ethics not filtering through to the dominant view, can be found in Haney's (1980) work. This is all worth noting and interesting; what I want to do is to examine in detail why women, as opposed to any old subordinate group, don't get into philosophy, as opposed to into any other unspecified so-called 'Good Thing' in society.

In doing this one can look in two directions – first at women's psychological–social–political–economic position. In doing this I'm not going to delve in detail into the issues of determinism or inevitability, save to note that feminists will have a tendency either to say there is no inevitability and/or to stress the particular worthwhile contribution that women have to make. (Here one can look at Ruth's suggestion (1979, p. 56) that men and women express their different consciousness in what and how they think and that is perhaps how it should be.) The other direction – for which the preceding section was background in so far as it opened up the idea of the many variations on a philosophical theme possible – is to look at how philosophy might be thought to be such that women won't fit in.

There are claims that because of women's special psychological or social position they'll be excluded from philosophy. Le Doeuff is concerned to argue that women's chances of getting taken seriously in philosophy and their chances of getting to take philosophy seriously have been and are curtailed by the fact that women have often approached philosophy through a 'tutor-lover' – they see only his philosophy, they don't enter it fully themselves, and being confined to this relationship don't go beyond it to be fired by that disappointment that spurs one on to produce one's own philosophy (Le Doeuff, 1977). So women are excluded from the starting post. Janice Moulton (1983) criticises the aggressive 'adversary method' in philosophy, where a certain style of reason associated with the sex-linked psychological trait of aggression, reinforced by social pressure, both limits philosophy and serves to exclude the non-aggressive, notably women. Freya Mora (1980) considers a speculation that because of the social relations between the sexes, women's psychological development inclines them to certain philosophical results, namely to a position of subjective idealism in philosophy which, although useful to appreciate, will lead to stultification if not passed beyond. These are just outlines and I'm not saying that I agree with these positions, but noting the sort of claims possible.

In looking at these considerations about the nature of women and their lack of fit to philosophy, how should philosophy be taken? Mora seems to accept that certain areas of philosophy, to which women are said to gravitate, are 'soft' (e.g. ethics), and to accept certain positions as philosophically conservative, with a note of optimism that these positions could be transcended. In other words, given that women might be excluded from philosophy or from certain areas of it, one may either want to accept philosophy as it is – and adjust women? – or see through the situation and suggest that change should come from within philosophy. Criticism is possible and frequent – found in Ruth, in Lloyd, in Moulton, and others, along lines such as: philosophy on the whole, as it now is, is biased to a picture fitting men best: 'reason' should be conceptualised so as not to be so sharply divorced from emotion; and philosophical arguments should not proceed as if beating off the most vicious opponent imaginable.

Now let us consider ways in which women have been said to philosophise differently; a commoner claim, and in many ways just a shift of perspective, one overlapping with the claim that women are excluded, if their own approach to philosophy exists and is undervalued.

There are suggestions that women's philosophy differs from men's in not being quite so good (this generally fitting in with an uncritical acceptance of philosophy as it is now). It may be claimed that women lack some necessity for truly great thinking.[4] But the major stress is on personal experience – how women bring this into philosophy; how it should be brought into philosophy; how personal experience and, in particular, that of women as an oppressed and unheard group (and, some say, the first and most fundamental of oppressed groups) should be consciously adopted and fed into philosophy.

Various problems then arise: the problem of the inevitability and accessibility of this experience, expressed through issues such as that of false consciousness; whether women have to discover and express these experiences themselves; and all the problems of gulfs or meetings of experience between the sexes. All of this feeds into the issue of what is to be done with this experience? What role exactly does this have in philosophy, what role should it have? That is, then, what value could there be in all this women's philosophy?

Ruth (1979) ends her article thus:

> the feminist scholar, against weapons economic, political, and psychological, must trust her woman's consciousness and insights, must insist upon status in the 'mainstream', must resist the quest for the male seal of approval, and assert her right to philosophise as philosophy, not the philosophic establishment, means her to. (p. 61)

Here, then, personal experience is stressed; women have had little or no part in philosophy, philosophy is biased to the male (in ways such as rationality superseding feeling). Let me survey some more claims that women, because of their experience, have valuable things to offer.

In methodology: I have already referred to Moulton's work on the adversary method and her suggestion that this is linked with male psychology; women's experience of discussion with each other and of their own thought could, it's suggested, lead them to a more fruitful approach, or to a wider range of approaches. In questions raised in philosophy, women do seem to gravitate to certain areas – e.g. ethics – perhaps because of their experience and concern with the interpersonal domain. Here Haney's (1980) view is interesting, that different questions in ethics will be raised by women who are aware of their oppression and see it as pivotal in an ethical theory: questions, for instance, about the place of nurturance in an ethical theory. I've mentioned earlier that scepticism will enter into philosophy differently from different points of view, and adoption of the adversary method includes the idea that the worst form of sceptic must be kept at bay.

It has been claimed that a stress on women's experience will affect philosophical results: Haney's article carries the claim that women (and other oppressed groups) will have a good idea of the content of an ethical theory to be proposed as an alternative to the dominant theory, an alternative which includes their own experience. Held (1985) stresses the pervasiveness of gender and how human interests colour knowledge and the type of picture of the world a person will draw, quoting Hintikka and Hintikka (1983) on the relevance to epistemology of the finding that boys stress individual discrete units, girls stress interdependencies – from the way they experience their world, so they draw their philosophical pictures of the world. Annette Baier (1985) claims to have found that women do produce different work in ethics along the lines of Carol Gilligan's findings of different ethical understanding between the sexes. So I end this survey with a remark from Carol Robb (1981):

> Those developing feminist ethical theory are overwhelmingly inclined to refer to lived experience as the source of ethical claims, granting the complexities of this method.   (p. 52)

I shall now consider some of those complexities.

Some results so far: experience is needed, women's experience is needed explicitly, and that experience may be lost in some way. This brings me on to a point brought home by Freeman and Jones (1980), that women may to some extent be in false consciousness, so that a woman's experience of her experience may not be all that was hoped. They stress the need for women in groups to share experience and for consciousness-raising. This brings in the issue of women's philosophy and feminist philosophy – which may be self-conscious women's philosophy, and perhaps one may doubt if there is such a thing as women's philosophy at all, if isolated women in false consciousness may not fully or partially appreciate their position as women. Women need to get to their experience even though it may be blocked in some way. Yet women will still experience something, of course. This could be used, and could be a basis for philosophy or for grouping women together in philosophy. Common psychological experiences leading women to develop differently from men may be pointed at, perhaps, but in addition to this the pressures on women to adopt the dominant worldview of a patriarchal society must be taken into account. So, precisely because women may have special experiences previously shut out of philosophy, we may expect any account of women's experience as a whole to be in such ways messy. This again is an answer to those who find the area messy and conclude there's no fine detail there to be discerned.

One may express doubts, modify or make more sophisticated the claim that women will automatically have access to, and use, experiences which could rejuvenate or vitalise philosophy. One may likewise ask: is it women who have to do this? By this I mean to raise the issue of how far another group can understand and represent the experiences of women. Freeman and Jones (1980) discuss the view that as an oppressed group women have privileged access to this knowledge, and the issues of how women themselves have to be led to an awareness of this and how much men can understand and empathise – the less they can, of course, the more women are needed for the task. I'd guess that women were, to put it gently, at least pretty useful for the task of discovering these experiences, but the claim that men simply can't understand them is rather misguided. And this not just because it is a position of despair for all save separatists, not only because some men are members of oppressed groups too, and so may share some types of experience, but because this claim seems generally to be based upon a shaky conception of understanding. Freeman and Jones (ibid., p. 434) refer to an analogy with pain, that only I can experience my pain, only I can experience and understand my oppression.

But such logically private internal phenomena as pain have a special first person/third person asymmetry of their own and are only a small part of what is to be embraced in the understanding of another person. It simply isn't true that only I can know that I am depressed, only I can have any understanding of it – a friend or doctor may know before I do. Understanding comes in degrees and others may at least have some glimmerings. The pain analogy breaks down when the incompleteness of self-knowledge in other areas – which false consciousness illustrates – is considered. But if I fail to know something about myself it doesn't follow that everyone else's comprehension of it must be even dimmer. Although, of course, various sensitivities are needed for understanding.

This links with how the results of women's experience are to be incorporated into philosophy, how they are to link with the dominant, with the male. A common theme is to abandon male bias, to stop seeing the male as the human absolute. Perhaps this maleness should be seen as just simply male, or perhaps rejected as distorted by patriarchal bias, as one might want to encourage away the unexamined experiences of women in false consciousness. Some philosophers are unclear, I find, as to whether they want perhaps a synthesis of men's and women's philosophy or merely some sort of balance. Carol Robb (1981) suggests challenging the weight and sufficiency of data and this suggests balance or throwing some of the 'male' stuff away completely. Haney (1980, p. 120) suggests bringing masculine confidence and courage together with feminine nurturance. Those impressed by a picture of the genders as complementary – as I am – could think that along such lines will be found the best approach. Annette Baier (1985) for me provides perhaps one of the best expressions of this in her claim that women will do moral philosophy with different emphases, but will want to make a theory accessible to all. She suggests a way women could build on their male predecessors with an ethic of 'appropriate trust', obligation and love brought together from male and female, to form a human whole.

*   *   *

How am I to round up these issues? There may still be a question of whether experience should have this role in philosophy. What I've said about the opening up of philosophy to admit points of view, and in particular what different philosophers will bring in terms of their own assumptions, and questions around assumptions, should make a connection with experience clear. But one may still entertain doubts about claims such as this:

> Yet might it not be possible, for example, that belief in a supreme deity is correlated with perceived ability to control one's future? . . . Belief in a deity would benefit, would be rational, for the very young, the very old, the poor and the helpless. But for others, with experience of being able to control their own lives and surroundings, the difference in experience would give rise to a different belief.   (Moulton, 1983, p. 162)

Is experience just used to produce useful beliefs, ones that fit in with one's life? And is this what it is to be rational? This can't be right – this can't be beneficial to philosophy. Still needed is some critical probing and a certain ability to remove oneself from one's experience whilst not alienating oneself from it. For if experience leads a person to find different assumptions problematic, one should likewise be aware of one's own assumptions and not simply complacently note them and organise beliefs around them for convenience and reassurance.

Experience should have a role – the virtue of feminist philosophy, of women's philosophy, is not only in bringing in the experiences of a group previously only dimly heard, or hazily interpreted through centuries of male bias, but in emphasising the whole idea of the need for experience in the first place. But it must be treated carefully. And now to consider a resultant thought. If it is necessary to consider personal experience in general, will this ultimately merely trivialise the issue of a women's philosophy? Will there be a suburban 40-year-old housewife's philosophy, a myopic, lower middle class, war veteran's philosophy, a left-handed, ginger-haired, bisexual's philosophy? Will all experience crowd in? Whilst stress on personal experience needs to recognise personal differences, I don't think the issue of women's philosophy will disappear under this deluge. For one thing, there is the entirely reasonable claim that one should pay special attention to women's experience as there is so much evidence that it has been ignored for so long. Furthermore, the man/woman, masculine/feminine dichotomies are so pervasive that they will still be visible and still useful. They have already shown themselves useful in ethics, as Baier (1985) amongst others has illustrated. And she suggests something else I would agree with and state clearly: that man/woman, masculine/feminine is for us a fundamental, useful and visible ordering of experience because it encompasses and divides the whole human world, because together in some balance or synthesis it is a basic way of explaining and describing all that is human, because in bringing the sides together we find, in some way, a human whole.[5]

NOTES

1. Man/woman could be distinguished from male/female. I'm trying to avoid too many complications without leaving out anything essential.
2. See, for example, Ruth (1979), particularly p. 58, where she lists various traits associated with the male and beloved of philosophy, and traits associated with the female and outcast; e.g. flight from ambiguity (very present in Austin's use of language) is 'male', humour and lightness, 'female'.
3. See, for example, J. L. Austin, *Philosophical Papers* (1961), at various points.
4. In so far as Freya Mora (1980, p. 378) claims that 'great female thinkers there are none . . . But privileged women have been registering for universities for generations. They enter; they make splendid examinees; and they mostly disappear', she illustrates this opinion, as does Le Doeuff in her claim that women seeing philosophy through their 'tutor-lover' will lack the spur to probe extensively and critically into philosophy. It's a view I have also heard expressed in various forms and degrees by a few professional philosophers.
5. I would like to thank students on the feminist theory course in Bristol University Philosophy Department 1985–6, who have provided me with endless inspiration.

REFERENCES

ANDOLSEN, Barbara Hilkert (1981), 'Agape in Feminist Ethics', *Journal of Religious Ethics*, vol. 9, pp. 69–83.

ATTIG, Thomas (1976), 'Why Are You, a Man, Teaching This Course on the Philosophy of Feminism?', *Metaphilosophy*, vol. 7, pp. 155–66.

AUSTIN, J. L. (1961), *Philosophical Papers* (Oxford: The Clarendon Press).

AYER, A. J. (1971), *Language, Truth and Logic* (Harmondsworth: Penguin).

BAIER, Annette C. (1985), 'What Do Women Want in a Moral Theory?', *Nous*, vol. 19, pp. 53–63.

CODE, Lorraine B. (1981), 'Is the Sex of the Knower Epistemologically Significant?', *Metaphilosophy*, vol. 12, pp. 267–76.

DIAMOND, Cora (ed.) (1976), *Wittgenstein's Lectures on the Foundation of Mathematics Cambridge, 1939* (Brighton: Harvester).

FILDES, Sarah (1983), 'The Inevitability of Theory', *Feminist Review*, vol. 14, pp. 62–70.

FREEMAN, Helen and JONES, Alison (1980), 'For Women Only?', *Women's Studies International Quarterly*, vol. 3, pp. 429–40.

GILLIGAN, Carol (1977), 'In a Different Voice: Women's Conceptions of Self and of Morality', *Harvard Education Review*, vol. 47, pp. 481–517.

HANEY, Eleanor Humes (1980), 'What Is Feminist Ethics? A Proposal for Continuing Discussion', *Journal of Religious Ethics*, vol. 8, pp. 115–24.

HARDING, Sandra (1982), 'Is Gender a Variable in Conceptions of Rationality?', *Dialectica*, vol. 36, pp. 225–42.

HARDING, Sandra and HINTIKKA, Merrill B. (eds) (1983), *Discovering Reality: Feminist Perspectives on Epistemology, Metaphysics, Methodology, and Philosophy of Science* (Dordrecht: Reidel).

HELD, Virginia (1985), 'Feminism and Epistemology: Recent Work on the Connexion between Gender and Knowledge', *Philosophy and Public Affairs*, vol. 14, pp. 298–307.

HINTIKKA, Merrill B. and HINTIKKA Jaakko (1983), 'How Can Language Be Sexist?', in S. HARDING and M. HINTIKKA (eds), pp. 139–48.

HOSPERS, John (1956), *An Introduction to Philosophical Analysis* (London: Routledge & Kegan Paul).

JASPERS, Karl (1954), *The Way to Wisdom: An Introduction to Philosophy*, trans. Ralph Mannheim (New Haven: Yale University Press).

JOAD, C. E. M. (1975), *Teach Yourself Philosophy* (London: English Universities Press).

LE DOEUFF, Michèle (1977), 'Women and Philosophy', trans. Debbie Pope, *Radical Philosophy*, vol. 17, pp. 2–11.

LLOYD, Genevieve (1979), 'The Man of Reason', *Metaphilosophy*, vol. 10, pp. 18–37.

LLOYD, Genevieve (1984), *The Man of Reason: 'Male' and 'Female' in Western Philosophy* (London: Methuen).

MORA, Freya (1980), 'Metaphysical Purdah', *Philosophy*, vol. 55, pp. 377–85.

MOULTON, Janice (1983), 'A Paradigm of Philosophy: The Adversary Method', in S. HARDING and M. HINTIKKA (eds), pp. 149–64.

PARSONS, Kathryn Pyne (1977), 'Moral Revolution', in Julie Sherman and Evelyn Beck (eds), *The Prism of Sex: Essays in the Sociology of Knowledge* (Madison: University of Wisconsin Press), pp. 189–227.

ROBB, Carol S. (1981), 'A Framework for Feminist Ethics', *Journal of Religious Ethics*, vol. 9, pp. 48–68.

RUTH, Sheila (1979), 'Methodocracy, Misogyny and Bad Faith: Sexism in the Philosophical Establishment', *Metaphilosophy*, vol. 10, pp. 48–61.

SOBLE, Alan (1983), 'Feminist Epistemology and Woman Scientists', *Metaphilosophy*, vol. 14, pp. 291–307.

WITTGENSTEIN, Ludwig (1958), *Philosophical Investigations*, trans. G. E. M. Anscombe (Oxford: Blackwell).

WITTGENSTEIN, Ludwig (1980), *Culture and Value*, trans. Peter Winch (Oxford: Blackwell).

Index

DATE DUE

2/16/08	